POSTCOLONIALISM:
A GUIDE FOR THE PERPLEXED

The Guides for the Perplexed Series

Continuum's *Guides for the Perplexed* are clear, concise and accessible introductions to thinkers, writers and subjects that students and readers can find especially challenging – or indeed downright bewildering. Concentrating specifically on what it is that makes the subject difficult to grasp, these books explain and explore key themes and ideas, guiding the reader towards a thorough understanding of demanding material.

Related titles include:

Beckett: A Guide for the Perplexed, Jonathan Boulter
Deleuze: A Guide for the Perplexed, Claire Colebrook
Derrida: A Guide for the Perplexed, Julian Wolfreys
Eliot: A Guide for the Perplexed, Steve Ellis
Existentialism: A Guide for the Perplexed, Steven Earnshaw
Literary Theory: A Guide for the Perplexed, Mary Klages
Tolstoy: A Guide for the Perplexed, Jeff Love

POSTCOLONIALISM:
A GUIDE FOR THE PERPLEXED

PRAMOD K. NAYAR

continuum

Continuum International Publishing Group
The Tower Building   80 Maiden Lane
11 York Road   Suite 704
London SE1 7NX   New York, NY 10038

www.continuumbooks.com

British Library Cataloguing-in-Publication Data
A catalogue record for this book is available from the British Library.

ISBN: 9780826437006 (hardcover)
            9780826400468 (paperback)

Library of Congress Cataloging-in-Publication Data
Nayar, Pramod K.
Postcolonialism : a guide for the perplexed / Pramod K. Nayar.
p. cm.– (Guides for the perplexed)
Includes bibliographical references and index.
ISBN 978-0-8264-3700-6 (hardcover)
ISBN 978-0-8264-0046-8 (pbk.)
1. Postcolonialism in literature. 2. Postcolonialism.
3. Literature, Modern–20th century–History and
criticism–Theory, etc. 4. Developing countries–Literatures–
History and criticism–Theory, etc. I. Title. II. Series.

PN56.P555N39 2010
809'.933581–dc22

2010000465

Typeset byNewgen Imaging Systems Pvt Ltd, Chennai, India
Printed and bound in Great Britain by the MPG Books Group

CONTENTS

PREFACE

This is a quick introduction to a vast topic. 'Postcolonialism' as a critical-analytical approach, way of thinking and academic project now spans multiple disciplines in the social sciences and humanities, from film studies to literary criticism. This book is rooted in the written – as opposed to say, film – postcolonial, drawing its arguments and case studies from literary and discursive texts from Asia, Africa and South America – regions whose history includes long periods of European colonization.

The book is a primer, a compact but (hopefully) lucid explanation and explication of several of the themes, concerns, images and motifs that characterize the work of influential writers such as Salman Rushdie, Marjane Satrapi, Nawaad El Saadawi, Chinua Achebe and Jackie Huggins. As far as possible this book has addressed common themes among postcolonial cultures and literatures, and excluded specialized or isolated ones. As case studies in 'colonial cultures' it has restricted itself to two examples, education and religion. Other domains – sports, arts and crafts, law and literature – have also been subject to postcolonial scrutiny, but have not been included here. An exhaustive bibliography directs the interested reader towards further explorations and more specialized studies.

A section of the chapter on cosmopolitanism is due to appear as an essay, 'The Postcolonial Parasite: The Transnational Indian Novel in English' in Gonul Pultar (ed.), *Del Construction of Ethnicity and Nationhood in the Age of Globalization*. Parts of the chapter have also appeared as 'Spaces of "Home": Boman Desai's *Asylum, USA*'. *ICFAI Journal of English Studies* 1, 4 (2006), 63–72. Parts of chapter 7 were delivered in abbreviated form as the keynote address, 'Postcolonialism, Suffering and Affective Cosmopolitanism' at the 'International Conference on Postcolonial Literatures and the Transnational', 7–9 April 2010, Chaudhary Charan Singh University, Meerut, India. Some of the arguments in this book were rehearsed, in different and abbreviated form, in my earlier work, *Postcolonial Literature: An Introduction* (2008).

ACKNOWLEDGEMENTS

My thanks to all those who made this book possible, contributing to it in plentiful, prompt and pertinent ways:

My parents, for their blessings, prayers and constant support;

Nandini and Pranav for the necessary time away from libraries, books and the PC (in the latter's case, such time being spent discussing Batman, Asterix or Transformers), their unstinted affection and care (often in the face of my obstinacy in falling ill);

Ai and Baba at Nagpur who remain puzzled yet polite at my workaholism;

Colleen Coalter at Continuum for her advice and suggestions.

Friends and fellow-academics: Anindita Mukhopadhyay (for her own work on colonial law), Brinda Bose, Rita Kothari, Walter Perera, Raghuramaraju (for sharing his papers on colonialism and modernity), Nandana Dutta, Walter S. H. Lim (who invited me to revisit an old haunt – colonial cultures – by suggesting I contribute an essay on early modern colonial travellers), Narayana Chandran (who directs me to interesting reading from assorted postcolonials, and for sharing his Sahgal essay on the 'schizophrenic imagination'), and Akhila Ramnarayan (for directing me to Lau's paper on 're-orientalism');

The American Library, Chennai, especially its phenomenal Librarian, Mysore Jagadish, for their exceptional service;

Neeraja S. for procuring essays at short notice and comments on my chapters, and S. Vimala for sharing her colonial texts with me and supplying references.

This one is for Anna, friend and colleague, whose intellect and affection plans books for me to write, and then makes my reading interesting, the writing both possible and pleasurable.

CHAPTER ONE

INTRODUCTION: POSTCOLONIAL THOUGHT

Postcolonialism is the academic, intellectual, ideological and ideational scaffolding of the condition of decolonization (the period following political independence for nations and cultures in Africa, Asia and South America). Postcolonialism as a theory and a critique emerged from within anti-colonial activism and political movements in Asia, Africa and South America. Intellectuals and political leaders among 'natives' – a term used, throughout this book, to reference non-European cultures and peoples of Asia, Africa and South America – interrogating colonial practices in these movements generated ideas that eventually coalesced into a body of thought within academic practices. Gandhi, Cesaire, Tagore, Senghor, Cabral, Fanon were anti-colonial activist-thinkers whose political views metamorphosed into political and literary-cultural theories. It is this political context that provides much of postcolonialism's critical edge and social concerns. Race is the key prism through which all postcolonial analysis is refracted.

TERMS AND DEFINITIONS

Postcolonialism deploys a set of terms as part of its lexicon and conceptual framework: colonialism-imperialism, postcolonial-postcoloniality, postcolonialism, neocolonialism, decolonization and postcolonial theory.

Colonialism is the process of settlement by Europeans in Asian, African, South American, Canadian and Australian spaces. Colonization was a violent appropriation and sustained exploitation of native races and spaces by European cultures. The European nation established itself primarily as a military-administrative power in the 'colony'. Military-political conquest and domination were accompanied, in all cases, by a close *study* of native cultures: anthropological-ethnographic studies, codification of native laws and detailed documentation of native histories and arts, to produce a colonial archive of knowledge about the natives. Finally, having acquired in-depth knowledge of native cultures, the colonial power proceeded to modify and control the social and cultural practices and beliefs of the natives in the guise of 'reform' and 'welfare'. New systems of schooling, architecture and even agriculture forced the colonized natives to acquire new skills and methods. Colonialism was never just as an exploitative political or economic process, it was also a *cultural conquest* of the native whereby the native's forms of knowledge, art, cultural practices and religious beliefs were studied, classified, policed, judged and altered by the European.

Colonial discourse is the construction of the native, usually in stereotypical ways, in European narratives, images and representations in a variety of modes and genres such as the arts, literature, the law, science writing and administrative reports.[1] The native is *constructed* as primitive, depraved, pagan, criminal, immoral, vulnerable and effeminate in colonial discourse. Such a discourse then constructs a reality where future European administrators would not only see the native *through* the lens of this discourse, but also enact policies or initiate political-administrative measures because they believe in the truth-claims of the discourse. Discourse becomes, in other words, the mode of perceiving, judging and acting upon the non-European.

Imperialism refers to the practice of governance of Asian or African nations through 'remote control', *without* actual settlement in the non-European spaces when European or American powers control financial, military, political, cultural activities in Asian, African or South American nations. It generally refers to a system of economic domination and exploitation, though political and military domination often accompanies the economic one. Imperialism is the *ideology* that recommends, furthers and justifies colonial rule. Imperialism situates the Asian or African region on the periphery, with the control resting with the European centre. Imperialism is the theory and colonialism is the practice, where both are based on racial difference.

Neocolonialism is the continuing economic exploitation of Asian and African nation-states by the former colonials – Europeans – and American powers. In most cases, neocolonialism is achieved not merely through state control by Euro-American powers but by a nexus between the economic (embodied in the banking and financial systems of the Euro-American 'First World'), the nation-state (embodied in the politician and governments) and the business house (embodied in multinational corporations), often accompanied by insidious threats of trade sanctions and military action. Neocolonialism, therefore, may be the more insidious and dangerous form of colonialism.

Postcoloniality refers to the historical and material conditions of formerly colonized Asian, African and South American nations. It refers to the economic and political conditions in countries such as India after the European ruler handed over political power to the native population. Since the last decades of the twentieth century, 'postcoloniality' increasingly emphasizes the impact of global geo-politics, globalization and economic shifts upon material conditions in Asian and African nation-states. Thus 'postcoloniality' signals late twentieth-century contexts of

- the continuing use of 'Third World' labour in the Information and Communications Technology (ICT) revolution,
- the reception accorded to Asian and African migrant workers,
- the new economic policies (including trade agreements, IMF controls, economic embargos) of import-export of 'Third World' products and
- military campaigns and wars in Arab, Asian, South American nations as a mode of acquiring territorial and natural resources like oil or minerals.

'Postcoloniality' maps a continuum between their former colonized state and the present neo-colonized one. Postcoloniality as a condition and term is allied with 'decolonization'.

Decolonization is the process whereby non-white nations and ethnic groups in Asia, Africa and South America strive to secure freedom (economic, political, intellectual) from their European masters. 'Postcoloniality' and 'decolonization' are used, especially in postcolonial theory to describe resistance, particularly against class, race and gender oppression. Decolonization seeks freedom from colonial forms of *thinking*, to revive native, local and vernacular forms of knowledge by questioning and overturning European categories and epistemologies. Thus decolonization has resulted in the revival of mysticism and spiritualism – which had been rejected by colonialism's scientism as primitive – as forms of knowledge in post-colonial societies. Decolonization is thus a critical methodology.

Postcolonialism, the theoretical and intellectual arm of the postcolonial condition, refers to a mode of reading, political analysis and cultural resistance that negotiates with the native's *colonial history* and *neocolonial present*. Leela Gandhi defines postcolonialism as a

> theoretical resistance to the mystifying amnesia of the colonial aftermath. It is a disciplinary project devoted to the academic task of revisiting, remembering and, crucially, interrogating the colonial past. (1999, p. 4)

Postcolonialism invokes ideas of social justice, emancipation and democracy in order to oppose oppressive structures of racism, discrimination and exploitation. But it also emphasizes the formerly colonized subject's 'agency' – defined as the ability to affect her/his present conditions and future prospects – in the face of *continuing* oppression. It is a set of critical approaches, ideas and critical methodologies that enable us to 'read' colonial/colonizing practices and structures.

Postcolonial theory is a complex analytical strategy that foregrounds *racial difference* in the relationship – political, social, economic and cultural – between First/Western and Third/Eastern worlds. It is a reading practice that is determinedly political when it examines

- how the First/Western world represented the non-European native/world,
- how colonial histories, anthropology, area studies, cartography were rooted in a racial discourse,
- how the native was feminized, dehumanized and marginalized in both, representations and real life in the period of colonialism,
- the psychological effects of colonialism on colonizer and colonized,
- the 'instruments' of colonial domination: English literature, historiography, art and architecture,
- the rise of nationalist discourse that resisted colonialism.

The remainder of this chapter traces the history of postcolonial thought. I have opted to zero in on influential thinkers rather than undertake an exhaustive survey of every trajectory, minor and major, in postcolonialism. While this runs the risk of homogenizing and hierarchizing the diversity of Asian, African and South American histories and postcolonial ideas, it also enables a sharper focus on the development of key ideas that have sustained through postcolonial theory in general.

It must be emphasized that colonials from France, England, Spain or the Netherlands were *not* one unified category ('West'). 'Coloniality' is a highly context-specific process where local institutions, people, groups, social and economic conditions and even the landscape inform the nature of that coloniality. One of the problems of postcolonialism's colonial critique has been, as Frederick Cooper points out in a recent essay, 'story plucking' where

One can pluck a text or a narrative from Spanish America in the sixteenth century, or from the slave colonies of the West Indies in the eighteenth century, or from a moderately prosperous twentieth-century cocoa planter in the Gold Coast, and derive a lesson that conveys a generalizable meaning. (2007, p. 405)

As Cooper points out, colonial power depends on the 'specific resources of those involved' and we should be alert to how people 'confronted the forms of power they faced' (p. 405).

THE BEGINNINGS: GANDHI, FANON, CÉSAIRE, CABRAL

Postcolonialism as an intellectual project finds its origins in the thoughts and theories of anti-colonial movements. Anti-colonial struggles in Africa and Asia generated ideas of political independence, colonial exploitation and identity politics which eventually grew into a substantial body of ideas in postcolonial theory and studies. These anti-colonial sentiments and thought often relied upon a nostalgic reverence for their (native, non-European) pre-colonial cultures, a pride in their culture and a fierce xenophobia. However, it would be wrong to see anti-colonial thought as simply positing the 'good' native culture in antagonism to the 'bad' European culture. In what is an important reminder, Raghuramaraju points to figures in Indian philosophy such as Gandhi and Vivekananda, who 'while making a case for India in the face of colonial onslaught . . . have neither hidden nor ignored defects within Indian theories and realities'. He adds: 'their criticism of the British either immediately followed or even preceded their admission of internal problems' (2009, p. 355). As Fanon was to illustrate in his own work, a fair amount of self-reflexivity and what Raghuramaraju calls 'internal criticism' has marked postcolonial thinking.

Contributions to postcolonial thought have come from diverse sources: Asia, Africa and Latin America, initially, and a more Euro-American 'literary theory' tradition since the 1980s. José Carlos Mariategui (Peru), Oswald de Andrade (Brazil), Nestor Canclini (Argentina), Che Guevara (Cuba) from South America dealt with their colonial legacy in ways that are radically different from Gandhi (India) or Fanon (Algeria). This rich diversity and intersection of Asian, African and Latin American postcolonial thought inspires Robert Young (2001) to describe it as 'tricontinentalism' (a reference to the 'Tricontinental Conference of Solidarity of the Peoples of Africa, Asia and Latin America' in Havana, Cuba, 1966).

In this section, I examine the postcolonialism of four influential thinkers: Mahatma Gandhi, Frantz Fanon and Aimé Césaire.

Mahatma Gandhi

Mohandas Karamchand Gandhi, better known as Mahatma Gandhi or 'the apostle of non-violence' orchestrated one of the most wide-spread anti-colonial struggles of the modern world. Gandhi's ideas on native culture, modernity and colonialism, spread across several essays and writings constitute, along with his political praxis, a major contribution to postcolonial thought.

The anti-colonial struggle in India was of a very different nature from that of other colonized nations, and Gandhi entered it after it had been underway for sometime. Trained in the law, and exposed to the 'centre' of colonial culture, London, and apartheid South Africa, Gandhi brought to the anti-colonial struggle a new ideology.

Gandhi's resistance to colonialism began with a critique of Western modernity. His emphasis on *swadeshi* (economic self-reliance) and *swaraj* (self-rule) were forms of cultural nationalism that he projected as the answer to soulless Western modernity. Gandhi's vegetarianism, support for local languages (influenced by Welsh linguistic nationalism) and culture, and anti-industrial stance also constituted his cultural nationalism.

Gandhi's major contribution to postcolonial thought can be best identified as a *moral* one (hence he does not fit into the predominantly

Marxist postcolonial theory, Young 2000, p. 320). His overarching goal was the attainment of a moral superiority, of both the colonized nation and the colonized individual, over the colonizer. Gandhi's 'satyagraha' system of protest was an indigenous form of struggle that was based on the moral principle of non-violence. Passive resistance, personal discipline, fasting and non-violence contributed to the *moral* stance. Gandhi's genius was to embody the native's *agency* and *resistance* not in violence but in passivity, not in revolution but in moral positions.

Gandhi saw how colonialism was embedded in European capitalist modernity. His anti-industrial stance was born out of the belief that capitalism is inherently exploitative. His early moves in the experiments in anti-colonial struggle were therefore class struggles: peasant and working-class resistance in Kheda and Bardoli.

Taking recourse to Hindu values he would also appropriate European discourses of the degeneration of society to plead for a moral rebirth and rejuvenation of India as an answer to colonialism. This principle evolved out of his belief that the English civilization was degraded and degenerate, and the only way India could throw out the colonial was to acquire a higher moral position.

Ashis Nandy in his study of Gandhi (1983) has persuasively argued that Gandhi developed a response to the ultra-masculine colonial. Gandhi did not offer a counter-masculinity. Instead, what he did was to propose a masculinity that also took into account a certain feminization. This nearly androgynous, child-like femininity in Gandhi was also aligned with his support of notions of *shakti* ('power', but also feminized *shakti* in Hinduism) as non-violence. Thus Gandhi countered the machismo cult of colonialism with a feminized one. This gendered resistance – not without its problems, though – would later reappear in the feminist dimensions of post-colonial theory.

Gandhi's use of religion and cultural practices was, indisputably, effective in the anti-colonial struggle. It produced a strong sense of national and cultural identity, but also ran the risk of either homogenizing different cultural practices ('Hindu' practices becoming a code for 'Indian' practices when it was simply a majority practice) or alienating minority practices (Muslim, Sikh, native Christian). Anti-colonial cultural nationalism, as later thinkers like Frantz Fanon and others discovered, very easily swerved into intolerant xenophobia, nativism and 'tribalisms'. Gandhi's Hinduized cultural nationalism and anti-colonial thought has, for this reason, not suited postcolonial theory very well because the latter seeks a more secular version (Chakrabarty 2000).

What is often overlooked in Gandhi is his syncretism, the mix-and-match method of his ideas. More recent work (Nandy 1983, Parekh 1999, Young 2000) has argued for a 'hybridity' in Gandhi, where, they propose, he adapted and adopted Western thinkers (his fondness for Ruskin and Thoreau, for example) along with Hinduism (but a Hinduism without the scriptural tradition). Gandhi spoke of the assimilation of cultures. In *Hind Swaraj* he famously declared: 'the introduction of foreigners does not necessarily destroy the nation, they merge in it' (1909, online). This aspect of Gandhi's postcolonial thought would resonate through several generations of critics as diverse as Homi Bhabha and Ashis Nandy.

Frantz Fanon

Frantz Fanon was writing during Algeria's struggles against French colonialism during the 1940s. As a psychiatrist Fanon had several opportunities to observe the psychological effects of colonialism on the (black) native, and this was the foundation of his classic studies of the colonial condition: *Black Skin, White Masks* (1967a), *The Wretched of the Earth* (1963) and *Toward the African Revolution* (1967b).

Fanon argued that the black man had lost his culture and his past. The resulting inferiority complex is the direct result of years of dehumanization in the colonial context where he sees himself only as the white man sees him. That is, the black man sees himself as inferior because he looks at himself through the white man's eyes. The white man has constantly portrayed the black as less-than human, an 'object' without a soul, an animal and years of such indoctrination have made the black man believe this to be true. The colonial set-up has settled into 'the very centre of the Algerian individual and has undertaken a sustained work of cleanup, of expulsion of self' (1967b, p. 65). For the white man, the native is always the negative, primitive Other: the very *opposite* of what he and his culture stand for. The black man is always the 'darkness' inside the white man that the white man seeks to expel and deny.

Fanon was responding to the work of Octave Mannoni (*Prospero and Caliban: The Psychology of Colonization* 1956). Mannoni argued that the colonized suffered from a 'dependency complex' and was prone to a feeling of abandonment by the colonial father figure. The colonizer came to the colony with an inherent inferiority complex. In the colony, given the chance to dominate and oppress over the blacks, the colonizer over-compensated for his inferiority complex. Mannoni argued that these complexes were the *pre-condition* of all colonial relations: it was in the very nature of the native to be colonized and in the very nature of the white man to colonize. Fanon argued against this line of thought by suggesting that the native's dependency complex was the direct *effect* (and not the cause, as Mannoni seemed to think) of colonization. When the white master constantly treats the black man as simply the means of hard labour, the relationship between the two is of only one kind: white master-black slave. This enslaved condition contributes to the black man's inferiority complex.

As a result of colonization, the white man becomes the epitome of perfection and the black man seeks to emulate him – a 'white mask' over his 'black skin', in Fanon's unforgettable phrase. For the native the term 'man' itself begins to mean 'white man' because he (the black man) does not see himself as a 'man' at all. In terms of culture, the native extends this accepted notion to believe that the only values that matter are those of the white man. The black man seeks to escape his blackness. Fanon writes: 'in the man of color there is a constant effort to run away from his own individuality, to annihilate his own presence' (1967a, p. 60). The native takes on Western values, religion, the language and practices of the white colonial and rejects his own traditions. But at the same time his own traditions and customs continue to exert a powerful pull on the black man. The result is a schizophrenic condition, torn between the white man's culture that he seeks to appropriate and his own culture that he is reluctant to let go. The neurosis and psychological crises experienced by the black man were, therefore, less a pure mental condition than the effect of the social and economic realities of colonialism. This was Fanon's major contribution: to locate African mental illness within the exploitative and cruel conditions of colonial domination.

The build-up of this sense of inadequacy in the native's psyche, argues Fanon, results in violence as a form of self-assertion. When the native discovers that he cannot hope to become truly 'white', or even expel the whites, his violence turns against his own kind. Violence becomes a channel for aggression and frustration to flow out: 'for the last resort of the native is to defend his personality vis-à-vis his brother', as he puts it (1963, p. 54). Fanon sees tribal wars as an instance of such violence where the 'wretched' natives turn upon each other because they are haunted by their failure to turn against the colonial master. He notoriously described violence as a 'cleansing force' (p. 94) arguing that it unifies a nation. Fanon argues that violence generates a new social consciousness and builds alliances against the colonial master, even attributing therapeutic properties to it: 'this violence becomes the absolute line of action . . . the colonized man finds his freedom in and through violence' (pp. 85–6).

Fanon recognized the significance of cultural nationalism when he propounded the idea of a 'national literature' and 'national culture' in *Wretched of the Earth* leading to a 'national consciousness'. 'National culture' had to be a greater, pan-African sensibility, and not just a narrow, sectarian-tribal one. Fanon differentiated between a racially (tribal, ethnic) defined nationalism and a wider antiracist national consciousness which would 'open out . . . [to] the truth of the world' (1967c, p. 44). The blacks had to create their own history and write their own stories to break free of the colonial shackles in what Fanon envisaged as a deeply *humanist* project. A national culture, believed Fanon, must take return to African myths and cultural practices so that black identity can be resurrected. Intellectuals have a major role to play in this, but for this they need to first abandon their colonial inheritance. They need to stop thinking of the masses as 'unthinking', and elicit and reinforce their self-esteem and belief in their own ideas.

A 'national culture' is constructed in three stages. In the first, *assimilationist* phase, the native intellectual is under the influence of the colonizer's culture, and seeks to emulate and assimilate it by abandoning his own. The poetry and prose written in this phase imitates the colonizer's and has abandoned its native roots. In the second stage the native discovers that he can never become truly white for the colonial master to treat him as an equal. He therefore returns to his own culture but this is often romantic rather than critical. This is the stage of *cultural nationalism* where a new sense of pride in his own culture begins to assert itself. In the third, *nationalist* stage the native intellectual undertakes a careful analysis of his own culture, abandoning the dated or unjust elements of his own culture so that a new future after colonialism is possible. He proceeds to 'shake the people' (1963, pp. 178–9). Fanon warned that the idea of a 'national literature' and 'national culture' might result in xenophobia. 'National culture' had a limited value: it could help define native culture against colonial rule. For national culture to be effective, it has to remedy the conditions of the working classes. Fanon argued that culture must be dynamic and open to change to suit changed historical circumstances and ensure justice for all.

Aimé Césaire

Césaire's pithy summary of the colonial condition has reverberated through postcolonial thought:

> colonisation works to decivilise the coloniser, to brutalise him in the true sense of the word, to degrade him, to awaken him to buried instincts, to covetousness, violence, race hatred, and moral relativism . . . (1972, p. 13)

What Césaire is stating is the paradoxical nature of colonialism. Colonialism projects itself as a civilizing mission, but in reality it brutalizes both the white man and the native. It was never a benevolent enterprise because it was spear-headed by the pirate, the opportunist, the adventurer and the merchant.

Césaire argued that community-centred, anti-capitalist native cultures were destroyed by the colonial's capitalist one. The sustained presence of the colonial meant that the native was in despair about ever finding his own identity. Native cultures are rejected by the colonial and, Césaire argued, the only response possible was 'negritude'.

Negritude is the *cultural* response of the native to the onslaught by colonialism's culture. Negritude is the attempt of the black, colonized people to retrieve their cultural heritage and identity. Influenced by the Harlem Renaissance of African Americans and the Black Arts movements in the USA, Césaire's negritude was characterized by a *cultural* separatism that rejected assimilation of the colonial's culture by Africans. This separatism was necessary because, Césaire and later Leopold Senghor argued, the native needed to find his own roots and culture which the colonial experience had destroyed. Negritude therefore must be seen as an anti-colonial and postcolonial political project that retrieves cultural identity.

Amilcar Cabral

Cabral was one of the co-founders of the Movimento Anti-Colonista of Africans and later of the Popular Movement for the Liberation of Angola and the African Party for the Independence of Guinea and Cape Verde. Thus Cabral's political theories were the direct result of his activism. In his speeches and writings from the 1960s and '70s, Cabral argued fervently for the diversity of the African peoples, refusing to accept a homogenized 'Africa'.

Cabral was certain that any liberation struggle and anti-colonial movement must draw upon the real conditions of *local* populations and cultures. He was also clear, after his work with the local populace in these regions, that Western development models and practices were unsuitable for the Africans. The cultural and material lives of local populations must constitute the basis for any models, he argued.

Cabral is also interesting as a postcolonial thinker because he treated anti-colonial struggles as a platform for waging a war against *all* forms of foreign domination, including neo-colonialism. In order to battle neo-colonialism, argued Cabral, the native populations must turn to socialism. Thus Cabral emphasized not only a struggle against the colonizing power, he also stressed the need for an internal restructuring of the colonized society through local development models and socialism. Cabral declared:

> The neo-colonial situation . . . is not resolved by a nationalist solution; it demands the destruction of the capitalist structures implanted in the national territory by imperialism, and correctly posits a socialist solution. (quoted in Young 2000, p. 287)

Finally, Cabral also foregrounded cultural resistance and cultural nationalism. When faced with foreign cultures and subdued by a foreign power, native cultures need to 'return' to their own histories, he argued. Political independence from the colonial was possible only through a strengthening of their own cultural roots and sustained cultural resistance. Since all colonial domination was built upon a cultural imperialism, all anti-colonial struggles would also be the fight to save one's own culture. Cabral also put a great deal of faith into the resilience of native *culture*, arguing that these were indestructible even if the military and political structures of native societies were destroyed.[2] Cabral also filled an interesting caveat (something which reminds us of Fanon's arguments about native elites who assimilate the colonizer's culture): it is the masses that preserve native cultures even if their leaders, elites and intellectuals assimilate the white man's.

'READING' COLONIALISM AS 'ORIENTALISM': EDWARD SAID

In 1978, a Palestinian immigrant Professor of English at Columbia University, Edward W. Said, published a curiously titled book, *Orientalism*. The book turned out to be the text many academics and scholars in the Third World, and several studying colonialism in the First, were waiting for. This epoch-making book may be said to have officially inaugurated the field of postcolonial studies as a discipline and postcolonial theory as a critical method.[3]

'Orientalism' can be defined as *the theory, poetics and practice of representation, by Europeans, of the Arab world, Asia, China and Japan* (together dubbed 'the Orient'). Orientalism begins as the act of story-telling, fictions and fantasies about the Orient by European travellers, writers and artists. It generates a desire to see and then *possess* the Orient. Thus Orientalism is a style of narrative that instills a desire to conquer and control. We can term this the politics of the Orientalist narrative, where representation becomes (i) the source of particular images of wealth, barbarism and emptiness of the Orient and (ii) the preliminary moment to European intervention in these lands. Said dates the major Orientalist period as 1815–1910 when entire institutions – universities, learned societies – in Europe were dedicated to Oriental studies.

Orientalism *begins* with imaginative narratives but then moves into a project of enquiry, discovery and knowledge-gathering. The East is written about in diverse ways – in the form of fictionalized creations as well as 'authoritative' commentaries, personal memoirs of Western experiences in the East and the administrative study. Orientalism includes scientific modes of writings about the East, including census and archaeological surveys, botanical expeditions and medical geographies. These scientific texts support the project of conquest and control. Said showed how *literary* texts encoded formulaic representations, stereotypes and clichés about Oriental religions, cultures and peoples as part of a larger colonial project. Orientalism was a grand narrative, an overarching story told by Europe about all non-European cultures. Said therefore shows how literary and narrative projects have a material-political consequence. The Orient, as Said puts it, was a 'textual universe' (p. 52).

Said defined 'Orientalism' throughout his work as

'a way of coming to terms with the Orient that is based on the Orient's special place in European Western experience' (p. 1);

'a Western style for dominating, restructuring, and having authority over the Orient' (p. 3).

'a library or archive of information' (p. 41);

'a manner of regularized writing, vision and study, dominated by imperatives, perspectives, and ideological biases ostensibly suited to the Orient . . . The Orient is taught, researched, administered and pronounced upon in certain discrete ways' (p. 202);

'a system of representations framed by a whole set of forces that brought the Orient into Western learning, Western consciousness, and later, Western Empire'. (pp. 202–3)

Said proposed that the Orient was contained and represented by dominating frameworks, and the literary and political frameworks informed and influenced each other.

Orientalism takes three main forms:

a. It generated more awareness about the Arab and Asian world through newly discovered texts in translation,
b. It produced more commentaries, researches and institutions (Royal Asiatic Society, the American Oriental Society, etc.), specialized periodicals (such as the *Asiatick Researches* from the *Asiatic* Society established in Calcutta in 1784) and created a 'modernization' of Orientalism,
c. It restricted and influenced how the Orient was imagined/written about.

What Orientalism did was to polarize the Westerner in opposition to the Oriental. That is, it created binary opposites, situating the West as the very contrast to the East. In doing so, it subsumed all Western cultures – with its diversity and differences – into just one homogenous category: 'the West'. Likewise, it merged Arab, Chinese, Japanese cultures into one single category, 'Oriental'. Binarisms operated on a principle of essentializing and homogenizing where internal differences in Asian cultures were ignored. This was done so that the Asian culture's diversity was never a threat: it was simpler to comprehend Asia or India if it was treated as one undifferentiated, homogenous mass.

Orientalism became a field of study based on a geographical, cultural, linguistic and ethnic unit. The Orient was the object of study, and the West did the studying. In effect, therefore, there was a clear power relation between West and East, where the East was the passive, inert object of study and the West effected the studies and made pronouncements and judgements about it. Thus 'Orientalism' is a form of thinking, talking about and examining Asian or Arabic cultures that then leads to imperial policies and action. What Said wants us to understand is that imperial practices are built upon (i) imperialist dreams and unconscious desires and (ii) imperial discourses and ways of talking, representing the non-European.

Said argued that Orientalism created an 'imaginative geography' (pp. 49–73), where the West drew the distinction between 'our' lands and barbarian lands (the barbarian was not required to ratify this). This imaginative geography emphasized and dramatized the cultural differences between 'us' and 'them'. Said writes:

> This universal practice of designating in one's mind a familiar space which is 'ours' and an unfamiliar space beyond 'ours' which is 'theirs' is a way of making geographical distinctions that can be entirely arbitrary . . . imaginative geography of the 'our land-barbarian land' variety does not require that the barbarians acknowledge the distinction. It is enough for 'us' to set up these boundaries in our own minds. (p. 54)

But Orientalism also produced the Orient as a stage, on which the spectacle of the Orient was performed to be viewed by the West. It combined accurate knowledge with myth and fantasy – a *theatre* of the Orient. The task was to confirm what was already believed about the Orient, where the belief itself came from an entire archive of prejudiced and flawed representations.

Said traces Orientalism back to the thirteenth-century poet Dante, where the first vocabulary of the Orient begins to emerge: Orient as cruel, barbaric; Islam as evil, the Prophet as impostor; the Hindu as weak but treacherous. All subsequent representations, Said notes, used this same vocabulary. There is no correspondence between the language used to depict the Orient and the Orient itself because the language is not trying to be accurate: it aims to provide a ready-made vocabulary for all subsequent understandings and writings of the Orient. In other words, the language of representing the Orient need not match the Orient's material reality; it was enough to provide a ready-made language in which the Orient could be described by any Westerner.

However, Orientalism also sought as accurate a *knowledge* of the Orient through Oriental 'projects' – of translation, codification of Oriental texts, information (of oriental laws, for example). The colonial administrative and military structure needed information about their subjects in order to govern them effectively. William Jones, appointed Governor General of British India in the last decades of the eighteenth century, in fact drew up a personal list of domains in which he hoped to acquire competence so that he could rule India better. Jones writes:

The objects of enquiry during my residence in Asia:
   I. The laws of the Hindus and Mahomedans.
   II. The history of the ancient world.
  III. Proofs and illustrations of scripture.
  IV. Traditions concerning the deluge, etc.
   V. Modern politics and geography of Hindustan.
  VI. Best mode of governing Bengal.
 VII. Arithmetic and geometry and mixed sciences of Asiaticks.
VIII. Medicine, chemistry, surgery. And anatomy of the Indians.
 IX. Natural products of India.
  X. Poetry, rhetoric and morality of Asia.
 XI. Music of the Eastern nations.
XII. The She-King or 300 Chinese odes.
XIII. The best accounts of Tibet and Kashmir.
XIV. Trade, manufactures, agriculture and commerce of India.
 XV. Mughal constitution
XVI. Maharatta constitution.
     (Memorandum 12 July 1783, quoted. in S. N. Mukherjee 1987, pp. 68–9)

Jones evidently wished to be intimately acquainted with most matters Indian.

Said's thesis is simple enough: in the case of the colonial encounter, knowledge was power. The more the European 'knew' the colony, the better could be the forms of administrative, legislative, social and political control. To return to William Jones, we can discern this very real connection between colonial knowledge and colonial control in his speech to the Asiatick Society – an organization founded in 1784 to gather information – on 24 February 1785. Jones begins by asserting the superiority of Western knowledge, but he also suggests that knowledge of the East might prove useful:

> although we must be conscious of our superior advancement in all kinds of useful knowledge, yet we ought not therefore to contemn the people of *Asia,* from whose researches into nature, works of art, and inventions of fancy, many valuable hints may be derived for our own improvement and advantage. (Jones 1807, III, p. 11)

He then proposes a justification for acquiring such knowledge:

> The Jurisprudence of the *Hindus* and *Muselmans* will produce more immediate advantage; and, if some standard *law-tracts* were accurately translated from the *Sanscrit* and *Arabick*, we might hope in time to see so complete a Digest of *Indian* Laws, that all disputes among the natives might be decided without *uncertainty,* which is in truth a disgrace, though satirically called a *glory,* to the forensick science. (Jones 1807, III, pp. 11–23, emphasis in original)

Such projects of translation, codification, historiography and social history, argues Said, were accompanied by military and other projects (e.g. De Lesseps and Suez reduced the metaphoric and literal distance of the Oriental world from the West). Textual and military, cultural and political projects went hand-in-hand in Orientalism.

Later travellers and soldiers went into the Orient accompanied by this same textual knowledge, with information about the place they were about to visit, live in and administer gathered from earlier

Orientalist texts that, by the early nineteenth century, begins to acquire the magnitude of an imperial archive. Thus their attitudes, responses, policies and interactions with natives were mediated by and shot through with the 'knowledge', prejudices and stereotypes they had acquired through the Orientalist texts. Thus *texts constructed their very experience of the reality of the Orient*. What Said was emphasizing was the *textual* and *discursive* nature of colonial power and domination.

Orientalism was thus a Western projection onto the East. It codified the East into a set formula, a set of characteristics and detail that was treated as fixed and unchanging in time and place. By 'authoritative' commentary, Orientalism essentializes the Oriental as a dehumanized being, fixes him/her in a stereotype. Thus the stereotypes of the 'treacherous Brahmin', the 'effeminate native', the 'child-like native' and the cruel Muslim king were unified, unchanging constructions of the natives that, for administrative and political purposes, 'captured' the Easterner. The stereotype, by the very fact of being 'unchanging', was therefore easily governed.

Ethnology as a discipline that classified the Oriental emerged during the nineteenth century. We thus see a typology of the human race emerging: 'wild men', the Europeans, the Asiatics, etc., where physiological and moral characters are merged. The task of the Orientalist was to 'reveal' the Orient secularized forms through philology, history and anthropology, and thus making Orientalism itself a 'scientific' discipline.

Orientalism is 'cumulative', and achieved through the mixture of traditional learning (the classics, philology), public institutions (governments, trading companies, geographical societies, universities) and generically determined writing (travel books, books of exploration, exotic descriptions, fantasy). Said notes that the age of Orientalism is also the period of greater territorial expansion. Thus the academic study of the Orient went hand-in-hand with the *use* of the knowledge in conquest and dominance.

However, it must be noted that Orientalism itself changed its form. By the late eighteenth and early nineteenth century Orientalism acquired a popular form in addition to the academic one (the latter being the domain of the Chairs of Oriental or Sanskrit studies in British and European universities). John MacKenzie's work on imperial popular culture (1989) demonstrates how magazines, newspapers and other popular forms seemed to have worked through Orientalist views for the 'common' British reader. Nigel Leask's work (1993) demonstrates how English Romantic poets, Wordsworth, Coleridge, Shelley and Southey, show clear signs of being interested in and influenced by India-themes. In terms of popular representations, the Orient was linked with idyllic pleasure, intense energy, terror and sensuality, a place of romance and danger, but also adventure, vast fortunes and the opportunity for the Westerner to acquire fame. Martin Green (1980) shows that it was the Orientalist adventure tales of R. M Ballantyne and Rider Haggard, that inspired young English men to go out and seek their fortunes in the East.

Said discerns two forms of Orientalism. There is a 'latent Orientalism', which is an unconscious set of views about the Orient full of stereotypes, fantasies and fears. Then there is a 'manifest Orientalism' which is Said's term for the *stated* and articulated views about Oriental society in history and literature. While the form or manifest Orientalism may change, the unconscious remains the same. That is, the stereotypes and cultural beliefs about the Orient remained more or less consistent throughout the imperial age, even if the form of their expression changed.

Orientalism had a 'worldly' effect on the white man. The white man was an idea as well as a reality – one thought, behaved and spoke in certain ways. It was a form of authority and a view of the world. It was a policy towards the world, where the white man, instilled with (Orientalist) views of Western superiority or racial difference, developed a set of attitudes towards the Easterner. What Said is arguing is that Orientalism resulted in colonial attitudes, as well as colonial policies. The white man thus functioned within a policy/vision of a binary: us and them. 'Us' was defined by particular forms of art, history, ideas and rationality. 'Them' was the object studied by the Occidental/white man. Orientalism allowed the Orient to be spoken of in certain ways and every author/text fitted into this tradition of speaking. All writing therefore belonged to a recognizable and authoritative convention – one put in place by Orientalism.

While every traveller/individual White Man assumed that his view of the Orient came from a personal/individual encounter with the Orient, it actually proceeded from a larger and more general field. This imbrication of the personal with the cultural-general furthered the Empire and imperial projects: the white *individual* out in the Orient observed the Orient and imbibed knowledge about and put it to *use* in the cause of his country's conquest, control and expansion. This is the 'instrumental' attitude within Orientalism, especially visible from the mid-nineteenth century, the heyday of Empire. Thus Said emphasizes that it is not simply the 'discursive' aspect of Orientalism but its *material* and *institutional* presence that is crucial. To phrase it differently, Orientalism is a system of representation that operates for a purpose. Every individual Orientalist provided Orientalist discourse with what it needed at the moment (the idea of 'discovery' in the sixteenth and seventeenth centuries' period of exploration, or the idea of the barbarism of Oriental religion in the nineteenth-century age of reform). That is, Orientalism responded to certain cultural, national, political and economic demands of the imperial age.

In the twentieth century, especially after 1970s, the Arab Muslim becomes the site of the biggest Orientalist project. Popular images and social science representations showed him as a threat. Propaganda worked with this set of images, and cultural-relations policy was influenced by these representations. Western attitudes after 9/11 show a continuity of this tradition whereby the 'inscrutable' Arab is now a threat (Salaita 2005). Indeed, as Richard Cimino shows (2005), the discourse on the primitiveness and 'inherent' violence of Islam in American evangelical discourse after 9/11 shows remarkable – and frightening – continuities with nineteenth-century Orientalist thought.

Said's reading of colonialism as Orientalism influenced the first wave of postcolonial studies. These exhibited a more or less steadfast adherence to Said's view of Orientalism as a dominating, powerful mode of controlling the non-European. Texts from scholars like John MacKenzie (1988, 1989), Anne McClintock (1995), Jenny Sharpe (1993), Peter Hulme (1992), Stephen Greenblatt (1991) and Sara Suleri (1992) built on the Saidian paradigm and focused on *colonial discourse* – the narrative unified what represented and influenced colonial relationships. These studies were characterized by a focus on

- forms of colonial discourses in various settings (Australia, America, Asia, Africa);
- forms of colonial domination and control while ignoring resistance and schisms in colonial discourse;

- stereotypes of natives, representations of exotic Others, the dismissal of native culture, the demonization of native religion, the subtle representations of colonial control and authority;
- language, narrative and literary-cultural practices.

MacKenzie shows how the English popular press or the wildlife/nature conservation movements in nineteenth and early twentieth century represented the native animals and humans in particular so that it justified stricter laws, British imperial surveys and controls. Suleri shows how Edmund Burke's speeches at the impeachment of Warren Hastings combined the aesthetic theories of the sublime with colonial discourse to represent an unknowable, obscure India. Anne McClintock and Jenny Sharpe show how colonial discourse used the native woman as a boundary-figure: the safety of the native woman becomes, in this discourse, the European man's prerogative and duty because the native male was either the oppressor (of the native woman) or was effeminate. Greenblatt demonstrates how, using a rhetoric of wonder, Columbus manages to trope the 'new world' as empty and ready for conquest.

CRITICAL RACE THEORY AND STUDIES

Critical Race Theory and Race Studies have fed into postcolonial thought in direct as well as indirect ways. The overlaps and intersections are both understandable and necessary, since both deal with the centrality of race to identity-formation, political matters and literary representations. Critical Race Studies (CRS) foregrounds race and ethnicity as key categories in the analysis of law, history, politics and culture.

Race has served as a marker of difference, a difference that leads to slavery, exploitation and death. While biological evidence for the superiority of one race or another has not emerged, the social and political fields are rooted in discourses that consistently deploy race as difference. Critical Race Studies examines these discourses and representational strategies of racial marking. Critical Race Studies includes various components since the 1980s: Black Feminism, Aboriginal and First Nation peoples' studies, Mestizo and 'mixed race' studies. In this section I shall quickly survey these main strands in Critical Race Studies.

Cornel West has located a genealogy of racism:

- Greek antiquity through the early modern period to the 1600–1800,
- The period of emerging botanical, phrenological and other 'scientific' theories and,
- The Enlightenment and nineteenth century.

West locates racial theories as discourses that link social theories with science and economic theories in order to show the history of racist discrimination (West 2002). Race therefore is a marker of *difference*. Racial difference marks distinctions of language, beliefs, artistic traditions but also natural attributes such as athletic ability.

A related strand within Critical Race Studies is the emphasis, from the 1990s, on First Nation peoples and Aboriginal cultures. The turn to native studies is affiliated with social, legal and political movements seeking aboriginal rights, land rights, welfare and recognition. These studies note how Aboriginal writings emphasize the interconnected-ness of all life, the domination of white settlers, the exploitation of their lands and the suppression of their way of life. I have elsewhere argued that Aboriginal writing might be categorized as 'postcolonial' along with other cultures from Asia, Africa and South America because they have been conquered and oppressed and their cultures marginalized (Nayar 2008a, p. 89). Aboriginal and First Peoples cultures must be read as an instance of the *literature of the exploited, the culture of resistance* and the *cultures of revival*. Aboriginal writing gestures at cultures of oppression (settlers) and their binary opposite, 'cultures of survival' (aboriginals) and recent critical theories emerging from within such a writing foregrounds survival, nature, spirituality, home/lands as concerns informing First Peoples cultures.

'Mixed race' studies emerged from three major intellectual and social contexts: poststructuralist literary-cultural theory of the 1970s and 1980s accompanied by historical research, heightened migration and the formation of multicultural cities and populations and the rise of black and non-white public intellectuals. These included not only high-profile, and recognizable, artists and authors like Toni Morrison, Michael Jackson and Maya Angelou, but also university professors like Stuart Hall, Cornel West, Kwame Appiah, bell hooks (black) Edward Said, Gayatri Spivak, Homi Bhabha (Asian) and Gloria Anzaldua and Cherri Moraga (Chicano). Since the late 1990s 'mixed race' has shifted more towards identity politics in complex multiracial formations and populations. Thus Danzy Senna (2004) speaks of a 'Mulatto Nation' where there could be any number of variations on the 'mulatto' theme, including Jewlatto (Jews *and* Blacks), Gelatto (Italia American *and* African American), Cablinasian (mix of Asian, American Indian, Black and Caucasian), among others (2004, pp. 205–8). Artists and theorists like Gloria Anzaldua and Cherrie Moraga have spoken of Chicano/a identity as border-crossing, *mestizaje*. The *mestiza* is the hybrid, the site of cultural encounter, cross-breeding and conflict. Alfred Arteaga (1997) explores the 'impure' state of bodies, borders and border-crossing in his study of Chicano/a poetry, treating Chicano/a subjectivity as a 'site of cultural interaction' (p. 9), always already contaminated and hybridized. Thus *mestizo* theories and poetics opt for difference, multiplicity, hybridity and ambiguity and cultural diversity. As we shall see in the chapter on cosmopolitanism, 'mixed race' studies have reoriented postcolonial theory and studies.

A specific strand focusing on the intersection of race and gender in Critical Theory is that of Black Feminism.

Born Gloria Watkins, bell hooks is one of the leading commentators on gender and race matters in contemporary literary and cultural theory. Her *Ain't I a Woman? Black Women and Feminism* (1981) was one of the early articulations of a problematic relationship – that between race and gender. Do black women experience sexism the same way as white women do? Does 'race' become a critical category in the relationship between women? How does feminism appeal to white and black women?

hooks argued that sexism combined with racism during slavery in America and contributed to the double marginalization of black women. The black woman was marginalized on account of her race and her gender, and consigned to the lowest strata of American society and culture. hooks argued that for white feminists the white woman was the norm and standard, always depicting her as the virgin, the goddess or the wronged one. This ignored the conditions of black women because black femininity was treated as promiscuous, impure and immoral. hooks suggests that this demonization of the black woman justified rape, oppression and slavery of the black woman, even when the white women were fighting for equal rights.

Building on the work of bell hooks, a new version of the feminist movement emerged in the 1980s: black feminism. Black feminism was oppositional to both patriarchy and racism, to both sexism and white feminism. bell hooks writes:

> black feminists found that sisterhood for most white women did not mean surrendering allegiance to race, class, and sexual preference . . . we witnessed the appropriation of feminist ideology by elitist, racist white women. (1981, pp. 188–9)

Black feminism emerges with a double agenda, to

- Question the *masculinist-patriarchal* ideologies of the Black movement
- Question the *racism* in the feminist movement.

The writings of Patricia Hill Collins, Hortense Spillers and Hazel Carby in the 1990s, marked the beginnings of black feminist critical theory. The aim here was to create forms of knowledge built upon the lived experiences of black women that had thus far been marginalized within mainstream (white) feminism. This entailed the creation of an archive, the compilation of a tradition of black women's writing, oral traditions, folk lore and other forms of cultural practices (as a result the researches uncovered Ma Rainey, Bessie Smith, Billie Holiday and Blues). It also meant a reappraisal and critical scrutiny of early forms of black writings (Hazel Carby's critical work on nineteenth-century black women novelists 1987, for instance).

Black feminism unraveled stereotypes of mammies and matriarchs, arguing that these stereotypes constructed the black woman as the Other. The black woman is either the faithful family servant (the mammy) or the sexual object. However, Hazel Carby argues (2000), notions of family, patriarchy and reproduction critiqued by white feminism mean very different things for *black* women: black men have not always held the same positions of power within the black family, black women have headed households and they have often laboured within both black and white households.

In the chapter on 'gender and sexuality' we shall see the emergence and expansion of postcolonial feminisms.

POSTCOLONIAL 'THEORY'

From the 1990s race has been one of the most influential categories in cultural analysis. Postcolonial 'theory' is a method of interpreting, reading and critiquing the cultural practices of colonialism, where it proposes that the exercise of colonial power is also the exercise of racially determined powers of representation. It argues that race and racial discourses enable colonial powers to represent, reflect, refract and make visible native cultures in particular ways preliminary to ordering and controlling these cultures. Postcolonial theory is an analytical-critical approach that treats colonial writing, arts, legal systems, science and other socio-cultural practices as racialized and unequal where the colonial does the representation and the native is represented.

The complex relation of race and Empire within colonial discourse and arts has been studied for various regions (Asia, Africa, South America, Ireland and the settler colonies of Australia and Canada). The first major theorists, Edward Said, Gayatri Spivak and Homi Bhabha 'read' colonial texts for the implicit and explicit colonial ideologies. Later critics expanded their work to analyse figures of native resistance, native collaboration and internally divided colonial discourse.

Gayatri Chakravorty Spivak

Spivak's work is situated at the intersection of several critical approaches: poststructuralism, feminism and Marxism. Spivak argues that subjects are constituted *through* discourse. An individual develops an identity because she/he is the subject of a discourse over which she/he may have little or no control. Such a subjugated subject is what Spivak terms the 'subaltern' (a term she adopts from the Italian political theorist Antonio Gramsci). The subaltern is one who has no position or sovereignty outside the discourse that constructs her as subject. In her most-quoted essay, 'Can the Subaltern Speak?' (1985), Spivak rejects the idea that one can access a 'pure' subaltern consciousness because the subaltern cannot speak, and is hence spoken *for*.

She argues, via a reading of a woman's suicide in early twentieth-century India, that the structure of colonialism prevents any speaking.

This structure is *doubly* strengthened in the case of the native woman, who is silenced through both patriarchy and colonialism. That is, she is *silenced for her gender as well as her race*. Hence, reduced to silence by these structures, the woman writes her body. Spivak argues that the subaltern wrote her body, because there was no other way of speaking. The subaltern woman has no position of enunciation: she remains within the discourse of patriarchy and colonialism as the object of somebody else's discourse. All notions and representations of 'subaltern' consciousness or 'Third World' women, are in effect constructions of Western discourses. These discourses construct the subaltern and give it a voice.

This interpretation of course produced a body of work that has sought to, alternately, agree with and disparage Spivak. There is, however, an urgent need to respond ethically to the voice of the subaltern. Spivak proposes that the subaltern can figure only in an ethical relation where there is the deliberate creation of a space for the voice of the radical Other.

Homi Bhabha

Bhabha's work makes a significant departure from the Saidian paradigm by revealing how colonial discourse was often internally flawed, contradictory and divisive and often *failed*. His work has also been instrumental in revealing native subversion of what has always been taken as a monolithic and seamless power structure (the Empire and colonial discourse).

Bhabha notes how identities in the colonial encounter are never stable or fixed but function as *transactions* between colonizer and colonized. The European in the colony can construct his identity only through a relationality based on difference. Bhabha proposes that identities are based on differential relations: the colonizer establishes his identity by positioning himself against and in opposition to the native. 'I am white because I am not this brown man' – it is this structure of relational, and race-determined difference that helps the white man construct his identity.

From this it follows that the colonizer does not possess a self-identical identity: he needs the colonized-native for contrast. In other words, it is the presence of the brown or black Other that creates the white man's identity. Bhabha suggests here that we cannot see colonial identity as fixed or monolithic: it is unstable, relational and dependent upon the native. This is a major shift in the way we deal with colonial discourse because Bhabha is suggesting that the white man depends on the native for his own identity.

Bhabha proposes that colonial discourse is actually ambivalent. The colonial master is actually informed by two contradictory psychic states: what Bhabha terms 'fetish' and 'phobia'. Bhabha argues that the festish/phobia structure of colonial relations results in a condition where the white man both fears *and* desires the Other (the black or brown native), while at the same time wishes to erase the difference. The colonizer is both fascinated by the difference and also repulsed by it. This 'ambivalence' of the colonial results in stereotypes such as that of the unknowable native and the vulnerable, innocent or childlike native. In the first stereotype the colonial power is baffled and fascinated by the inscrutability of the native and in the second he is a knowable subject of the all-powerful colonial master. Bhabha thus proposes a *divided* colonial discourse, and a *native subject* whose subject-position, like the *colonial master's*, is never stable or automatic. The repetition of stereotypes (such as the ones mentioned above) is not a sign of the power of colonial discourse. Rather, it is a sign of its *instability*. Stereotypes are invoked and repeated not because they are stable but because, unless repeated, they lose their power and validity *as* signs.

As an example of this repetition Bhabha uses the 'English book', the Bible, in his essay, 'Signs Taken for Wonders'. Bhabha argues that the Bible functioned as a sign of colonial power: the authority to disseminate the book throughout the colony. However, Bhabha notes, the *sign* (or book) is ambivalent as soon as it is disseminated. Bhabha suggests that the book is 'translated' by natives into their own contexts, a process that often involves subversion and sometimes resistance. There is no 'original' Bible that can reflect colonial authority totally because the natives have transformed it into what they see fit and which suits them at that time. When the native repeats the English book, she/he does so with variations. Thus the book acquires a wholly different form and loses its authority as a colonial sign becoming instead a sign that has been rewritten by the native. The 'authority' of the book, in other words, is not what the colonial intends, but what the *native* makes of it (Bhabha 2009b). This is the inherent instability of colonial discourse, and the potential for resistance. Bhabha uses the term 'ambivalence' to describe this *rupture* between the hoped-for original authority of the English book/sign and the effect of repetition and difference.

In his next key move to demonstrate the instability of colonial discourse, Bhabha proposes the idea of 'mimicry' in his essay 'Of Mimicry and Man'. Mimicry is the disciplined, conscious imitation of the white man by the colonized and supposedly subservient native. The native has been taught that he must ape the white man and immerse himself in the white man's culture. Western education, religion and structures are modes through which the native is trained to think/behave *like* the white man. Bhabha argues that this act of mimicry is a site where colonial authority, rather than being reinforced, actually breaks down. The native becomes Anglicized but is never truly white. He is a mimic who can now respond in English and argue rationally (rather than sentimentally, which would be a stereotypical 'native' or Oriental form of argumentation) because of Western education. When Raja Rammohun Roy argues in favour of English education in his letter to Lord Amherst (1827), he appropriates a rational argument rather than a sentimental one: he appeals to the English in the language of logic, reason, administrative convenience and expediency. The 'mimic man' here appears to have adopted the white man's authority but in effect fractures and disrupts it. Mimicry here reveals the incomplete and fractured nature in the colonial discourse which can therefore *never be total in its authority* (Bhabha 2009a).

This mimicry also fails because the colonial master wants the native as similar to himself as possible and yet wishes to retain the difference between himself and the native. That is, the colonial wishes to *both erase and reinforce difference*. Similarly, the native repeats or mimes the master, but with subtle variations and nuances. The mimicry of the native often consists of both a *superficial* obedience and a *deeper* disobedience and mockery (what Bhabha terms 'sly civility', 2009c). The native seems to express servility but in fact articulates resistance. This dual state of mimicry by the native is what Bhabha terms 'hybridity'.

This hybridized native who refuses to acknowledge the colonizer's authority, is placed in a position of *in-betweenness*: between 'adopted' Englishness and the 'original' native condition or identity, between obedience and resistance. This hybridity creates a 'third space' where

- colonial identity and native identity meet and often contest,
- colonial discourse is both asserted *and* subverted,

- there is deference *and* difference,
- there is a split and a negotiation (within colonial discourse),
- where mimicry *and* mockery occur.

Bhabha's work therefore shows the failures of colonial discourse. He shows how native resistance emerges because colonial discourse is incomplete.

Paul Gilroy

Paul Gilroy's work on British and Black identities in *There Ain't No Black in the Union Jack* (1987 [2002]) and *The Black Atlantic* (1993) has added a new dimension to postcolonial theory: that of diaspora, multiculturalism and cosmopolitanism. Here race studies refuses to treat black or native cultures as simply the Other of white-colonial cultures. Gilroy's efforts have been to show how each culture learns from and is constitutive of the Other. Gilroy argued that British identity was built by consciously excluding the black presence within it: Asians and blacks who, since the fifteenth century, were central to the very idea of Englishness, English identity and the colonial construction of England as a nation in the nineteenth century are ignored when speaking of a 'pure' English identity. Englishness came to be associated the white culture be erasing black presences. Gilroy argued that the Atlantic and American culture was the consequence of black cultures in contest and contact with white ones. The '*black Atlantic*', as he terms it, is the space of diasporic, transnational and *hybrid* cultures.

Gilroy argued that hybrid spaces emerge when African cultures meet European ones and vice versa. Right from the time of the slave trade Africans moving towards the 'new world' became diasporic, with a consciousness of *both* European and African cultures. This double consciousness is a productive cultural condition. Gilroy suggests that *black Atlantic* and 'transculturation' (Marie Louis Pratt's term, 1992) works both ways: Africans learn from and adapt to European cultures and Europeans seeing, recognize an Other culture.

Gilroy shows how African American authors exhibit this double consciousness. Gilroy argues that we must see displacement, the trans-Atlantic voyage and interaction, the origin-new world binary as culturally productive in its hybridity. These are not simply 'home versus away' displacement narrative but fertile sites of cultural hybridity. One cannot, therefore, see African American culture as rooted in the mythic African 'home' cultures perhaps because the trans-Atlantic experience has always been a part of Black consciousness.

Arif Dirlik

Paralleling Gilroy's work on hybridity and transculturation is the work of Arif Dirlik.

Dirlik's famous debut in postcolonial theory came with his now-classic 1994 essay, 'The Postcolonial Aura'. Dirlik argued that the epistemological claims made by postcolonial intellectuals are at odds with the realities of cultural and political domination. Postcolonial intellectuals working in Western universities make strategic claims about their independence of thought, when these are made possible by their presence within neocolonial and racialized structures of Western culture and academia. Ethically speaking, Dirlik suggests, the postcolonial intellectual cannot write from within this position. In other words, postcolonial theory is the result of class privileges granted to 'Third World' academics by First World academia: '[postcolonial theory happens] when Third World intellectuals have arrived in the First World' (Dirlik 1997, p. 294). Leela Gandhi points out that Dirlik's metaphor of 'having arrived' suggests an opportunism where the intellectual flees the material conditions of the Third World 'into the abstraction of metropolitan theory' (Gandhi 1999, p. 58).

In his more recent work Arif Dirlik has argued that ethnic writers have been burdened with the task of providing an ethnography of culture for Western consumption. Dirlik suggests an interesting turn is visible in ethnic writing today. The

> appropriation of politics for literature implies also a privatization of history . . . replacing politics conceived as public activity by politics conceived as identity politics . . . a displacement of political questions to the realm of culture. (2002, p. 214)

Dirlik suggests that the crucial marker of ethnic writing today is its problematic negotiation between history and literature. For Dirlik, this burdens the writer with tasks that undermine her or his autonomy. Such ethnic writing is bestowed the task of addressing a collective identity. The writer has to mediate between different times and spaces, to translate from its 'original' or national idiom which now includes many languages. This is the 'burden' of the transnational literary text, for Dirlik.

Aijaz Ahmad

Dirlik's claims – and accusations – against the postcolonial intellectual anticipates Aijaz Ahmad's critique of Edward Said in his 1995 essay 'The Politics of Literary Postcoloniality' in which Ahmad claims that there is the luxury of shifting identities and hybridity afforded to the postcolonial intellectual situated in the *West* when real people in the postcolonial society struggle with their social and material identity, often in conditions of abject poverty. Ahmad argues that cultural hybridity is deemed to be 'specific to . . . the migrant intellectual, living and working in the western metropolis' (1997, p. 286). Such an intellectual is, in Ahmad's words, 'remarkably free of gender, class, identifiable political location' (p. 287). Such a position, argues Ahmad, denies the real material conditions of the postcolonial in the Third World – who is still caught in caste, class and gender identities. 'Only the privileged [migrant] can live a life of constant mobility', writes Ahmad (p. 289). Postcoloniality, sums up Ahmad, is 'a matter of class' (p. 289).

Ahmad and Dirlik provide a necessary corrective to the excessive emphasis on escaping identity in Bhabha's theorizing and the fiction of Salman Rushdie. The living postcolonial condition is tied (down) to caste, class and gender identities. Institutional support for the postcolonial intellectual – which allows him/her to theorize – is very different from the low-paid, poorly supported academic in the Third World university.

Michael Hardt and Antonio Negri

Aligning 'conventional' colonialism and colonial ideologies with contemporary globalization, Hardt and Negri in their *Empire* (2000) offer insights into new forms of colonial domination that emerge since the 1980s. Hardt and Negri define the new Empire thus:

It is a decentered and deterritorializing apparatus of rule that progressively incorporates the entire global realm within its open, expanding frontiers. Empire manages hybrid identities, flexible hierarchies, and plural exchanges through modulating networks of command. The distinct national colors of the imperialist map of the world have merged and blended in the imperial global rainbow. (2000, pp. 12–13)

Traditional colonialism was based on a clear binary: 'us' (as in white, European) and 'them' (as in brown or black, non-European). European metropolises sent in armies to conquer and control parts of Africa, Asia and South America. In the 'new world order' imperialism and colonialism take a very different form. The 'Empire' is now diffuse, without a real political centre or periphery. Interest groups, business conglomerates and international organizations (NATO, IMF, G8) create policies that affect the financial, social and political decisions of all other countries, even when they are not always signatories to these decisions and treaties. Such an Empire is more 'total' than earlier regimes because it lacks a specific centre – such as London used to be for the British Empire – that can be attacked.

Nation-based power structures collapse in the globalized era, and power is 'centred' elsewhere. Borders and regulations collapse so that finance flows from the new colonies (the postcolonial states) to the Microsoft or McDonald's coffers continues what earlier colonialism did. The new Empire is therefore ghostly, phantasmatic because its structures are not clearly visible, its leaders not knowable and its headquarters never identifiable. There is no real visible ruling class either. The Empire shifts shape and nature, spreading across military, political, economic and social domains. The new Empire is a series of such flows. Instead of the map (the dominant tool of colonial Empires) we now have a *route* of flows. Instead of national and regional territories during colonialism we now have global networks. Global economic inequalities exist, of course, and power remains in the West. The difference of course is that the *colonial power is not state-based* (in the nineteenth century the British Empire was based in the nation-state of Britain, as were the Dutch or French Empires). It is amorphous, free-floating and shifting.

Globalization puts in place specific economic, cultural and juridical structures. Hardt and Negri have detailed, with immense perspicacity, some of these structures. Even the notion of a 'global civil society', they argue, 'evoke the values of globalism that would infuse the new international order' (p. 7). The idea of a 'just war', they suggest, grants legitimacy to the military apparatus and treats military action as a means to achieve peace (p. 13). The new juridical apparatus of Empire also appears in the guise of 'global order' or 'justice' and 'right'. 'We are forced', write Hardt and Negri, 'increasingly to feel that we are participants in this development . . . the external morality of every human being and citizen is by now commensurable only in the framework of Empire' (p. 19).

Hardt and Negri identify three 'principles' of the new Empire: US nuclear supremacy represents the new monarchy, the economic wealth of the G7 and transnational corporations the aristocratic, and the Internet the democratic principle. Empire now, encourages multiculturalism – it is inclusionary, a 'machine for universal integration' (p. 198), so that there is no resistance or conflict. It affirms differences as a mode of imperial control. As Hardt and Negri put it: 'many official promotions of traditional ethnic and cultural differences [come] under the umbrella of universal inclusion' (p. 199). In other words, differences are subsumed into a gigantic machine of uniformity, and retained as non-threatening differences that are exclusively cultural and not political.

* * *

Postcolonialism as a form of cultural criticism has much to offer:

1. emancipation from restrictive forms of thinking,
2. a political consciousness of literary and cultural traditions of the Third World,
3. an alertness to the ways in which non-European/non-white races and their cultures have been represented and 'naturalized' by colonialism and neocolonialism for consumption,
4. an engagement with continuing forms of intellectual (as well as economic) dependence of the Third World upon the First,
5. a consciousness of the new forms of colonialism emergent in globalized conditions, among others.

It is, above all, *political criticism* in the sense it is alert to the power structures and struggles within the cultural domain. While it is true that much postcolonial thought continues to rework colonialism into its main agenda, it has also moved on to addressing and scrutinizing larger questions and domains of human rights, environment, neocolonialism, diaspora, globalization and techno-capitalism. Pride in native/local cultures has been resurgent under postcolonial thought, even as nativism and cultural nationalisms have come under suspicion for encouraging xenophobia and retrogressive parochialisms (especially in the wake of the events in Rwanda or Sudan and the rise of religious fundamentalisms in various postcolonial nations). While postcolonialism does foreground questions of race and ethnicity it has increasingly turned away from the traditional 'master race/ victim race' binary of the early postcolonials of the 1980s. Indeed, postcolonialism does see empowerment in racial difference now. This agenda of postcolonialism as a form of thinking that helps emancipation, empowerment and enlightened engagement is best summarized by Henry Louis Gates Jr's evocative comment:

We must now look beyond the I-got-mine parochialism of a desperate era. We must look beyond that over-worked master-plot of victims and victimizers. (1992, p. 151)

CHAPTER TWO

COLONIAL CULTURES

*Female children are regarded with dislike and dread . . . For genera-
tions the practice has prevailed of reducing, by more or less violent
means, the unwelcome moiety of the population . . . Efforts to check
the barbarous habit have been made by the British Officers, in various ways, for the last seventy years . . . in 1870 it was found necessary
to pass an Act for the application of special regulations to districts
or villages suspected of the practice.*

(Memorandum of the Census of India,
1871–1872 (1875), pp. 5–9, 10–19, 19–37)

Postcolonialism demonstrates how colonialism had its impact not
only in the political and economic arena but in the cultural domain
as well. Colonial domination of regions as diverse and expansive
as India was possible not only because of their (England's) superior
military strength but also because of their clever ways of manipulat-
ing the *cultural* domain: literature, the arts, architecture, the law, education, history-writing, anthropology and ethnography. Colonialism
studied, categorized, archived and disseminated native cultures
before enacting laws, affecting changes and undertaking 'reform' in
these domains. Colonialism masked its exploitative structures under
the guise of paternalistic benevolence, coding colonial domination
as acts of generosity, reform, 'development', welfare and stability.
Over a period of time, these 'codes' sedimented as beliefs among
the natives who then began to see the colonial masters exactly as
the masters wanted themselves to be seen: as gentle, firm, just and
benevolent protectors. These codes constitute the *ideology* of empire
and colonialism.[1]

Postcolonialism examines the cultural dimensions of the colonial project. It investigates how, in the colonial project:

- Political expansion, conquest and dominance had their effects and equivalents in the cultural domain.
- Ideologies of empire – dominance, difference, benevolence, the master-slave relationship, 'improvement' – found their most insidious expression in the cultural domain.
- Imperial ideologies were disseminated through the subject races through forms like the arts, education, religious instruction, the law or architecture so that they were cast as aesthetic, philosophical, literary or moral forms rather than as ideologies.
- Imperial ideology thus circulated became acceptable and 'natural' so that racism, imperialism and conquest were justified, legitimized and naturalized in the guise of philosophical, charitable or aesthetic principles.
- Imperial ideologies were internalized by the natives as 'true' representations, who therefore demanded, accepted and even supported the empire.

Edward Said summarizes postcolonialism's political reading of the colonial archive in *Culture and Imperialism*:

Neither imperialism nor colonialism is a simple act of accumulation and acquisition . . . Out of the imperial experiences, notions about culture were classified, reinforced, criticised, or rejected. (1994b, pp. 7–8)

Postcolonialism demonstrates that colonial cultures were instruments of imperial control and power but cast in roles/forms that naturalized them and made them acceptable. This chapter is a postcolonial exposition on colonialism's cultural practices and politics.

COLONIAL CULTURES AND THE CIVILIZING MISSION

To the state all eastern people look for enlightenment as well as protection. Unable to govern themselves, a strong government is to the people of India a condition of their very existence. Without the strong arm of the law to protect from robbers, India would fall into anarchy; and the tiger, and the jungle at last encroach on and expel man from the plain country.

(Anon 1858, p. 645)

Mr Goodcountry in Chinua Achebe's *Arrow of God* (1967) captures the essence of colonialism's civilizing mission: he wishes to 'save [Igbos] from the error [of their religious ways] which was now threatening to ruin them' (269). The white settler in Australia looks upon the harsh landscape and ascribes meanings: 'Horror can be ascribed and strange commissions given/to the fireless dooligarl' (Murray, 'Physiognomy on the Savage Manning River', 1992, p. 9). The 'civilizing mission' was visible in the colonial project from the latter decades of the eighteenth century. The 'civilizing mission' was the justification and legitimization of colonial rule but one which ran a risk: once the native had been civilized through colonial intervention then the justification for the colonizer remaining in the colony would disappear.

The colonial's civilizing mission worked on particular principles and ideas:

- Rule of law and good governance,
- Christian charity,
- Morality, as defined by European standards and cultures,
- Hard work,
- Material and technological reform of the country,
- Moral reform of natives,
- Native incapacity to govern, improve, educate themselves,
- The absence of a tradition to which the native could turn.

These ideas and principles constituted a colonial *discourse* of the native in narratives, images and representations.

The civilizing mission of the European colonial was another (more acceptable, less brutal-looking) name for intervention. This colonial intervention was often two-fold:

- Material-technological
- Moral

The first aimed at a radical and visible change in the condition of native cities, economy, the infrastructure and the institutions (railways, medical practices, navigation). The second aimed at a change in belief systems, native ways of thinking, 'character-building' of the natives and such 'abstract' domains. The second brought in Christianity, European principles of law, education, political theories and aesthetic ideas. Proceeding from the assumption that the natives were either primitive, barbaric and pagan in their beliefs, the colonials set themselves the task of reforming native religions, introducing Western principles of governance and Christianity. Battling the natives' social 'evils' thus became integral to the civilizing mission.

The cultures of the colonized were treated as primitive and in urgent need of 'development' by the Europeans. While white civilization had evolved and grown, the native cultures had remained stagnant in their old world:

> Australia is the present home and refuge of creatures, often crude and quaint, that have elsewhere passed away and given place to higher forms. This applies equally well to the aboriginal as to the platypus and kangaroo. (quoted in Ryan 1994, p. 121)

The description, by anthropologist Baldwin Spencer writing in 1927, is paradigmatic of a colonial view that envisaged development only as European intervention. In other words, the civilizing mission was based on the view that the native cultures could progress only through an *external* means, since the cultures had decayed to the point that they could not redeem themselves.

The 'civilizing mission' of colonialism was based on a clear distinction or binary: the primitive non-European versus the developed European. The native would be the pupil, child and servant to the European teacher, parent and master. This civilizing mission came into prominence mainly with the Evangelical movement from the last decades of the eighteenth century. Discipline, rigour and morality became the codes by which the colonizers were supposed to function, and of course, work to instil these same values in the wretched natives. 'Civilizing', therefore, was quite often interchangeable with 'Christianity' (though debates raged about the wisdom of proselytizing). William Bentinck, the Governor General of British India (1828–1835) argued that unless Hinduism and native beliefs were modified (or recast within a European framework, for example in Halhed's *Code of Gentoo Laws*, 1776) the social evils of the country could not be eradicated. Jeremy Bentham, James Mill and the Utilitarians believed that wholesale reform of Indian society was imperative for the empire to have any validity.

Aesthetics played a prominent role in the civilizing mission. Evaluating native cultural practices – music, painting, architecture – the colonizers found them wanting, pagan and hideous. Colonial aesthetes, architectural historians and critics documented native art forms, collected native 'curios' and offered detailed commentaries on native 'styles' in journals like the *Asiatick Researches*.

The civilizing mission was made possible through

- a thorough study of various aspects of native cultures,
- a detailed administrative appropriation of such studies for policy-making,
- a determined set of institutional structures to implement the policies.

'Colonial cultures' is the conjunction of these three aspects. The first, the study of native cultures, was made through certain 'ethnographies of the native'.

COLONIAL CULTURES AND ETHNOGRAPHIES OF THE NATIVE

We found them [the inhabitants of Tierra del Fuego] to be a short, squat race, with large heads; their colour yellowish brown; the features harsh, the face broad, the cheek-bones high and prominent, the nose flat, the nostrils and mouth large, and the whole countenance without meaning . . . All have a countenance announcing nothing but wretchedness.

(Johann R. Forster, 1778, p. 227)

Forster's observation is symptomatic of colonial cultures where the native is studied, categorized and judged according to European norms and values, and found wanting. In this section I discuss the various modes of organizing, studying and evaluating the natives in European colonial cultures.

The dominance of the colonial master depended upon

- accurate information about the colonized,
- a continuous spectacle before the native of the colonizer's 'superior' culture.

The first constitutes 'ethnographies of the native'. The second is the imperial spectacle embodied in the hunt or architecture. The first included extensive documentation of every aspect of the native's life. Religions, looks, customs and traditions, rituals and festivals, clothing, food habits, legal systems, art and architecture, women and children, domestic and public life, were studied in what Bernard Cohn has termed colonialism's 'investigative modality', knowledge gathering and the transformation of this knowledge into 'usable forms such as published reports, statistical returns, histories, gazetteers, legal codes, and encyclopedias' (1997, p. 5). Cohn's framework is useful to see how colonial cultures operated within such modalities of enquiry, study and control.

Local histories of African, Asian people were produced in massive quantities throughout the nineteenth century. These histories, exemplified best by James Mill's *History of British India* (1817), were meant to show specific colonial themes:

- The *primitiveness* of the native cultures,
- The *superiority* of the European,
- The *necessity* of European presence in the colony for the sake of the native.

Documenting native barbarism was a necessity for colonial order. Hence Arthur Gordon, the Governor of Fiji issued a fiat that any native disturbance must be recorded in writing and sent to the white administrator. Gordon wrote:

> If any sudden evil should arise in your district, write about it at once; let a true register of births and deaths be kept, and do not allow one to be unregistered. (quoted in Nicholas Thomas, 1994, pp. 110–1)

He further argued: 'the laws of the country may be compared to a net of very fine meshes, nothing can escape: it will cover all alike . . . Obey the laws' (quoted in Thomas, pp. 110–1). Gordon's orders gesture at both the historiographic and survey modality. In India, the history writings of Robert Orme (1782), Alexander Dirom (1793), James Mill (1817), Philip Meadows Taylor (1870) served a useful purpose: they introduced the country and its people to English readers, especially those training to come out to India. History-writing was therefore a powerful colonial instrument through which stereotypes of the lazy native, the primitive native, the seductive native woman, the barbaric Hindu religion could be circulated among prospective rulers. While it might not have been strictly to do with the 'government' or 'governance' (since many of these representations in colonial accounts could not be policed, as Nicholas Thomas argues, 45), they did play an important role in generating a particular colonial *imagination* about the colony.

It was not uncommon to see topographical and local geographic surveys being done in the form of 'histories'.

> The fort [Tipu Sultan's] thus situated on the West end of the Island, is distinguished by its white walls, regular outwork, magnificent buildings, and ancient Hindu pagods, contrasted with the more lofty and splendid monuments lately raised in honour of the Mohammedan faith . . . an extensive suburb or town, which filled the middle space between the fort and the garden, full of wealthy, industrious inhabitants, and it will be readily allowed this insulated metropolis must have been the richest, most convenient and beautiful spot possessed in the present age by any native prince in India.

Thus writes Alexander Dirom in his *Narrative of the Campaign in India, which Terminated the War with Tippoo Sultan, in 1792* (1793, p. 188). Lists of animals, plant species and items of 'curios' – all embodying what Cohn terms the 'survey modality' – are visible in European writings right from the seventeenth century. William Moorcroft and George Trebeck (1841, I, pp. 269, 291–2, 296) collected plant specimens, while William Carey (1761–1834) and Joseph Hooker (1817–1911) classified 'flora indica'. The Archaeological Survey of India and the Zoological Survey of India developed maps and descriptions of specialized domains.

Such surveys and histories offered stereotypes that fuelled imperial policies because these were accepted as true by the administrators. Here is an instance where the native is stereotyped as lazy and weak:

> The sailor no sooner lands on the coast, than nature dictates to him the full result of this comparison; he brandishes his stick in sport, and puts fifty Indians to flight in a moment: confirmed in his contempt of a pusillanimity and an incapacity of resistance, suggested to him by their physiognomy and form, it is well if he recollects that the poor Indian is still a man.

The muscular strength of the Indian is still less than might be expected from the appearance of the texture of his frame. Two English sawyers have performed in one day the work of thirty-two Indians: allowances made for the difference of dexterity, and the advantage of European instruments, the disparity is still very great . . .

This is Robert Orme in his *Historical Fragments of the Mogul Empire* (1782, pp. 297–306), stereotyping the weak bodied native and the superiority of European technology. From another context we have Mungo Park offering a profile of African tribes:

[The Feloops] are of a gloomy disposition, and are supposed to never forgive an injury . . . This fierce and unrelenting disposition is, however, counterbalanced by many good qualities: they display the utmost gratitude and affection toward their benefactors . . . During the present war they have, more than once, taken up arms to defend our merchant vessels from French privateers. (Mungo Park, 1799, pp. 16–21)

Park's analysis of native characters is one of the many such sketches that built the imperial archives. James Cook had this to say of the inhabitants of the Australian-New Zealand islands:

They live a wandering life never remaining long in one spot, and if one can judge from appearances and circumstances few as they are they live not in perfect amity one family with another, for if they do they do not form themselves into some society a thing not only natural to Man, but is even observed by the brute creation. (Cook, II, p. 134)

In all cases, Orme's, Park's and James Cook's, what we see is a *moral* and psychological evaluation of the non-European.

Histories and surveys were useful especially in documenting caste, class and religious organization of the natives. Meadows Taylor writes in his *A Student's Manual of the History of India* (1870):

Caste, as originally devised, was not supposed to extend to Brahmins, who, as the head of the four orders, are sacred, and professedly beyond its influence; but, in point of fact, it does exist among them . . . First, in the sections into which the Brahmins have become subdivided, which differ in an extraordinary degree, in every part of India . . . Secondly, from impurity of descent, or having mixed with aboriginal or secondary classes. These separations have virtually produced caste, which affects social relations . . .

Thus caste, it will be seen, has not an exclusively religious basis; nor is it, on the other hand, exclusively social in its aspect. It is a combination of both, serving to maintain the professed religious faith, and apart from that faith, to uphold the decent moralities of social life . . . (Taylor, 1870, pp. 24–7)

In other cases the enumerative mode offered the colony up as a set of 'usable' statistics. For example, a demographic survey of the Hindus and Muslims in India was drawn up in the form of a table-cum-description:

Classified according to religion, the population of British India is, in round numbers, divided into 140½ millions of Hindoos (including Sikhs), or 73½ per cent., 40¾ millions of Mahomedans, or 21½ per cent., and 9¼ millions of others, or barely 5 per cent., including under this title Buddhists and Jains, Christians, Jews, Parsees, Brahmoes, and Hill men of whose religion no census was taken or no accurate description can be given.

Hindoos	139,248,568
Sikhs	1,174,436
Mahomedans	40,882,537
Buddhists and Jains	2,832,851
Christians	896,658
Others	5,102,823
Religion not known	425,175
	190,563,048

(*General Report on the Census of India, 1891*, 1893, pp. 7–8, 86–92, 157–82, 182–8)

More obvious would be mapping projects that sought to create a database where people, boundaries and geographical features could all be easily accessed by the administrator (see section on 'Colonial Spaces' in Chapter 5). Here the map's *survey modality*, as Matthew Edney (1997) has demonstrated in his magisterial study, serves the purpose of colonial exploration as well as dominance.

The 'surveillance modality', integral to much colonial writing, had serious consequences for specific tribes classified as 'criminal'. For instance, W. H. Sleeman, who led a campaign against organized dacoits (called 'thugs'), in nineteenth-century India documented these groups so that they could be placed under surveillance. Sleeman writes in his *Rambles and Recollections of an Indian Official* (1893):

> These poisoners are spread all over India, and are as numerous over the Bombay and Madras Presidencie as over that of Bengal . . .
>
> The Thugs went on their adventures in large gangs, and two or more were commonly united in the course of an expedition in the perpetration of many murders. Every man shared in the booty according to the rank in which he held in the gang, or the part he took in the murders; and the rank of every man and the part he took generally, or in any particular murder, were generally well known to all. From these gangs, when arrested, we found the evidence we required for their conviction . . . (1893, I, pp. 101–6)

The survey modality was not the domain of the administrator alone. Civilians travelling through or residing in India often produced extensive documents in the form of observations, memoirs, travel diaries that gave the English reader a 'non-official' account of the colony. Written from a first-person point of view and in an informal style these travelogues constitute an important element within colonial cultures because they carried the burden of 'popularizing' the colony and the natives. Thus, in contrast to James Rennell's official mapping project, we see Katharine Anne Elwood in *Narrative of a Journey Overland from England, by the Continent of Europe, Egypt, and the Red Sea, to India* (1830) mapping the Indian landscape purely from a personal perspective and evaluating it in terms of comfort, safety and pleasure:

> Bombay: The rank vegetation, produced by numerous backwaters, rendered Bombay, at one time, so unwholesome, that three years were said to be the average of life at this Presidency. Now, however, the coconut trees which once covered the esplanade, and even the ground on which the present fort stands, have been cleared away . . .

Free from jungle, some parts [of the Nilgiris] are much cultivated, and many European plants and flowers are found there . . . [The hills] appear almost like a terrestrial paradise [because] extra-ordinary cures appear to have been effected by a visit to these salubrious hills . . . the Madras government patronises the establishment, the road up the mountain is already practicable for palanquins and loaded bullocks, and bungalows have been erected. (II, 85, pp. 317–8)

Documents produced by non-administrators also added to the fund of public knowledge – and fuelled their imaginations – of India. In other words, histories, travelogues and memoirs by civilians circulating in England also added to the colonial images of the colonies.

What is interesting is that several of these documents were also *critical* of the English in India. Thus we cannot see colonial cultures as only imperial in their stereotyping of the natives. Very often, the discourse was fractured, and observers and writers sharply uncom-plimentary of their fellow countrymen. Thus it is not uncommon to find passages like this in colonial writings:

There is nothing in the boys we send to India worse, than in the boys whom we are whipping at school, or that we see trailing a pike, or bending over a desk at home. But as English youth in India drink the intoxicating draught of authority and dominion before their heads are able to bear it, and as they are full grown in fortune long before they are ripe in principle, neither nature nor reason have any opportunity to exert themselves for remedy of the excesses of their premature power . . . Arrived in England, the destroyers of the nobility and gentry of a whole kingdom will find the best company in this nation, at a board of elegance and hospitality. Here the manufacturer and husbandman will bless the just and punctual hand that in India has torn the cloth from the loom, or wrested the scanty portion of rice and salt from the peasant of Bengal, or wrung from him the very opium in which he forgot his oppressions and his oppressor . . . Our Indian government is in its best state a grievance. It is necessary that the corrective should be uncommonly vigorous; and the work of men, sanguine, warm, and even impassioned in the cause. But it is an arduous thing to plead against abuses of a power which originates from your own country, and affects those whom we are used to consider as strangers . . .

This is the inimitable Edmund Burke, in the course of his famous speech in the House of Commons in 1783 (in Horn and Ransome, 1957, pp. 821–2). But similar sentiments about the crass, greedy, authoritarian Englishman can be found in private letters and narratives. Here is Maria Graham's disparaging (1812) description of the English society in Calcutta in the early decades of the nineteenth century:

> The civil servants to government being, in Bombay, for the most part young men, are so taken up with their own imaginary importance, that they disdain to learn, and have nothing to teach. Among the military I have met with many well-informed and gentleman-like persons, but still, the great number of men, the small number of rational companions, make a deplorable prospect to one who anticipates a long residence here. (p. 27)

There was of course a tendency to collect, organize and museumize the natives' cultures – what Cohn describes as the 'museological modality' (Cohn, 1997, pp. 9–10). Collection driven by the European's 'curiosity' (see Nigel Leask, 2002, on curiosity in European travelogues) and thirst for the exotic was a mode of

- cataloguing the colony into manageable categories, types and species,
- using the catalogue to generate discourses about the colony as though these categories and types were natural.

In other words, the museum was a space where the colony was organized in order to be studied for museums were modes of organizing and producing knowledge (Hooper-Greenhill 1992, Barringer 1998). The exotic, once at a distance, was now showcased. Botanical acquisitions and imports were, from the last decades of the eighteenth century, a component of the colonial expansionist project (see Brockway on the English botanical gardens and colonialism, 1979). The Royal Gardens at Kew, the British Museum and the stately homes of the English wealthy became museums of Asia and Africa because these were spaces where curios were displayed to visitors.

The museological modality partly ensured that colonial cultures were not restricted to the colonies, but extended back into the European metropolis and the European public's imagination: they could now see 'samples' of Indian or African cultures in stores, museums and manors. 'Tropical nature' (Stepan 2001), tropical objects and, frighteningly to the European imagination as Alan Bewell (1999) has brilliantly demonstrated, tropical diseases were suddenly within the metropole (Hall 2002). The colony had, in a sense, come home, was familiar and understandable because it was not at the periphery any more.

Colonial ethnographies, as postcolonial scholars have demonstrated

- prepared archives of every detail of the colonizeds' lives,
- this information-gathering was informed by racialized, imperial ideologies of difference and superior-inferior binaries,
- used these archives of information for administration and governance,
- deployed the information to train future administrators,
- constructed programmes of reform and change based on the information.

COLONIAL CULTURES AND INTERVENTION I: EDUCATION

As argued above, postcolonialism treats colonial cultures of information-gathering, historiography, translation and ethnography as preliminary moments to active colonial intervention in native cultural practices. Education is a domain in which colonial intervention was significant in Asia, Africa and South America. Postcolonialism therefore has been particularly interested in colonialism's use of education, language and pedagogic practices for its imperial purposes. Postcolonialism focuses on

i. the political and ideological contexts in which European education was introduced in the colonies,
ii. the uses to which European languages were put by the European colonials in the colonies,
iii. the uses to which these same European languages were put by the native elites,
iv. the continuance of English and other European languages in the postcolonial context.

Marxist critics like Antonio Gramsci, Terry Eagleton, Raymond Williams and Louis Althusser have shown how power works best when it is disguised and invisible. The 'subjects' then assimilate norms and systems of thought that reinforce the power structures. In other words, power works best when the subordinate classes or groups *readily accept* the structures of power unquestioningly by accepting the ideology-laden cultural practices – in the present case, education.

The middle classes that appropriated English in colonies often constructed themselves as a new community with its own cultural self-identity through English. It offered the native elite some minimal power. But it also taught them ideals of freedom and justice which therefore contradicted the actual material condition where the natives did *not* possess power.

The collaboration of the colonial and the native elites through English had significant social consequences. For example, it constructed new views of the Indian woman – chaste, oppressed and in need of 'rescue'. Hinduism had to be 'modernized' in accordance with then prevalent notions of gender and thereby entailing 'freeing' women from their oppression. The woman therefore becomes the 'subject' of both colonial and the native elite's concern (Ishwarchandra Vidyasagar, Rajarammohun Roy and the social reform movement in India, for instance, all of which focused on women). While the woman needed to carry the burden of continuity (as bearers of the native culture's traditions), they also needed to be reformed.

The cultural nationalism and 'renaissance' of colonized societies was therefore linked to the native elites' appropriation of English. In other words, the modernity and modernization of the natives was deemed to be possible only through their adoption of English. Bankimchandra Chatterjee, one of the great novelists of nineteenth century India, spoke with considerable pride of the 'two of the treasures we have culled from the rich mind of the English – love of Independence and the art of Nation building'. He added: 'the Hindu never knew what these two meant' (quoted in Jasodhara Bagchi, 1991, p. 155). The colonials, actively encouraged by local elites, saw their education project as part of their civilizing mission. The colonial state and its policies, in Africa, for example, were promoted as 'trustees' for native peoples.

Literary studies was often polarized between (a) literature as a creative enterprise and (b) literature as something which served *colonial* utility (Sangari 1991) – a theme to which I will return later.

Colonial Education and its Contradictions

For the British, an effective instrument of inducing such ready acceptance was English education. The 'discipline' of English studies served the purpose of disseminating particular modes of thinking about natives and the white cultures – modes of thinking that showed

- the native to be vulnerable, needing protection, incompetent, primitive and
- the European to be strong, competent, 'modern' and protector.

'Literature' is an important constituent of this colonial education. 'Literature', as Terry Eagleton has shown (1978), helped 'insert' individuals and groups of people into specific social roles ('mother', 'worker', 'slave') so that social order could be maintained through clear-cut distinctions between classes. 'Literature' gave a set of ideals, values and characters to be sought-after, modelled upon and emulated by the subject classes so that they remained *subjects*.

In the case of colonialism, English literary education after its institutionalization in the nineteenth century (in curricula, examination systems, pedagogic practices) sought the same thing: inculcating among the natives, a system of values that would help strengthen the British empire by rejecting their own (Hindu, Islamic or Sikh) beliefs and turning to Western/British ones. This action had two key 'codes', as deciphered by postcolonial studies:

- presenting the education of the natives as an act of bringing 'enlightenment' to barbaric natives,
- enabling the natives to serve as efficient cogs in the imperial machine because they now had English, Christianity and Western culture.

Charles Grant's 1792 document, *Observations on the State of Society among the Asiatic Subjects of Great Britain* made this point – and the 'codes' mentioned above – clearly:

> Hence the Hindus would see the great use we make of reason on all subjects, and in all affairs; they would also learn to reason, they would become acquainted with the history of their own species, the past and present state of the world; their affections would gradually become interested by various engaging works, composed to recommend virtue, and to deter from vice; the general mass of their opinions would be rectified; and above all, they would see a system of principles and morals. New views of duty as rational creatures would open upon them; and that mental bondage in which they have long holden would gradually dissolve. (Grant, 1999, p. 86)

Gauri Viswanathan's exemplary study (1989) treats the arrival and spread of English education as a *one-way* imposition, made possible by colonial structures and apparatuses alone. In Viswanathan's view, English education was the consequence of a powerful, unrelenting and insular colonial apparatus that needed no affirmation and brooked no resistance from the native subjects. Such a reading is, however, inadequate.

Alok Mukherjee's recent work, *This Gift of English* (2009) argues, I think correctly, that natives actively championed the cause of English language and literary studies. While there was some amount of apprehension about the role of Christian faith in the literary texts – Christianity as a system of thought that could 'convert' Hindus and Muslims – the natives, especially the elite, welcomed English. Thus Raja Rammohun Roy, in his now famous 1823 'Address' to Lord Amherst declared that

> we look forward with pleasing hope to the dawn of knowledge, thus promised to the rising generation . . . we already offered up thanks to Providence for inspiring the most generous and enlightened nations of the West with the glorious ambition of planting in Asia the arts and sciences of Modern Europe . . . As the improvement of the native population is the object of Government, it will consequently promote a more liberal and enlightened system of instruction . . . (Anderson and Subedar, 1921, pp. 106–8)

Roy's enthusiastic reception (if we take it as a reflection of other Indians' views as well) of English seems to suggest considerable native complicity in the arrival and dissemination of English education.

Mukherjee sees the arrival and spread of English education as composed of two separate but interrelated moves:

- The colonial system which saw English education as a way of imposing and reinforcing their dominance (what Mukherjee terms 'colonial hegemony'),
- The natives who saw it as a means to empower themselves and acquire better positions in the new colonial administrative machinery (what Mukherjee terms 'alternative hegemonies').

In Mukherjee's view, therefore, the native elites were an integral component of the apparatus of English education in India. It served the interests of both the colonial rulers and the Indian elites (and it continues to serve the latter even in postcolonial India, shows Mukherjee): 'the introduction of English in colonial India and its continued presence after independence reflect the hegemonic agendas of both the British colonial rulers and the Indian elite' (p. 50). The native elites, consisting very often of the Brahmins (as Mukherjee shows) and upper middle classes, created its own cultural self-identity as a nationalist intelligentsia because of their adoption of English (Joshi, 1991, pp. 5–6). In the case of Burma a similar phenomenon was visible: the new Western educated elite worked with Buddhist monks and with other Burmese.

The two positions (Viswanathan's and Alok Mukherjee's) seem antithetical. Viswanathan sees colonial domination in the cultural domains as a uni-directional process that did not require native assistance, while Mukherjee sees colonial domination as requiring native collaborative structures.

Viswanathan's postcolonialism is keen to exploring the modes through which colonial policies were *formulated* and executed (a mode favoured by postcolonialism's colonial discourse studies approach). Mukherjee focuses on the *effects* of these policies, discourses and structures.[2] English education, both agree, went hand in hand with colonial policies of reform and improvement of the natives of Africa, South America and Asia.

The first task of any colonial empire, Walter Mignolo has eloquently argued in his *The Darker Side of the Renaissance* (2003), has always been to establish a linguistic hierarchy and hegemony. Elio Antonio de Nebrija told Queen Isabella in 1492 – an epochal year for other reasons, specifically, one Columbus – while presenting her with a book on Castilian grammar:

> Now, Your majesty, let me come to the last advantage that you shall gain from my grammar. For the purpose, recall the time when I presented you with a draft of this book earlier this year in Salamanca. At this time, you asked me what end such a grammar could possibly serve. Upon this, the Bishop of Avila interrupted to answer in my stead. What he said was this: 'Soon Your Majesty will have placed her yoke upon many barbarians who speak outlandish tongues. By this, your victory, these people shall stand in a new need; the need for the laws the victor owes to the vanquished, and the need for the language we shall bring with us'. My grammar shall serve to impart them the Castilian tongue, as we have used grammar to teach Latin to our young. (quoted in Mignolo, 2003, p. 38)

All European colonials imposed their languages over native once. For instance in India English became the 'language of command' replacing both Persian and Sanskrit as the official language. This meant, for natives to acquire respectability and recognition from the colonials, they needed English. In turn the colonials acknowledged that the English language is the 'key which open to them [natives] a world of new ideas', as Charles Grant put it in his *Observations* (1792, quoted in Alok Mukherjee, p. 112). Mechanics, the law, agricultural sciences were all taught to the natives through English. Reform was needed, argued the British, to prevent further exploitation of the natives by their kings and religions, and social chaos. England was here in India to protect the natives and help them.

Reform policies had their origins in major academic endeavours dating back to the last decades of the eighteenth century. The 'Orientalists' were a group of English statesmen and administrators with a strong interest in 'knowing' India. William Jones (who founded the Asiatic Society in Calcutta in 1784), H. H Wilson, Charles Wilkins, Nathaniel Halhed and Henry Colebrooke studied Asian (including Arabic) and Indian legal texts (both Hindu and Islamic), literary traditions, caste and religious systems and made extensive notations for their English readers back home. The documentation project that such Orientalists represented also produced another result: it furnished stereotypes, myths and legends about Indian culture. For example, the view that all Indian rulers were despots came from within the Orientalist writings of this period. Many of the Orientalists came to appreciate and admire Indian cultural forms and actively championed Indian literatures and traditions. They were opposed to the English-only policy of education, and were supporters of teaching the native their own languages and literatures as well. The Orientalist argument was that teaching them [the natives] the errors of their own cultures would enable them to better accept the Europeans'! Chairs of Oriental studies were established in British universities and the Orient became a respected field of study. Within this field, of course, there were treatises on the Indian 'character' and morals.

The idea of 'national' literatures was given to the natives by the colonials. Vernacular and native literatures could be developed, they argued, only through English. As Charles Trevelyan puts it:

the languages of India will be assimilated to the languages of Europe as far as the arts and sciences and general literature are concerned . . . When English shall everywhere be the established as the language of education, when the vernacular literature shall everywhere be formed from materials drawn from this source . . . We shall leave a united and enlightened national where we found a people broken up into sections. (1838, p. 124)

Native writings and literature did indeed reveal English influences, even though stronger influences from Sanskrit and Persian remained. Many Indian authors did indeed battle the English influence (Bharatendu, the Hindi writer was one such, see Trivedi 1991) and turned to other European and American models as an act of resistance. In sharp contrast to the Orientalists, the Anglicists (led by Lord Cornwallis) argued that natives must not be allowed to 'contaminate' the ruling English classes. Cornwallis decreed that Indians cannot be allowed into the administrative services: what was needed, in his view, was more of the strong British steel.

A related development from 1813 was the extensive evangelical movement – perhaps the single largest contributor to English education in the colonies. Missionaries spread far and wide across South and Southeast Asia, and merged proselytising with education – and marked the first steps in English education in India. In 1819 when the

East India Company established its trading post at Singapore, the London Missionary Society immediately transferred its base there from Malacca. The Anglican Church had established its presence in Myanmar by 1826 (for a history of colonial missionary work in Southeast Asia, see Goh 2005). The early educational efforts by missionaries such as William Carey, Joshua Marshman and Alexander Duff were directed at exposing the 'flaws' in native religions (mainly Hinduism) and, concomitantly, the glories of Christianity.

James Mill's *History of British India* (1817), and his son, J.S. Mill's works, all contributed to English education in significant ways. However, postcolonial scholars have pointed out that the English approach to educating the Indians was by no means coherent or unified – there were dissenting voices within the ranks. For example, James Mill thought it necessary to encourage native/vernacular literatures because, he believed, these were integral to and drawn from their own lives. Lord Minto also favoured the encouragement of native learning and literatures. Others like Horace Wilson argued that English/Western knowledge could not be adapted to an older civilization like India because Indians would be reluctant to abandon their natives systems which had been in place for centuries. He wrote:

> By annihilating native literature . . . by rendering a whole people dependent upon a remote and unknown country for all their ideas and for the very words in which to clothe them . . . we should degrade their character. (Viswanathan, pp. 41–2)

Such debates about the necessity, means and political repercussions of English education reveal, postcolonialism shows, the schisms within colonial thought.

Postcolonial scholars are almost unanimous in treating Lord Macaulay's 1835 'Minute' on education as a benchmark of colonial ideas and politics (and not just within the field of education). Macaulay made it abundantly clear that 'in India English is the language spoken by the ruling class. It is spoken by the higher class of natives at the seats of Government. It is likely to become the language of commerce throughout the seas of the East' (Alok Mukherjee, p. 141). What is clear from Rajaramohun Roy's fervent espousal of English is that this argument was accepted by the native elites as well.

Macaulay dismisses works produced in the native languages (what he scathingly terms, 'the dialects spoken among the natives') as useless because, as he put it, these 'contain neither literary nor scientific information, and are moreover so poor and rude that, until they are enriched from some other quarter, it will not be easy to translate any valuable work into them' (Anderson and Subedar, 1921, p. 113). On native literatures Macaulay was even more caustic:

> I have never found one [Orientalist scholar] . . . who could deny that a single shelf of a good European library was worth the whole native literature of India and Arabia . . . All the historical information which has been collected from all the books written in the Sanskrit language is less valuable than what may be found in the most paltry abridgments used at preparatory schools in England. (Anderson and Subedar, 1921, p. 113)

This peremptory dismissal of both language and culture logically led Macaulay to the argument that what Indians needed was not their own literature or cultural traditions, but *English* language and literature to prepare the natives as better servants of the empire: 'a class of persons Indian in blood and colour, but English in tastes, in opinions, in morals and in intellect' (Anderson and Subedar, 1921, p. 120). Postcolonial scholars note that what Macaulay wanted English education to do was to produce Indian *clerks* for the empire. In like fashion, policy-makers argued in the case of Australia that education of the natives must be seen as a social investment that would eventually help the economy of the empire (Clatworthy 1969). But, as we shall see, in the process, it also enabled particular kinds of political culture to emerge among the natives.

This English education had to be Christian. Alexander Duff, for instance, was opposed to secular education for Indians. While he accepted that the natives' belief systems (Hinduism and Islam) were in and of themselves opposed to 'proper' Christian education, secular educational institutions were equally to blame for moral anarchy. English education should, at one go, throw out both native literature and native religions. In his *India, and India Missions*, Duff declared that peace in India could only be achieved through the evangelical-educational project. The purpose must be, he wrote, 'the intellectual, moral, and spiritual regeneration of the universal mind; – or, in the speediest and most effectual manner, the reaching and vitally imbuing the entire body of the people with the leaven of Gospel truth' (Duff, 1839, p. 284). He thus recommended studying the great analytical philosophers (Bacon, Locke) but alongside the Bible. Duff and his compatriots believed that an ordered and peaceful civil society in India could emerge only when it had become Christian.

J.S. Mill, in contrast to his father and Macaulay, was far less dismissive of the native traditions in the subcontinent. Mill also did not believe that English ideas could be spread among the subjects only through English language. He accepted that Indians once had a great civilization but it had unfortunately stagnated. Instead, he suggested, the colonial administration should train a small group of Indians who 'having derived from an intimate acquaintance with European literature the improved ideas and feelings which are derivable from that source, will make it their occupation to spread those ideas and feelings among their countrymen (Alok Mukherjee, p. 155). This group of Indians must be from the 'learned class: men of letters by birth and profession' (pp. 156–7). Years later Sister Nivedita (Margaret Noble) would write of Calcutta in her *The Web of Indian Life*:

> It was a world in which men in loin-cloths, seated on door-sills in dusty lanes, said things about Shakespeare and Shelley that some of us would go far to hear. (1904. http://www.sacred-texts.com/hin/wil/wil03.htm)

Sister Nivedita is gesturing proudly at the native appropriation of Shakespeare, even as a certain incongruity is discernable in her ironic description of 'culture'.

By the latter part of the nineteenth century such a group of Indians as J. S. Mill envisaged was being trained to think independently. Wrote a major Hindi author, Bharatendu Harischandra, from the period:

> The English gave us the nectar of knowledge to drink . . . The English by getting us interested in knowledge drew our mind to politics, not that they gave us true knowledge either, and this is the reason why we were entranced by their *maya* [illusion] and could not see our own harm. (quoted in Trivedi, 1991, p. 191)

Reading the English Romantic writers also contributed to a far greater imagination than the colonials would have wanted their subjects to acquire. The upshot was: the Indians were being trained to understand concepts of freedom and the equality of all humans, but were also discovering that none of the ideals embodied in Milton, Shakespeare or Wordsworth applied to their position as subjects to Britain! When Duff and the others sought (and believed) that reading literature would inculcate virtues and morals they found that literature also taught the Indians concepts of freedom and justice. They saw secularist education as creating greater chances of evil among the Indians, and hence something that must be replaced with the Christian religion. Native literary traditions were imprecise, aesthetically crude and morally depraved. English literature, on the other hand, exhibited, according to these same Anglicists, intellectual rigour, reasoning and excellent aesthetic sense (this was paradoxical because much of the literature that they wanted taught to the natives had strong religious themes). Thus the entire native literary tradition of the subcontinent was dismissed (by Anglicist educationists) as aesthetically, morally and politically dangerous to the empire. Much the same arguments were used in the late nineteenth century to reject Irish literature and culture as a subject of study. Declan Kiberd notes that in the case of Ireland arguments were floated about how it was 'almost impossible to get hold of a text in Irish which is not religious, or that is not silly or indecent' (2001, p. 466).

There were thus two strands of thought within English policy-makers on education for the Indians: should the English language alone be the medium of instruction and English literature the key area for studies? (a position supported by the Anglicists and opposed by the Orientalists), or should the vernaculars be supported alongside English language and literature? The solution, argued some, was to first train the natives in reading carefully selected English texts until such time as there was a 'suitable' body of native literature.

Thus the debates around education for Indians (and in other colonies) were organized around various binaries:

- rational/secular versus religious/Christian
- imagination versus empiricism
- literature versus religion
- English language versus native/vernacular language

- Romantic versus Classical
- Indigenous versus cultural imports.

The debates in education were not exclusively about literary texts. Native intellectual and political writings were rejected out of hand by the European. The entire tradition of Hindu philosophy, Islamic jurisprudence, medical systems and aesthetic theories in both were deemed primitive and 'unsystematic'. This furthered the cause of European textual cultures because every domain of colonial social, cultural, legal and scientific life required a European stamp or text to validate it.

English Education and its Postcolonial Nativization

Even as the European/English education system progressed through the colonies oppositional voices were raised against it. Anti-colonial movements also absorbed many of the ideals of freedom and deployed it against their colonial masters. In this sense, 'English' was nativized. New models of education in schools in the colonies ensured that there would be little time for religious instruction. However, this step also had an interesting native response: parallel and counter movements relying upon religion sprang up (the Arya Samaj and Brahmo Samaj in India, the Muslim Brotherhood in Egypt are examples. The last was founded in 1928 and by 1950 had nearly 2000 branches).

Postcolonialism, however, rejects the idea that English education completely decimated the native. In fact, critics like Homi Bhabha (1994) have demonstrated how English education created hybrid natives whose affiliation and loyalties (not to mention their accents) remained far more complex than the British could imagine. There existed, notes Ania Loomba, 'a fundamental contradiction at the heart of the attempt to educate, "civilise" or co-opt the colonial "other"' (1998, p. 91). As noted above, English literary and other texts might have been intended as disciplining tools, but they also produced some politically conscious citizenry. Contemporary post-colonial criticism and creative writers have seized upon this 'funda-mental contradiction' within the colonial educational cultures.

This 'fundamental contradiction' is exploited by the native writer when she/he modifies English to carry her/his own culture to his own people. English does not remain the colonial master's language any more – a truly unforeseen effect of English education! Thus Chinua Achebe writes:

> But it [the English language] will have to be a new English, still in full communion with its ancestral home but altered to suit its new African surroundings. (quoted in Loomba, 1998, p. 91)

V. S. Naipaul sees the hybridized postcolonial – the product of English education – as a philistine in *The Middle Passage*.

> A peasant-minded, money-minded community, spiritually cut off from its roots, its religion reduced to rites without philosophy set in a materialistic colonial society: a combination of historical accidents and national temperament has turned the Trinidad Indian into a complete colonial, even more Philistine than the white. (1969, p. 89)

This is Naipaul's description of Caribbean society in *The Middle Passage*. If Naipaul is suspicious of the hybridized postcolonial condition, Derek Walcott tries to come to terms with his dual heritage in 'A Far Cry from Africa':

> Divided to the vein
> How choose
> Between this Africa and the English tongue I love? (1986 [1962], pp. 17–18)

Others like Ngugi wa Thiong'O have argued that English literature and language cannot be at the centre of postcolonial education. In his famously controversial 'On the Abolition of the English Department' (1972) Ngugi argued that African literature and its allies, African American and Caribbean must be at the centre. Ngugi wrote: 'the primary duty of any literature department is to illuminate the spirit animating a people, to show how it meets new challenges, and to investigate possible areas of development and involvement' (1999, p. 439). Ngugi is explicitly situating education and literary studies as a *nationalist* project here. John Docker, an Australian postcolonial scholar, makes the case for centring Australian literature and culture within education on the same lines as Ngugi. Docker argues that even if the teachers have interests in Australian literature, their actual teaching remains 'anglocentric, dominated by the assumption that English literature is central and necessary to a student's critical education' (1999, p. 445).

The consequence of these debates and policies was the arrival of English education, its spread and also the concordant spread of new ideas that were appropriated by native elites. While the colonials saw education as a means of retaining their control over the natives, the natives saw English and its structures as a means of acquiring power under the new masters. As Alok Mukherjee puts it, 'English education was an ironic meeting point for the two hegemonic agendas' (p. 159).

COLONIAL CULTURES AND INTERVENTION II: RELIGION

It is the peculiar and bounden duty of the Legislature to promote, by all just and prudent means, the interests and happiness of the inhabitants in India; and that for these ends, such measures ought to be adopted as may gradually tend to their advancement in useful knowledge, and to their religious and moral improvement.
(Journal of the House of Commons *48 (1793), p. 778)*

Religion was the realm in which the largest – and most controversial – interventions took place. Colonial discourses about native religions described them as barbaric, primitive and in urgent need of renewal through an introduction of Christianity. Hinduism, in particular, came in for heavy criticism as a religion whose practices and rituals were cruel and barbaric. Thus the Jagannath Yatra, an annual procession in Orissa, Eastern India, came in for attention as iconic of native primitivism. As early as 1638 William Bruton had recorded his horror at the Hindu festival of Jagannath thus:

I went to view the city in some part, but especially that might pagoda, or pagod, the mirror of all wickedness and idolatory: unto this pagod, or house of Satan (as it may rightly be called) do belong 9000 brahmins or priests, which do daily offer sacrifices onto their great god Jagarnat [Jagannatha] . . . Here they also offer their children to this idol, and make them to pass through the fire, and also they have an abominable custom to cause or make them pass through the water as sacrifices unto the said ungodly God.

This idol is in shape like a great serpent, with seven heads . . . They have built a great chariot that goes on 16 wheels of a side, and every wheel is five foot in height, and the chariot itself is about thirty foot high. In this chariot (on their great festival days at night) they do place their wicked God, Jagannath, and all the Brahmins (being in number 9000) do then attend this great idol, besides of ashmen and fakirs some thousands (or more than a good many) . . . this chariot with the idol is also drawn with the greatest and best men of the town, and they are so eager and greedy to draw it, that whosoever by shouldering, crowding, shoving, heaving, thrusting, or any other violent way can but come to lay a hand upon the ropes, they think themselves blessed and happy. And when it is going along the city there are many that will offer themselves a sacrifice to this idol, and desperately lie down on the ground, that the chariot-wheels may run over them, whereby they are killed outright; some get broken arms, some broken legs, so that many of them are so destroyed, and by this means they think to merit heaven. (William Bruton, 1638, pp. 29–31)

David Smith, Bengal's Sanitary Commissioner recorded his disapproval of the pilgrimage in his *Report on Pilgrimage of Juggernauth in 1868* thus:

[Hindus] enslaved by priestcraft, steeped in idolatory, determinedly tenacious of caste, bewildered by frivolous superstitions and legendary fables, strongly prejudiced against education, and content to look forward to their periodically recurring festivals, at which they are despoiled of all they possess . . . Many of the religious forms and ceremonies to which the Oriyas fondly cling, either involve fatigue, fasting, penance, and pain, or, on the other hand, they lead to fasting, dissipation, sensual excesses, reckless orgies, and great mental excitement. These two sets of influences probably account for much prevailing sickness, and even mortality. (quoted in Arnold 1996, pp. 187–8)

Then there were the standard reports on the horrific rituals of *sati* (where the widowed woman consigned herself to the flames on her husband's pyre) – a native custom that has had more written about it by Englishmen than any other custom – female infanticide, religious rituals and temples of India. Fanny Parkes records a *sati* she reportedly heard of from a reliable eyewitness, her husband:

A rich baniya, acorn chandler, whose house was near the fate of our grounds, departed this life: he was a Hindu. On the 7th of November, the natives in the bazaar were making a great noise with their tom-toms, drums, and other discordant musical instruments, rejoicing that his widow had determined to perform suttee, i.e. to burn on his funeral-pile.

The magistrate sent for the woman, used every argument to dissuade her, and offered her money. Her only answer was, dashing her head on the floor, and saying, 'If you will not let me burn with my husband, I will hang myself in your court of justice.' The shastrs say, 'The prayers and imprecations of a suttee are never uttered in vain; the great gods themselves cannot listen to them unmoved' . . . My husband accompanied the magistrate to see the suttee: about 5000 people were collected together on the banks of the Ganges: the pile was then built, and the putrid body placed upon it; the magistrate stationed guards to prevent the people from approaching it. After having bathed in the river, the widow lighted a brand, walked round the pile, set it [sic] on fire; she sat down, placing the head of the corpse on her lap, and repeated several times the usual form, 'Ram, Ram, suttee; Ram, Ram, suttee;' i.e. 'God, God, I am chaste.'

As the wind drove the fierce fire upon her, she shook her arms and limbs as of in agony; at length she started up and approached the side top escape. And Hindu, one of the police who had been placed near the pile to see she had fair play, and should not be burned by force, raised his sword to strike her, and the poor wretch shrank back into the flames. The magistrate seized and committed him to prison. The woman again approached the side of the blazing pile, sprang fairly out, and ran into the Ganges, which was within a few yards. When the crowd and the brothers of the dead man saw this, they called out, 'Cut her down, knock her on the head with a bamboo; tie her hands and feet, and throw her in again;' and rushed down to execute their murderous intentions, when the gentlemen and the police drove them back.

The woman drank some water, and having extinguished the fire on her red garment, said she would mount the pile again and be burned.

The magistrate placed his hand on her shoulder (which rendered her impure), and said, 'By your own law, having once quitted the pile you cannot ascend again; I forbid it. You are now an outcast from the Hindus, but I will take charge of you, the Company will protect you, and you shall never want food or clothing.' (Parkes, 1850, I, pp. 88–90)

William Bentinck, the Governor General responsible for banning *sati* wrote in his famous Minute of 1831:

Whether the question be to continue or to discontinue the practice of *sati,* the decision is equally surrounded by an awful responsibility. To consent to the consignment year after year of hundreds of innocent victims to a cruel and untimely end, when the power exists of preventing it, is a predicament which no conscience can contemplate without horror. But, on the other hand, if heretofore received opinions are to be considered of any value, to put to hazard by a contrary course the very safety of the British Empire in India, and to extinguish at once all hopes of those great improvements-affecting the condition not of hundreds and thousands but of millions-which can only be expected from the continuance of our supremacy, is an alternative which even in the light of humanity itself may be considered as a still greater evil. (Anderson and Subedar 1921, pp. 87–93)

Bentinck argued that 'from the native population nothing of extensive combination, or even of partial opposition, may be expected from the abolition [of *Sati*].' The 'first and primary object of my heart', wrote Bentinck, 'is the benefit of the Hindus. I know nothing so important to the improvement of their future condition as the establishment of a purer morality, whatever their belief, and a more just conception of the will of God' (William Bentinck, Minute on *Sati*, 1829, in Anderson and Subedar, 1921, pp. 87–93). Reform was the colonial's aim when faced with such rituals. Expectedly, the modes of reform were often disruptive.

Such depictions of native religious beliefs and practices were preliminary moments to colonial reform, evangelical proselytizing and 'civilizing'. The larger project of civilizing the native was a method therefore of not only imposing European interpretations on native customs but also seeking to convert natives into accepting these interpretations. As we shall see in the case of 'conversion narratives', colonial cultures' hegemonic success becomes visible when the native himself/herself

- *accepts* European evaluation of her/his native practices and beliefs,
- *rejects* her/his native practices and beliefs as a result,
- *turns* to European forms of thinking and beliefs.

Native practices and beliefs as interpreted by the European become the 'acceptable' or true tradition for the native. This is the most significant element of colonial cultures: the construction of convenient native traditions by the Europeans which

- the natives accepted and
- the Europeans could 'pronounce' (as Edward Said termed Orientalist discourse), legislate and pass judgements on.

Several postcolonial critics examine the processes through which colonial cultures constructed such 'pure' and 'acceptable' native traditions.

Postcolonial readings of India's *Sati* reform (Lata Mani 1998) have shown how the debates around *Sati* were not really about the woman. Mani argues that the aim was to identify the 'proper' and acceptable *Sati* as the Hindu scriptures defined it. Thus the debate was about the purity of Hindu traditions rather than about the woman herself. In other words, postcolonial readings of colonial reform show how reform was often not about the subject (the woman, or the child) but about interpretations of native traditions for their own purposes and within their own frames.

Conversion to Christianity meant gaining access into a new modernity and new social relations for the natives. Native Christians documented their experience of Hinduism and their 'new life' in Christianity – a mode of narrative that was actively supported by the colonial administration. Thus Baba Padmanji writes:

I fell lower and lower, till I reached the lowest level of superstition – that is, demon worship. My life was marked by the grossest inconsistencies; I believed in the most contradictory doctrines, and practised rites that could not possibly be reconciled with each other.

In all this I was quite sincere. My earnest faith in popular Hinduism left me a fetish-worshipper of the lowest kind. Such was the necessary result of my earnest faith in its teachings; for it enforced not only the worship of spiritual deities and virtuous men and women, but that of the most despicable vermin . . . (1889, p. 55)

He concludes:

Am I not a happy man! Yes, a most blessed man, in spite of my imperfect obedience and feeble resolutions . . . Even now I have Christ, and intimate communion with him, who is the fountain of all happiness. (p. 147)

More than the native's account of his conversion is the Englishman's view of the narrative's significance. J. Murray Mitchell in his prefatory note writes:

There is at this moment a terrible unrest in the mind of educated India. Will this honest and earnest narrative not serve to lead some souls that are tempest-tossed and like to suffer shipwreck, to see the one sure haven of refuge, Jesus Christ? (p. vi)

Mitchell expresses the hope that Christianity would quieten the Indian mind and prevent it from rebellion against the empire which was, to the colonial, a Christian one. The *Christian Missionary Intelligencer* was able to declare with confidence that 'Christianity strengthened lawful authority, concurs it with action, makes the man more loyal, more submissive to his superiors, more attentive to their commands' (quoted in Bolt, 1971, p. 159). Sarah Tucker, as early as the 1840s, is able to point to the advantages to be gained from the natives' conversion:

the moral influence of Europeans over this people is so great, that you might travel alone from Madras to Cape Comorin, and often find yourself thirty or forty miles from any European, without the slightest danger of any advantage being taken of your defenceless situation. (1842–1843, I, pp. 106–7)

Peace in the country, Tucker suggests, was possible when the natives had adopted Christianity. This image of the beautiful, peaceful and

Arcadian colony – the result of Christianity – is common to numerous colonial documents of the nineteenth century. George Pettitt notes that a mission-school in south India 'presented a far more pleasant sight than the native bazaar that occupied it before' (419). Another describes the transformation of the countryside

> The capital itself, once the seat of Eastern misrule and selfish luxury . . . henceforth we trust, if we do our duty, and God's blessing rests upon us, to be gradually leavened by Christian civilization – is almost girt by a belt of park-like country . . . (*Macmillan's Magazine* 4, 1861, p. 155)

William Clarkson speaks of a similar transformation of the countryside through Christianity:

> In the rural scenes of wells and watercourses, fields and orchards, and amid the rural operations of sowing and reaping, threshing and fanning, there was no lack of apt illustrations of those grand truths which relate to the regeneration of man . . . Oh for labourers in that and similar regions! Oh for labourers! (1850, p. 85)

In all these cases the native soul and the native land have both been transformed into something quiet, peaceful and controllable through Christianity. As I have argued elsewhere, missionary rhetoric conflates morals, religion, landscape and agrarian images in order to depict a landscape that is under control (Nayar 2008b, Chapter 4).

The colonized were moulded into citizens of a new political order through Christianity, English education and European cultures. When an observer notes that orphans in a missionary compound 'were neatly dressed, a little too much caricatures of English children, perhaps, but happy looking, well fed, well cared for', she/he is speaking of the 'Englishing' of native bodies ('One Long Resident in India', 1877). Viswanathan argues that conversion left the natives in a double bind:

> While they were treated as dead by their former religious community, the lease of life they were given by civil courts [colonial] was founded on an equally unreal fiction, a perverse denial of their adopted religious identity. (1998, p. 81)

Thus the natives were treated as outcasts by their Hindu and Muslim brethren, but were not accepted as fully, or truly, Christian by the colonials. Indian Christians remained less than true Christians for the colonials, who continued to treat them as Hindus:

> The missionaries, no less than British administrators, participated in the dislocation of Indian Christians from a larger community of Christians and continued to identify the customs, practices, and usages of native converts with those of Hindus. (Viswanathan, 1998, p. 93)

This is what Viswanathan terms as 'civil death'.

If conversion was a mode of ensuring pliable and amicable natives, postcolonial scholars have argued that the British emphasis on and studies of the Hindu caste system was also a mode of control. Nicholas B. Dirks (2003), for instance, argues – not without controversy – that while the caste system is anterior to colonialism, the British cleverly used it as a mode of organizing Indian society. Dirks proposes that it was under British rule that 'caste' became an organizing term, 'systematizing' India's diverse forms of social identity, community and organization.

What postcolonial critics like Lata Mani, Nicholas Thomas, Bernard Cohn, Gauri Viswanathan and Nicholas Thomas show is that ethnographies of the native, in the domains of education, religion and cultural practices were instruments of colonial domination because

- they codified the practices of the natives,
- they produced a 'pure' tradition of these practices by identifying the 'true' elements within it,
- they served colonial purposes of control by organizing native society into sections, segments and hierarchies which the colonials could understand.

Such colonial modes often ignored the complexities of native practices, and simply homogenized or categorized them as they suited the colonial administration at that point. Thus the meanings of familial, tribal or caste affiliations in African and Hindu societies were simply ignored when the Europeans set about classifying identities and groups. Bernard Cohn (1997) argues that the colonial 'conceptual scheme' 'reduced vastly complex codes and their associated meanings to a few metonyms' (p. 162). This 'reduction' was achieved by ignoring overlaps, contradictions and shared legacies within native cultures.

What postcolonial societies inherit as 'their' tradition, postcolonialism argues, was what *colonialism* identified, codified, valorized and thus produced as tradition. As Nicholas Dirks puts it in his work on caste and colonialism, colonialism 'played a critical role in both the identification and the production of Indian "tradition"' (2003, p. 9). Dirks elaborates: 'the congeries of beliefs, customs, practices, and convictions that have been designated as traditional are in fact the complicated byproduct of colonial history' (p. 9).

* * *

Colonial cultures created specific identities, categories and ways of 'knowing' the native. As this chapter has illustrated in the case of the civilizing mission, ethnographies of the native, education and religious reform, colonialism sought to impose structures – economic, social, political, geographical – in order to better understand and therefore control what they perceived as chaotic native cultures. They framed Indian, African and other identities in ways that were subtle by working within the cultural rather than political domains. These identities have spilled over into the postcolonial age, and newly independent nations in Africa and Asia in the twentieth century carry their legacies of colonial law, education systems, social policies, in addition to more obvious colonial structures like the railways or medical training. The cultural processes of the civilizing mission colonized the bodies and minds of the natives, and this aided the colonial project. This chapter has looked at ethnographies of the natives in colonial cultures, and two principal domains of colonial cultures of intervention: education and religion. Other domains in which colonialism made significant interventions have also been studied: railways (Kerr 1995), science and technology (Deepak Kumar 1995), architecture (Metcalfe 1989), medicine (Anil Kumar 1998, Harrison 1999, Edmond 2006), law and order (Mukhopadhyay 2006), communication (Bayly 1999) being some of them.

In short, colonial cultures were first and foremost, *colonizing* cultures.

CHAPTER THREE

NATION AND NATIONALISM

Nations and nationalisms demand our attention for three reasons:

- The nation is the largest of the collectivities with which the people possess an affiliation.
- The nation is the decisive unit of political allegiance.
- The nation is the decisive territorial collectivity. (Smith 2003, p. 3)

The nation is a sacred object for people across the world and the endurance of national identities can be explained by exploring 'collective beliefs and sentiments about the "sacred foundations" of the nation' (Smith 2003, p. 4). The work of political parties in many Third World nations has explicitly situated nationalist idea(l)s within religious traditions (India's Bharatiya Janata Party, e.g. has always argued a case for both, a *Hindu* nationalism and a *Hindu* nation).

Nationalism can be defined as the

relatively recent beliefs and practices aimed at creating unified but unique communities within a sovereign territory . . . [where] such forms of community are thought of as nations and sovereign territory is associated with the concept of the state. (Puri 2004, p. 2)

Nationalism could be patriotism (love and loyalty towards one's country) or become associated with militancy and fanaticism. Nationalism emerges when there is a transition from one kind of society to another, from agrarian societies (in which literacy was confined to a small elite) to an industrial society (which required greater communication between people). This need for communication generated the need for nations. Benedict Anderson argued in his influential *Imagined Communities* (1991, Rev. ed.) that nationalism was always, primarily, populist, akin to religion and myth, and appealed to the imagination. Nationalism emerges alongside capitalism and its technological developments (mainly print) and to the spread of the vernacular. Nationalism enables people to *perceive* themselves as connected to distant people whom they have never met. Nationalism is also a process of differentiation: about people who *feel* they belong together as opposed to other people. Feeling and nationalist *sentiments* were reinforced by cultural practices and forms such as the novel (see Anderson, Cheah, Brennan) by stimulating the national imagination in Europe. Storytelling, therefore, is integral to the formation of national identity.

Partha Chatterjee counters Anderson's thesis that nationalism draws upon (Western) 'modules' by arguing that if Third World nations have to choose even their nationalisms from 'modular forms already made available to them by Europe and the Americas', then 'there is nothing left for them to imagine' (1999b, p. 5). Subaltern scholars argue that it was Western humanism percolating down through colonial systems that generated feelings, ideas and beliefs about nationalism in Third World places/cultures. Partha Chatterjee also argues that nationalism has sought to continue the legacy of Enlightenment and hence fails (1999a). It is therefore necessary, proposes Chatterjee, to trace the *non-Western*, indigenous and subaltern voices that have been submerged within nationalist historiography.

Nationalism also becomes evaluated as 'good' or 'bad'. Jyoti Puri shows how, after 9/11, American nationalism becomes coded as 'patriotism', or 'good' nationalism and nationalism's negative connotations becomes the feature of the Third World. Michael Billig had summarized it thus:

'Our' loyalties to 'our' nation-state can be defended, even praised . . . 'Our' nationalism is not presented as nationalism, which is dangerously irrational, surplus and alien . . . 'Our' nationalism appears as 'patriotism' – a beneficial, necessary and, often, American force. (1995, p. 55)

Nationalism also draws on forms of identification: us and them, insider and outsider, friend and stranger. These forms of identification are very often based on biological (racial) and cultural differences. Thus after 9/11 American nationalism built on already existing suspicions, fears and dislike of Arab, non-white and Muslim cultures. Nationalism therefore remains inextricably linked, along with identification, to racism and xenophobia.

The nation comes into being as a system of 'cultural signification' (Bhabha 1995a [1990], pp. 1–2), narratives and practices. National-ism has its own language: myths, images, ghosts (of 'great leaders'), *cultural* practices, flags and other national symbols become common modes of expressing nationalist sentiments. In fact, national identity and its politics are very often almost entirely framed, contested or erased in the cultural domain, especially in postcolonial societies where the anti-colonial struggle for political independence had been fought primarily at the site of the *cultural* (see section below on cultural nationalism). Nationalism, national identity and national 'feeling' in *postcolonial* societies have thus appeared under various guises and aligned with various themes in their literary and cultural productions, that is, *narratives* (Bhabha 1995a [1990], p. 2).

Nationalism's contexts and discourses would include the following:

- material contexts such as land ownership and land reform – as in the case of Zimbabwean fiction such as Chenjerai Hove and Yvonne Vera, as argued by James Graham (2009),
- development and its politics, as in the case of Indian author Kamala Markandaya's *The Coffer Dams*,
- the future of multiculturalism, as explored in the novels of Salman Rushdie, Monica Ali, Hanif Kureishi, Frank Chin,
- the debates around inclusive national identity and an exclusionary one (seen in the work of minoritarian and marginalized writers such as Dalit writing from India, Chicanos from the USA),
- local myths and legends in the plays of Wole Soyinka, for instance, of First Peoples and aboriginals as seen in the plays of Jack Dawes

in Australia, of the Ananse story-telling tradition in Ama Ata Aidoo, the Hindu concept of *karma* in R. K. Narayan, and the idea of *yajna* (sacrifice) in Raja Rao,
* transnational/globalized identities, as explored by Hanif Kureishi, Timothy Mo and Pico Iyer.

In this chapter nations and nationalism in postcolonialism are studied under specific heads. In the case of postcolonialism, since many of the nations acquired the status of being 'nations' after an extended period of anti-colonial struggles with most such struggles being the direct manifestations of nationalist sentiments, there is an even greater need to study the phenomenon.

HISTORY AND POSTCOLONIAL NATIONALISM

Most people they met along the way had their bodies tattooed with their identities: that is, name, nationality and address. Some had engraved on their skins the reason why they had become who they were when living and others had printed on their foreheads or backs their national flags or insignia.

Nuruddin Farah (1999, p. 43)

Somalian novelist Farah is describing here a cultural practice: the *embodying* of national identity. It is through the medium of such cultural practices – art, poetry, fiction, songs, cultural memories – that a nation's history is handed down from the colonial times to the postcolonial age. History is perhaps postcolonialism's greatest single theme, and merits sustained attention.

Reclaiming History

In a paradigmatic postcolonial tale, Thomas King's, 'The One about Coyote Going West', Coyote wants to fix the world by telling stories. She says: 'I been reading those books . . . about that history . . . All about who found us Indians' (1996, p. 421). As the conversation between Coyote and the narrator goes on we discover several such stories being subverted in the retelling:

Maybe I tell you the one about Christopher Cartier looking for something good to eat . . . Maybe I tell you the one about Jacques

Columbus come along that river, Indians waiting for him . . . Everyone knows who found us Indians. Eric the lucky and that Christopher Cartier and that Jacques Columbus come along later. Those ones get lost. Float about. Walk around. Get mixed up . . . We got to find them. Help them out. Feed them. Show them around. (p. 421)

The 'discoverers', Jacques Cartier and Christopher Columbus are deliberately conflated into one and their names reversed. When the postcolonial rewrites history, King suggests, she does exactly what the colonials did to the natives: erase distinctions of 'black', 'brown' or the 'native'. The references to lost, wandering and incompetent explorers debunk the myth of heroic discovery. Instead, it is the natives who lead the explorer, direct him and even care for him. Post-colonial reclamation of history is this vigorous, parodic and satiric inversion of the traditional stories of the discovery of the Indians.

Writing about Turkey and Turkish nationalism in 1929, Tekin Alp praises Kemal Ataturk for emphasizing the role of writing a 'proper' history of the Turkish people. Alp argues that detailed and thorough research has resulted in very specific gains for a true 'Turkish' identity. Alp writes:

the age-old prejudice concerning the Mongoloid origins of the Turkish peoples has itself become past history. No one in Turkey believes it any more, and many Western specialists and men of learning . . . have become convinced that the Turks occupy a prominent position among the Indo-European peoples. (1970, p. 212)

This turn-around in the perception of the Turks by the Europeans and the Turks themselves, writes Alp, has been made possible because the culture's history has been rewritten:

The pioneers of the Kemalist revolution give long revolutions from the celebrated Persian poet Firdevsi, as well as from other Persian poems and epics which describe legendary Turkish heroes whose morphological characteristics have absolutely nothing in common with those of the mongols. (p. 213)

Alp goes on to describe the 'new' Turkish identity that emerges from such historical and archaeological researches.

In India, writing a few decades before Alp, Surendra Nath Banerjea, in an 1880 speech called for a study of India's 'noble history' by the Indians. What is needed, he argued, was a 'communion with the master minds of ancient India, with Valmiki and Vyasa, Panini and Patanjali, Gautama and Sankaracharya' (1970, p. 225). The novelist Raja Rao in an essay tellingly titled, '*The Meaning of India*' (1996), suggests that India's greatest offering to the world is *yajna* (sacrifice), treating it as a symptomatic and encapsulating myth. Rao also suggests in 'Mahatma Gandhi – Saint or Politician' that Gandhi is India's offering to the world, for 'without Gandhi, there can be no world of tomorrow' (1996 [1972], p. 77).

Writing at the time of Indian independence the Muslim scholar Choudhary Rahmat Ali identifies a specific territory as the centre of human civilization

land which lies in the northwest of the Continent of Dinia, otherwise known as the subcontinent of India; and which constitutes the age-old national stronghold of the people who represent the original core and content of the Millat living in the Orbit of Pakasia.

Ali goes on to argue that Pakistan was the birthplace of human culture and civilization, the 'earliest center of communal aggregation of human society' and the 'strongest citadel of Islam in the Continent of Dinia and its Dependencies' (1970, pp. 245–6).

What we see in all these writings from/about Turkey, India and Pakistan is the emphasis on antiquity, historical inquiry, myth and legend. Nationalism is the evocation of such common myths and stories about a people's past. These texts, written during anti-colonial and nation-building periods, gesture both at a culture's reclamation of their history but also at the myth-building that occurs around the idea of a nation.

Postcolonialism questions the European construction of native pasts and histories. Postcolonial critics argue that, for the Third World countries, their histories will always be produced by the West, within Western frames. Australian Aboriginal writer, Sally Morgan mourns:

All our history is about the white man. No one knows
what it was like for us. A lot of our history has been lost, people
have been too frightened to say anything. There's a lot of history
we can't even get at. (Morgan 1987, pp. 163–4)

Indian novelist Nayantara Sahgal asks: 'is "colonial" the new Anno Domini from which events are to be everlastingly measured?' (1992, p. 30). Such a view of history means:

- Secular 'modernity' becomes an ideal form of nation-building in Western frames, and this rejects non-European mysticism and spiritualism as inessential to history writing,
- The Third World nation's history is always dated around its colonization, almost as though there was no history before the European entry into the Third World colony,
- Within the discipline of history, Europe remains as the 'sovereign' subject and Third World historians feel compelled to refer to works in European history, and the history of the non-European peoples 'tend to become variations on a master narrative that could be called the "history of Europe."' (Chakrabarty 1997, pp. 223, 224)

Chakrabarty shows how history-writing itself not only marginalizes non-European histories but also the very modes of knowledge-making. Projected as a scientific discipline in the nineteenth century, history-writing, it was argued, was objective and eschewed moral and subjective interpretations. This enabled the European history-writer to claim objective truth-telling for himself, even when what he was writing was a subjective fiction. There could be no debates about the nature of historical interpretation because 'history', by definition, was accurate and true. Whatever the white man recorded was therefore promoted and believed to be a transparent reflection of true conditions. Thus when Robert Orme in his 1974 [1782] account of India described Indians as lazy and weak, it was deemed to be a clear and true picture of Indians. James Mill, whose *History of British India* (1978 [1817]) – a prescribed text for civil servants in India in the nineteenth century – built on Orme's interpretations. What we see is the effective use of history-writing to convey 'truths' that suited the colonial discourse of the time: the lazy and vulnerable native had to be improved through colonial intervention. Such colonial acts could be justified only when the myths and fictions were touted and accepted as true, and this was what history-writing precisely did. Jose Rabasa (1993) in an innovative postcolonial reading of European atlases shows how such myths were the incessant feature of all maps. The European map organized the world, Rabasa notes, into clear binaries: Europe was modern, masculine and Old World, while the rest of the world was ancient, New World and feminine. More importantly, maps along with histories erased older (pre-European) territorial possessions and boundaries. Maps reappraised space for European purposes: 'history . . . naturalizes particular natural formations and institutionalizes forgetfulness of earlier territorializations in the perception of the world' (1999, p. 362).

These arguments finds resonance in Australian writer Jackie Huggins who asks: 'Who has responsibility for what and whom? Who does what? Who takes responsibility for saying things for whom? Who does the saying and the writing?' (1998, p. 116). Huggins is calling for an investigation into the methods of *representation*, as a critique of European history-writing and non-European reclamation of history. This representation could be in anthropology, theology, history or myth-making. Take, as an instance, Edward Blyden who in his *The Negro in Ancient History* (1871) criticizes the historians for ignoring the African contributions to 'ancient works of science and art' (1970, p. 251). Blyden goes on to show, quoting anthropologists and philologists as evidence, that Blacks were integral to the glories of the ancient world and that it was through the mechanism of an 'unrelenting theology' that the Europeans 'consigned a whole race of men to hopeless and interminable servitude' (p. 271). Blyden is accusing theological and Church representations, as well as historians' writing, for twisting 'true' history in order to establish the superiority of the European and the concomitant inferiority of the black race. In similar fashion, Cheikh Anta Diop, writing in 1955, makes the claim that 'it is impossible to exaggerate what the whole world – and in particular the Hellenic world – owes to the Egyptian world' (1970, p. 275). Just as Blyden before him, and Surendra Nath Banerjea in the case of India, Diop is seeking a validation for non-European histories as well as non-European self-representation. Huggins' question about 'who speaks for whom?' has already been answered by these postcolonial writers: it must be the non-European who speaks for his/her *own* culture, for the European cannot be trusted to deliver other than a white version of native history. Walcott writes:

I met History once, but he ain't recognize me,
A parchment Creole. (Walcott, '*The Schooner Flight*', 1986, p. 346)

The purpose here is the construction of a local history, a vernacular mythography that can counter the colonial history. In Australia, for example, Thomas Keneally (*The Chant of Jimmie Blacksmith*, 1973), Peter Carey (*The True History of the Kelly Gang*) and Aboriginal writer Mudrooroo Narogin (formerly Colin Johnson) interrogate the European version of Australian history. These counter-histories are political acts of representation that enable the African and the Asian to reclaim her past for herself, freeing it from the myths, lies and subordination of the European. Diop's summary of why such reclamation is necessary also sums up the postcolonial project:

> The Negro should be able to recapture the continuity of his national historic past and to derive from it the necessary moral profit to enable him to reconquer his position in the modern world. (pp. 281–2)

An instance of Diop's native reclamation of history is seen in the rewriting of the 'discovery' narrative. While the 'discovery' of Australia or India or interior Africa is glorified by European writings, native histories treat this moment of 'discovery' very differently. Mudrooroo explains it thus:

> All New Zealand schoolchildren were taught about Captain James Cook's discovery of New Zealand and his historic landfall . . . They are told . . . that the reaction of the Maori people on shore was one of awe for the huge white bird, the floating island, and the multicoloured gods who had come on the bird . . .
> But what the schoolchildren are not told is that Cook's first landing was marked by the killing of a Maori called Te Maro, shot through the heart by a musket bullet, Monday 9 October, 1769. (quoted in Ralph Crane 2001, pp. 395)

Chinua Achebe's now-famous 1977 reading of Joseph Conrad's *Heart of Darkness* shows how the Congo becomes the very 'antithesis of Europe and therefore of civilization' (2001, p. 211). Achebe summarizes Conrad's depiction of Africa thus:

> Africa as setting and backdrop which eliminates the African as human factor. Africa as a metaphysical battlefield devoid of all

POSTCOLONIALISM: A GUIDE FOR THE PERPLEXED

recognizable humanity . . . the real question is the dehumanization of Africa . . . (2001, p. 215)

This too is an act of interpretive reclamation of a European classic. Nobel Laureate Derek Walcott in his now-classic work, 'Ruins of a Great House' reworks the English country-house poem (made famous by Ben Jonson's 'To Penshurst' and Andrew Marvell's 'Upon Appleton House') to devastating postcolonial effect. Walcott begins with referencing, in his epigraph, Thomas Browne's *Urn Burial*. The great house, once an icon of colonial domination and dominion, is now in ruins:

A smell of dead limes quicken in the nose
The leprosy of Empire

Walcott's explicit evocation of leprosy, which had a clear colonial history in that colonies were often linked to leprosaria and other tropical diseases (see Edmond 2006), is an ironic reversal of the colonial stereotype. Everywhere the house's magnificence lies in ruins, and Walcott not only describes the ruins but inscribes them in the brutal, petty and exploitative history of its builders: 'The imperious rakes are gone, their bright girls gone'. He meditates on the change where he conceives the 'great' English explorers and poets as mere 'murderers and poets' and where 'the ashen prose of Donne' burns his eyes. He then reverses the colonial's history:

I thought
Some slave is rotting in the manorial lake,
And still the coal of my compassion fought:
That Albion too, was once
A colony like ours. ('Ruins of a Great House', 1996, pp. 498–9)

Walcott here is against mere postcolonial bitterness and anger. Compassion is what informs a rewriting of colonial history. History, suggests Walcott, is to remember but moving on. As he puts it in his essay, 'The Muse of History':

The servitude to the muse of history has produced a literature of recrimination and despair, a literature of revenge written by the descendants of slaves or a literature of remorse written by the descendants of masters. (1998, p. 37)

The reclamation of history often takes the form of exploring alternative, hybridized and marginalized cultural practices. Wilson Harris (1999 [1981]) thus locates the origins of the Caribbean 'limbo' dance in the Middle Passage, where the slaves on the ships had very little space. It becomes, as Harris argues, a 'gateway' from the Old World to the New, from the African context to the American one. It gestures not only at the African past but marks 'the renascence of a new corpus of sensibility that could translate and accommodate African and other legacies within a new architecture of cultures' (Harris 1999 [1981], p. 380). Harris's is a move of postcolonial reclamation where he locates a specific cultural practice in its colonial history, but sees a hybrid culture as a positive consequence of history.

Australian poet A. D. Hope in his famous 'Australia' begins by acknowledging that his is a barren country, 'without sons, architecture, history' populated by 'second-hand Europeans'. Yet Hope concludes with a glad return to this backward place: 'Yet there are some like me turn gladly home.' He also hopes to see prophets rise in the country's deserts. It is the nature of such prophets that Hope underscores as being distinctly Australian:

Some spirit which escapes
The learned doubt, the chatter of cultured apes
Which is called civilization over there. ('Australia', pp. 193–4)

A. D. Hope echoes the sentiments of the first major Indian poet in English, Nissim Ezekiel, who concludes his 'Background, Casually' with a simple declaration: 'My backward place is where I am' (Ezekiel 1989 [1976], pp. 179–81).

Writing about Haitian historians, Joan Dayan (1995) notes how they needed to not only stay 'human' but also Haitian (slaves were not treated as human by Europeans, and non-humans of course do not write histories). Thus their claim to represent their 'native land' to foreign readers depended on their offering authentic evidence of their colour and that too in 'proper' language. Many often took recourse to mythic constructions – and thus merged literary and historical writing. Dayan points to the trope of the hero and the madwoman (the long suffering or mad *negresse* and the powerful *noir*) in numerous Haitian texts. As Dayan puts it, a Haitian *vodou* history must appropriate oral accounts, spirits and local mythic figures. It is only through such a reappropriation that can help the postcolonial 'destroy the illusions of mastery, circumventing and confounding *any* master narrative' (p. 93, emphazis in original), where the master narrative is the European history of the native.

It is also possible to see Diop's 'reconquering' exemplified in the *El Plan de Aztlán* prepared by the National Chicano Youth Liberation Conference of 1969:

> With our heart in our hands and our hands in the soil, we declare the independence of our mestizo nation. We are a bronze people with a bronze culture. Before all of North America, before all our brothers in the bronze continent, we are a nation, we are a union of free pueblos, we are Aztlán. (*Documents of the Chicano Struggle* 1971, p. 4)

It is the ancient, pre-colonial space – the Aztlán, the ancestral homeland of the Aztec – that is being retrieved here as a *metaphor* for the Chicano struggle for self-determination. The document is all that we have said of postcolonialism's version of history-writing: it maps the colonial period but also retrieves a *pre*-colonial past. Now it is important to understand that:

- This pre-colonial past might be a myth.
- This pre-colonial past cannot be retrieved uncontaminated by colonialism.
- This pre-colonial past had its own dominant and subordinate ordering of societies.

Mythic spaces serve the postcolonial purpose of economic self-determination, cultural identity and political freedoms. I now turn to the role of myth in postcolonial nationalism.

Myth-making, Nationalism, Disillusionment

Such myths serve the purpose of constructing an image of the nation for the postcolonial. Salman Rushdie sums up myth-making in post-independence India thus:

[Indian independence day] an extra festival on the calendar, a new myth to celebrate . . . a country which would never exist except by the efforts of a phenomenal collective will except in a dream we all agreed to dream . . . India, the new myth – a collective fiction in which anything was possible, a fable rivaled only by the two other mighty fantasies – money and God. (1982, p. 111)

The postcolonial novel was a space and form where such myths could be forged. The novel itself, as Benedict Anderson (1991) and Timothy Brennan (1995 [1990]) have pointed out, is linked to nationalist sentiments in Europe. In the case of Third World writers, Brennan notes, there is more than just nationalist sentiment. There are very often nostalgia, anti-colonial thought and a sense of exile in these authors. Brennan notes that in the case of Salman Rushdie, the aim is to explore 'postcolonial responsibility' (p. 63), to tell the story of 'an entire region slowly coming to think of itself as one' (p. 63). This is of course the linkage of the novel with nation-building. But, Brennan notes, Rushdie's *Midnight's Children* is about 'disappointment', because 'so little improvement has been made' (p. 63). What Rushdie maps is, according to Brennan, not national heroism, which is treated 'bitterly and comically', but the 'nationalist demagogy of a caste of domestic sellouts and power-brokers' (pp. 63–4). In Nigeria's Chimananda Ngozi Adichie's short story 'Cell One' she describes how university students join cults and cult wars erupt frequently on campus: 'guns and tortured loyalties and axes had become common' (2009, p. 7). Adichie's story deals with the descent into chaos and disillusionment as the postcolonial nation's spaces of learning are corrupted. In Ngugi's *A Grain of Wheat*, the leader of the anti-colonial movement, Kihika, acquires mythic status and Ngugi alerts us to the problems inherent in this when he refers to Kihika's self-aggrandizing 'visions of himself [as] a saint, leading Kenyan people to freedom and power' (1967,

p. 83) and his 'immense arrogance' (p. 89). In Ayi Kwei Armah's *The Beautyful Ones are Not Yet Born* (1988) Armah captures the promise of the decolonized state and the unbelievable collapse of all the postcolonial ideals:

> The promise was so beautiful. Even those who were too young to understand it all knew that at last something good was being born. It was there. We were not deceived about that. How could such a thing turn so completely into this other thing? Could there have been no other way? (1988, p. 85)

Like Rushdie, Armah is also appalled at what the postcolonial nation has become. In Isabel Allende's novel about a South American country, *Of Love and Shadows* (1994 [1987]) she describes a dictator-ship appalling in its cruelty. The General, believes Hilda in the novel, is 'possessed by Satan' and that it was 'possible to defeat him through systematic prayer and faith'. In order to end the trauma of the nation, Hilda takes to attending mystic evening sessions with a group of 'pious souls who were steadfast in their intent to put an end to the tyranny'. It was, writes Allende, 'a national movement, a chain of prayer' (1994, p. 103). Postcolonial nations also require national movements against their own governments sometimes, suggests Allende. In Rohinton Mistry's *Such a Long Journey*, the postcolonial nation-state has degenerated. The Indo-China war, calculated to arouse 'national feelings', becomes the context for political greed and opportunism:

> No Chinese soldiers approached Khodadad building. Instead, teams of fund-raising politicians toured the neighbourhood. Depending on which party they belonged to, they made speeches praising the Congress government's heroic stance or denouncing its incompetency . . . . (10)

In George Lamming's *In the Castle of My Skin* (1979 [1953]), Mr Slime's organization that sets out to fight the English, eventually forms the corrupt local elite, and betrays the anti-colonial cause. This is the *postcolonial novel of disillusionment* and gives the lie to the glorification of the nation by postcolonials themselves. The myths of glorious nation-hood have failed.

Political myth-making is a strong component of Third World literary fictions. However, such a mythification often derives from an exclusionary tradition, a selective history where, even the postcolonial society appropriates only *select* sections of its own past. This selective tradition is then presented as the national condition. To phrase it differently, postcolonial societies often adopt specific elements from their pasts while marginalizing some others and then present these selective elements as representing an entire national culture. These marginalized histories are subaltern histories, as we shall see.

LANGUAGE AND THE POSTCOLONIAL

One had to convey in a language that is not one's own the spirit that is one's own. One has to convey the various shades and omissions of a certain thought-movement that looks maltreated in an alien language. I use the word 'alien', yet English is not really an alien language to us... We cannot write like the English. We should no. we cannot write only as Indians. We have grown to look at the larger world as part of us.

(Raja Rao 1963, p. vii)

The postcolonial writer in English has always had to deal with the question: why write in English, the language of the former European master? Raja Rao's argues that it is impossible to capture native feelings and thoughts in the European language unless – and this is important for the postcolonial project – it is nativized. Recent debates revolve around this process of nativization.

I have already cited Achebe's reliance on Igbo proverbs. The use of such local expressions (as well as local legends and myths) alters the tone, style, usage and patterns of the European's language. If during the colonial period the nationalists used the foreign language as a means of articulating dissent and demanding freedom, in the post-independence period the postcolonial writer nativizes the European's language. That is, English and the European language gets hybridized by the native as his/her own. While some postcolonial writers and critics (Harish Trivedi, Ngugi) demand that the postcolonial writer should use only her/his native language, others argue that nobody 'owns' a language and as such the postcolonial could benefit from this dual inheritance of English and the native language. Often, of course, this results in a tension, as Derek Walcott captures it in the lines from 'A Far Cry from Africa' I have already quoted (in Chapter 2):

> Divided to the vein
> How choose
> Between this Africa and the English tongue I love? (1986, pp. 17–18)

The native writer's language is hybridized because the writer's identity itself is hybridized:

> I'm just a red nigger who love the sea(google)
> I had a sound colonial education,
> I have Dutch, nigger, and English in me,
> And either I'm nobody, or I'm a nation. (Walcott, '*The Schooner Flight*', 1986, p. 346)

Walcott, in particular, like Rushdie, has been at the forefront of forging new identities through hybridization. He accommodates and appropriates multiple sources and traditions in his work: Creole, Caribbean dialects and the colonial English.

As varieties of English emerge, we see 'Englishes' that are post-colonial, nativized and hybridized. 'Pidgin English', as these are known, combine English with a native language. Poetry, especially, has benefited from such a hybridization:

> You can make her out the way she speaks;
> Her consonants bludgeon you;
> Her argot is rococo, her latest 'slang'
> Is available in classical dictionaries . . .
> No, she is not Anglo-Indian . . .
> She is Indian English, the language that I use. (Keki Daruwalla, 'Mistress' 1982, pp. 22–3)

Another Indian poet, Kamala Das, asserts her right to English, especially her right to modify it to suit her needs:

> Don't write in English, they said,
> English is not your mother tongue . . .
> The language I speak
> Becomes mine, its distortions, its queerness
> All mine, mine alone. It is half English, half

Indian, funny perhaps, but it is honest,
It is as human as I am human, don't
You see? It voices my joys, my longings,
My hopes . . . ('An Introduction', in Thieme 1996, p. 717)

In each case the postcolonial writer asserts her identity not in an abandonment of the former European master's language, but in its appropriation. A postcolonial identity is forged, in many cases, not in a return to a pre-colonial language or a 'pure' form, but in a hybridization where political independence means that the postcolonial is empowered through the colonial past to fashion a new identity. While it is possible to argue that this makes postcolonialism a derivative discourse and form, it is also clear that hybridization is an act of agency and freedom where the writer creatively uses English – Rushdie's mix of English with Hindi film songs is an instance – in order to show how the crucial weapon of colonization can become the weapon of the postcolonial as well.

CULTURAL NATIONALISM AND NATIVISM

National liberation is necessarily an act of culture.
Amilcar Cabral (quoted in Cheah 2003, p. 11)

In Canadian Aboriginal writer Jeanette Armstrong's *Slash*, an old medicine man tells the young Indian boy:

It is not the [native] culture that is lost. It is you. The culture that belongs to us is *handed down to us* in the sacred medicine ways. Our strength lies there . . . That is not lost. It is around us here *in the mountains and in the wild places.* It is in *the sound of the drums* and in *the sound of the singing of the birds.* (1985, p. 191, emphasis in original)

The old man's admonition captures postcolonialism's nostalgic cultural nationalism as much as it does the embeddedness of native cultures in the landscape and environment. In Australian Judith Wright's 'Nigger's Leap, New England' even the dust and rocks are seen as carrying the history of the Aborigines:

Did we not know their blood channelled our rivers,
and the black dust our crops ate was their dust?

Wright concludes with the erasure of Aborigine history:

> Night floods us suddenly as history
> that has sunk many islands in its good time. (1972, p. 15)

Here of course a white poet is seeking to bring to public attention the cruelties perpetrated by her ancestral whites on the Aborigines.

Cultural nationalism and nativism, both integral components of anti-colonial struggles as well as postcolonialism, are characterized by

- the assertion of pride in a disappearing tradition
- nostalgia for the disappearing tradition
- attempts to adapt traditions to modern demands and contexts
- retrieval of folkloric and indigenous methods of storytelling or lifewriting within the new contexts of global publishing.

What is important in the case of postcolonial societies is that nationalism is a *cultural* phenomenon. Thus Caribbean poets, writes Edward Kamau Brathwaite (1999 [1984]), are influenced by 'nation language' – the language 'which is influenced very strongly by the African model, the African aspect of our New World/Caribbean heritage' (p. 311). This 'nation language', Brathwaite notes, has its roots in African oral traditions and is a performance in the sense the poet-singer requires an actual audience. It is therefore a performance that works within a community and is thus a shared cultural practice as opposed to reading. Here Brathwaite makes a fascinating postcolonial move:

- He links a cultural practice to a historical genre/context.
- He explicitly references this practice to a shared experience.
- He shows how this shared witnessing of the cultural practice can serve as the basis of a national identity.

This is postcolonialism's insistence on nationalism as a cultural phenomenon.

The experience of individuals, groups and communities in specific territories often take recourse to long-standing cultural 'root metaphors'. Dipankar Gupta (2000) has argued that cultural spaces relate to each other through nation-state *metaphors*. Such metaphors help nation-states to overcome identity conflicts involving language, religion or caste. *Sentiments* towards one's roots metaphors – especially of the nation-state – enable an identification with the nation-state. As Gupta demonstrates, the task for many postcolonial societies has been to transform such sentiments into a *structure*. The best example of the role of sentiment in the building of nations is to be found in cultural nationalism.

One of the first to theorize cultural nationalism was Frantz Fanon. Fanon argued that anti-colonial struggles can be best fought at the level of culture. Within anti-colonial struggles we can discern the possibilities of what Fanon termed a 'national culture'. In this the victory over the colonial must be seen as the work of the people and not only of the national elite, a victory that will aid the rise of a true nationalism. There is a risk, Fanon argued, that nationalism could degenerate into ethnic, tribal strife and even racism. Fanon's *The Wretched of the Earth* instead proposes that anti-colonial struggles must result in an awakening of the intelligence and consciousness of the people. This will allow the birth of true nationalism and a national culture. As Fanon put it:

> The awakening of the whole people will not come about all at once; the people's work in the building of the nation will not immediately take on its full dimensions. (*Wretched* 135)

What Fanon does is to shift the focus from nationalism to a national *consciousness*. Such a consciousness, he argues, will possess an 'international dimension' (p. 247). This will require a clear and concrete linkage between the intellectuals and the masses. In other words, Fanon foresees national consciousness as the consequence of the awakening of the masses. This will make them extremely self-conscious, and self-consciousness is a prime requirement for a national consciousness, according to Fanon.

A revival of native cultural forms and identities was essential to the anti-colonial struggle as we have seen above. Pan-Africanism and Negritude were cultural movements directed at reclaiming black pride, tribal cultures and their local histories. Negritude and nativism are examples of a consciousness and cultural practice that builds upon a collective sentiment and investment in practices regarded as essential to a group's identity. When Leopold Senghor referred to the 'sum of the cultural value of the black world' (1994, p. 28) he was appealing to a sentimental and native vision of African identity. Nativism is a form of literary creation and postcolonial criticism that

> Demonstrates not only the innate strength of native traditions and the capacity of such traditions to offer alternatives to received knowledge-systems, but also the awareness that a continuing dependence on Western modes of criticism and scholarship, even when apparently helpful in our struggle for selfhood, are ultimately self-defeating. (Paranjape 1997a, p. xi)

In postcolonialism and especially postcolonial intellectual work nativism assumes a different aspect. Literature, CL Innes has demonstrated (1996), is the space where nationalism, especially cultural nationalism, finds very strong expression. Literature often:

- offers native cultures that are distinct from colonial cultures,
- locates cultural practices in very material conditions like the landscape and environment,
- offers resistant readings of canonical European texts by showing how these texts have misrepresented the natives (see the discussion of Achebe's reading of Conrad above) and
- foregrounds issues of ethnic/tribal or national pride.

Nativism focuses on local as opposed to foreign cultures, indigenous knowledges as opposed to received ones and the vernacular rather than European (in Third World nations with a history of colonial rule). Nativism is a form of postcolonial cultural practice that seeks a 'return to roots' as a means of battling the foreign presence, cultures and forms of thinking. Nativism in postcolonialism asserts the primacy of and pride in native cultures as a means of self-empowerment and emancipation from foreign intellectual and cultural domination.

Nativism as an intellectual and cultural movement capitalizes on sentiments like pride in one's native cultures, while it also warns against a simple 'revivalistic cultural nationalism . . . a mere atavistic retrieval of an ethnic separatism' (Satchidanandan 1997, p. 16). It seeks to foreground tradition and inheritance, but is cautious about the *nature* of the tradition being retrieved. Nativism emerges when local cultures begin to see their cultural practices as being marginalized under any of the three contexts of colonial domination, globalization and neo-colonialism and 'national' discourses of development and modernity.

Nativism in postcolonial critical practice

- is a form of cultural nationalism that calls for a preservation of native cultures in the face of such threats,
- seeks to retrieve native histories, folklore, local traditions and customs as alternate forms of knowledge.
- opposes native traditions and forms of thinking as a counter to colonial and even postcolonial ideas about modernity.

The nativist movement has, according to Debjani Ganguly, the

> ethical responsibility of decontaminating our *bhasa* [vernacular, local, as opposed to mainstream Sanskrit, Westernized] traditions from both colonialist (European) and mainstream (Sanskrit) literary historiographies and conceptual apparatuses. (1997, p. 131)

Nativism is 'postcolonial' because it

- resists Western traditions of thinking
- returns to the 'roots' of 'little' or local traditions
- resists even mainstream, 'national' traditions for being exclusionary, elitist and selective.

Nativism seeks a return to ethnic and local traditions, but, when critically edged, is careful to examine the *nature* of the traditions themselves. Retrieving unjust and socially exploitative traditions such as a feudal way of thinking is a very real risk in nativism – and one that practitioners warn us against (see Paranjape et al. 1997a, 1997b). As K. Satchidanandan puts it:

> Nativism is progressive in so far as it fights this revivalistic destruction of our native plurality; it can also be regressive if it just creates an alternative past and obstructs the growth of genuinely modern perceptions and attitudes, for nothing is necessarily good because it is native. (1997, p. 20)

Nativism can become, Debjani Ganguly warns us, 'retrogressive cultural nationalism' (1997, p. 132). Makarand Paranjape (1997b) rightly points to the key problems within nativism: that nativism posits local cultures as static and unchanging. But cultures – even local, vernacular ones – have always adapted and assimilated other cultures. Paranjape notes, citing another Nativist critic Balchandra Nemade, that one cannot valorize a tradition, merely because it is homegrown (1997b, p. 162).

Yet there is also the suspicion in some quarters that the postcolonial culture's attempted emphasis on 'authenticity' somehow ends up exoticizing their cultures for First World consumption. The use of native traditions, forms of language, folklore, myth, argue critics like Graham Huggan (2001) serves as the 'postcolonial exotic'. Here it is the native who does the exoticizing, a process Lisa Lau has termed 're-orientalism' (2007). Meenakshi Mukherjee, in what has turned out to be an influential and controversial argument, has argued that Indian authors who write in English, and especially those who cater to a cosmopolitan audience, often exhibit an 'anxiety of Indianness'. This anxiety, Mukherjee argues, results in a

homogenization of reality, an essentializing of India, a certain flattening out of complicated and conflicting contours, the ambiguous and shifting relations that exist between individuals and groups in a plural community. (2000, pp. 171–2)

The writer therefore fills her/his work with excessive markers of Indianness to prove that writing in English can also be truly Indian. This anxiety occurs because, unlike the 'regional' writer, the Indian writer in English is uncertain about his target audience (p. 172). Mukherjee's point that the Indian English author is at least partly addressing the West is indisputable. However, the accusation that this causes the Indian (or any postcolonial) author in English seek greater authenticity as compensation for writing in a foreign language is an unfair one (as novelist Vikram Chandra, 2000, was quick to point out in his response titled provocatively 'the cult of authenticity'). Does writing in one's mother tongue make one more authentic? And, by extension, does writing in English with markers of Indianness make it less so? Mukherjee is not a nativist critic, but her emphasis on striving for a totalizing authenticity in her critique of Indian writing in English smacks of unease with the *global recognition that only writings in English seem to achieve*. Regional literatures, she correctly argues (as does Rajeswari Sunder Rajan in her response to the debate, 2001a and 2001b), remain regional in the sense they cater to a smaller audience, make almost no money, attract few awards and even when translated, remain in a ghetto.

The 'native' is often set in opposition to the 'nation' (Kumar 1997) because they see the nation as being hegemonic and destroying native/ local traditions (Paranjape 1995). As Kumar points out, the native is what constructs the nation: 'the native . . . gives rise to the national, conversely, the native can also be appropriated as a mere item in the so-called national literature' (1997a 1997b, p. 124). It is with these tensions *within* – of nativism being itself exclusionary, xenophobic, anti-'nation' – that nativist criticism and thought has worked within postcolonialism. Jean-Baptiste Tati-Loutard, the Congo poet, is accused of *not being native enough* in what is characteristic of nativist ideology's fear of pluralism and cultural appropriations:

Now I carry inside me so many foreign lands
So many loves passed through in such scattered climes
That at home they think me grown less native to my place.
('Return from Ethiopia', p. 102)

In Australian literature the Jindyworobak movement of the 1930s was a nativist movement. The aim of this movement was to produce literature that could be readily identified as Australian. Poets like Rex Ingamells, Ian Mudie, William Hart Smith, Mary Cato and James Devaney turned to two major themes:

• Australia's distinctiveness from its 'roots' – Europe
• The Aboriginal cultures of Australia

But the movement was created almost entirely by white Australians, and hence their 'nativism' was often controversial for ignoring (or merely exhibiting) Aboriginal culture.

In more contemporary instances, nativism might be best exemplified in the works of Aboriginal, tribal and First People's writings. Indigenous cultures have traditionally been represented as exotic, primitive and in urgent need of both museumization and 'improvement' by the colonials. Aboriginal writing from Australia, New Zealand and Canada, and Dalit writing from India has acquired a significant readership because, in typical nativist fashion, these texts foreground an identity politics. They represent a resistance to homogenization in the postcolonial era where the Dalit, the Native American and the Aboriginal seek to exhibit their difference from the rest or mainstream postcolonial cultures.

Nativism in indigenous writing often relies upon a culture's *oral traditions*. In *Anthills of the Savannah* Achebe emphasizes the role of storytelling. The elder addressing his audience says:

> It is only the story can continue beyond the war and the warrior. It is the story that outlives the sound of war-drums and the exploits of brave fighters. It is the story, not the others, that saves our progeny from blundering like blind beggars into the spikes of the cactus fence. The story is our escort; without it, we are blind. (p. 124)

Oral traditions are treated as pre-colonial and therefore the novels of Mudrooroo Narogin (Aboriginal writer from Australia), Sivakami and Bama (Dalit writers from India), Thomas King and Alexie Sherman (Native American) use folk songs and myths as part of their storytelling. Proverbs and aphorisms are a routine element in Achebe's works. The significance of the use of proverbs in Igbo everyday life is made clear in the opening sections of *Things Fall Apart*:

> Having spoken plainly so far, Okoye said the next half a dozen sentences in proverbs. Among the Ibo the art of conversation is regarded very highly, and proverbs are the palm oil with which words are eaten. (1969 [1958], p. 10)

Passages like these explicitly reference a usage that everybody in that community immediately understands: 'I don't know why my tongue is crackling away tonight like a clay-bowl of ukwa seeds toasting over the fire' (Achebe 1988, p. 126). The novel functions here as a near-ethnographic narrative detailing the culture of the people, but *not*, as Dennis Walder has argued about Achebe, exoticizing them (1998, p. 9). Nativism here becomes a mode of retaining older cultural forms within the ambit of Western genres (the novel) and structures (publication in English).

Postcolonial Aboriginal writers have also produced a vast body of life writing. What is crucial is that many writers refuse to privilege the individual over the community, and hence the individual's story is embedded within the story of a tribe, a community or an ethnic group. While this problematically shifts the focus from the singularity of an individual's experience – and this singularity, as several scholars have shown, is the basis of (Western) human rights discourses (Ignatieff 2001) – to the shared experience of a more or less anonymous community. Such life writing texts became popular from the 1970s. Beverley Hungry Wolf's *The Ways of My Grandmothers* (1998), Florence Edenshaw Davidson and Margaret B. Blackman's *During my Time* (1992) and other texts became classics, and acquired some kind of cult status within feminist and postcolonial curricula.

However, in the postcolonial context nativism also turns reactionary and retrograde as *a response to the perceived marginalization of specific cultures in postcolonial contexts*.

NATIONAL IDENTITY, SUBALTERNIZATION AND MINORITY DISCOURSE

The marginalization of specific groups in postcolonial nations after acquiring political independence has resulted in cultural dissent, fundamentalisms, secessionist-separatist movements and political unrest. Postcolonial nations replicate structures of oppression and inequality and create subalterns of their own.

Subaltern Histories

The 'Subaltern Studies' group, consisting of David Arnold, Ranajit Guha, Dipesh Chakrabarty, Partha Chatterjee and, for a time, Sumit Sarkar, became interested in the 'lower' side of historiography. The term grew out of Italian Marxist Antonio Gramsci's vocabulary, where the 'subaltern' was a 'subordinate' or 'dependent'. 'Subalternity' was 'the general attribute of subordination in South Asian society whether this is expressed in terms of class, caste, age, gender and office or in any other way' (Guha 1982a, p. vii). Subaltern historiography has, building upon this ideological position, attempted to capture 'the small voice of history' where people developed their own forms of nationalism in 'defiance or absence of elite control' (Guha 1982b, pp. 2–4). Peasant actions, spontaneous rebellions and scattered acts of violence are re-read for their counter-histories. Using techniques developed by structuralism and narrative theory, the Subaltern group examines the archives where official records, individual memoirs and administrative reports have presented history in certain ways. Gyan Pandey explored how communalism was constructed in colonial India (1992), and David Arnold showed how European medicine colonized the native's body (1993) as Subaltern

Studies tried to uncover the layers of elite and colonial historiography, to get to the local (tribal, women, peasant and working
class). It is a *history from below*, and often utilizes resources in *native*,
that is *non-colonial, non-official* languages such as folk songs, ballads,
stories, etc., for its purposes.

The aim was to *re-read* these narratives from history. The group
was interested in representational strategies that could offer new
perspectives on anti-colonial resistance or rebellion. The problem of
course was that such a reading retrieved notions of 'consciousness'
and 'will' when speaking of subalterns. Here the influence of Gayatri
Spivak's collaboration with the Subaltern group – 1988 saw the
publication of *Selected Subaltern Studies*, co-edited by Ranajit Guha
and Spivak – is most visible. Spivak's essay in the volume, 'Subaltern
Studies: Deconstructing Historiography', located the Subaltern
Studies project within literary theory, especially deconstruction and
poststructuralism.

In a later (and more famous) essay, 'Can the Subaltern Speak?'
(1988) Spivak argued that subjects are constituted *through* discourse.
An individual cannot develop an identity without being the subject
of a discourse over which she/he may have little or no control. Such
a subject-subaltern cannot speak, and must be spoken *for* by scrupu-
lous historians. The subaltern woman, in particular, has no position
of enunciation: she remains within the discourse of patriarchy and
colonialism as the object of another's discourse.

Gyanendra Pandey (1999) has tellingly argued that a nation
constructs specific communities as marginal even as it claims
political independence. Minorities and specific ethnic groups feel
subalternized when they are disenfranchised. Postcolonial societies
which began with anti-colonial movements so as to empower
themselves end up doing the very *exclusions* they fought against.
Aijaz Ahmad writes in a critique of the postcolonial state itself:

> What we witnessed was not just the British policy of divide and
> rule, which surely was there, but our own willingness to break up
> our civilizational unity, to kill our neighbours . . . The major
> fictions of the 50s' and 60s' – the shorter fictions of Manto, Bedi,
> Intezar Hussein; the novels of Qurrat ul Ain, Khadija Mastoor,
> Abdullah Hussein – came out of that refusal to forgive what we
> ourselves had done and were still doing, in one way or another, to
> our own polity. (1987, p. 22)

Aboriginals in Australia and Canada, Dalits in India, the Chicano/ as in the USA, ethnic minorities, the women and the poor everywhere are the subalterns whose location within the postcolonial is always fraught, risky and threatened. In the fiction of Rohinton Mistry one sees the Muslims and Parsis under constant threat from a presumably secular India. Salman Rushdie's fiction does the same. Immigrants living lives of anxiety in First World cities are the subjects of Kiran Desai, Hanif Kureishi, Timothy Mo, Buchi Emecheta, Monica Ali and other postcolonial writers who offer insights into the immigrant experience.

Subalternization, as I have argued elsewhere (Nayar 2008a), is the process through which postcolonial nation-states valorize certain identities and marginalize certain others. Inter-ethnic and tribal conflicts leading to genocide, as evidenced by Rwanda, Sudan, Somalia and the Congo are extreme instances of this subalternization. Neil Lazarus, in an exemplary reading of postcolonial African literatures (1990), has argued that postcolonial thought cannot account for the marginalization of the natives by the postcolonial nation-state.

The problem of postcolonial intellectual work, Lazarus argues in a later essay (1994), is one of representation and the question of speaking for the subaltern. Reading the work of Gayatri Spivak, among other postcolonial theorists, Lazarus acknowledges that postcolonial scholars have homogenized the postcolonial people, something they accused the Orientalist-colonials of doing (p. 218). Lazarus accepts that any 'counternarrative of liberation' (a phrase he picks up from Henry Louis Gates, Jr.), would have to avoid Eurocentric 'bourgeois humanism' (p. 219). That is, any 'counternarrative of liberation' from the postcolonial might require an abandonment of humanism as articulated in the European tradition where it treated only the European as the universal human and ignored other varieties. Instead, suggests Lazarus following Fanon, postcolonial intellectuals would have to think of a *new* humanism. The postcolonial standpoint, he writes, must be universalist of a different kind, 'nationalitarian, liberationist, internationalist' (p. 220), so that it can speak for *all* humanity.

Subalternization in the colonial period meant marginalization of non-white races by European colonial masters. In the postcolonial age this *marginalization of tribals, minorities and specific groups is done by dominant ethnic groups, classes and castes, often with the active collusion of the newly-independent nation-state*, a process I term 'continuing colonialism' (Nayar 2008a). When the minorities have their laws modified by the majority, when corporate and economic control rests with a select ethnic group or tribe (as happened in the case of the Tutsis in Rwanda, who then reduced the Hutus to the status of menials), we see 'continuing colonialism' at work.

Continuing colonialism or postcolonial subalternization involves the following:

- The *cultural* marginalization of specific ethnic groups and communities whereby their cultural practices are mocked, legally proscribed or made difficult to practice,
- The *economic* marginalization of groups where employment and trade are restricted to dominant groups,
- The *political* disenfranchisement of groups through stringent laws of voting, housing or employment.

Subaltern groups in postcolonial societies rarely enjoy the benefits of independence. Kath Walker's 'We Are Going' captures this disenfranchised state of the Aboriginals, the original inhabitants of what became the settler colony of Australia. In the poem the Aboriginals come into a small town and sit around. They cannot express what they are really thinking:

We are as strangers here now, but the white tribe are the
Strangers.
We belong here, we are of the old ways . . .

The poem concludes with the clearly elegiac sense of Aboriginal history:

'The scrubs are gone . . .
The eagle is gone . . .
The bora ring is gone,
The corroboree is gone.
And we are going' (1996, pp. 223–4)

Much of Rohinton Mistry's fiction (*Such a Long Journey*, *A Fine Balance*, *Family Matters*) deals with Parsis as minorities in India, an ethnic group that is traditional, conservative, religious-minded in the context of a 'secular' modern India.

Some of the most politically significant work within postcolonialism in recent times has been directed towards subaltern writing and what Abdul JanMohamed and David Lloyd termed 'minority discourse' (1987, also 1990). Muslims in India, the Hutu-Tutsi battles in Rwanda, the conditional of the Aboriginal, it could be argued, can be productively read around the theme of minority discourse. Any ethnic culture, writes David Lloyd in a later elaboration, which is usually turned inwards towards its own traditions and histories, is transformed into a minority culture 'only along the lines of its confrontation with a dominant state formation which threatens to destroy it by direct violence or by assimilation' (1994, p. 222). Lloyd argues that we cannot see ethnic cultures as merely aesthetic. Instead we need to see them as ways of life that are social, and therefore *political*. Hence we need to articulate ethnic culture as caught in the *dialectic* of ethnic and minority identity: *ethnic culture which is turned inwards and minority culture when it becomes subordinated to another*. In other words we must see how ethnic cultures are *constructed* as subjects to a dominant cultural formation: Muslims in India, Tutsis in Rwanda, Aboriginals in Australia, Native Americans in the USA. Democracies and the state, argues Lloyd, work through hegemony. And it is the hegemonic nature of the state that makes some ethnic cultures minority. When the *state seeks to assimilate the ethnic groups into 'mainstream' or national culture, it constructs the ethnic groups as minoritarian that can be assimilated*. We see this often in the case of the museumization of ethnic crafts and cultures, the ghettoization of the ethnic into the narrative of the nation. Further, the very term 'minority' signifies *numerical* representation, a political act that reduces cultures to numbers. Lloyd suggests that resistance to such minoritization – or what I have termed subalternization – can occur in the form of a different conceptualization of the ethnic culture. This requires seeing the ethnic community itself as an 'alternative kind of public sphere'. The 'assimilative state' must be resisted not through establishing of ghettoes but questioning the very terms by which the state is brought into existence. This requires creating conditions where 'radical self-determination' of various social formations can be made possible (p. 235).

What minority discourse does is to articulate positions from which economic, cultural and political diff*erence* can be respected. The economic rights of tribals to their ancestral land – a constant source of political tension in India – asserted within political discourse are an instance of minority discourse. While the state's discourse posits a unilateral, linear idea of 'progress', which also implies assimilation, it refuses to treat tribal cultures as alternate public sphere. Instead it characterizes them as 'minority' cultures in terms of numbers and 'history' within a development scheme. Thus, tribal narratives constitute a 'minority discourse' in the sense that tribal cultures are relegated to a position of subordination by the dominant narratives of the nation. The tribal, otherwise confident of her/his culture, is made to feel a sense of disappearance through rejection or assimilation: then we can discern a minority discourse at work in their writings and cultural practices.

In Douglas Lockwood's *I, the Aboriginal* (1978 [1962]), arguably, the first Aboriginal autobiography, Waipuldanya says:

A belief in our own kind of voodooism is strong in the heart of every tribalized Aboriginal, and of most of those who have been detribalized.

I have been living with white men and as a white man for ten years, but I still have not conquered the innate fear and inherent conviction I have of existence of supernatural powers of certain elder tribesmen. (p. 15)

Here Waipuldanya is doing several things. He first locates a 'core' to Aboriginal culture: voodooism. He then argues that this 'core' is indestructible even when the Aboriginal individual has been 'detribalized'. Finally, he shows how even when 'assimilated' into white cultures he is unable to shake off his 'core' values. Waipuldanya then proceeds to reveal the inadequacy of the white man's processes of assimilation and attempts to 'understand' Aboriginal culture:

There comes a time during any white man's analysis of an Aboriginal act when logic fails disappears and he runs into a solid wall of superstitions. (p. 16)

Waipuldanya situates Aboriginal culture in opposition to white cultures not because they are truly oppositional but because he wants to emphasize how Aboriginal culture cannot be assimilated. When Waipuldanya concludes his narrative this is what he says:

We have accepted the alien faith so as not to offend the white men who have been good to us . . .

Yet if they try for another five hundred years they will never take the deeply religious Kunapipi and Yabudurawa from us. (p. 239)

Minority discourse is this resistance to erasure and assimilation and emerges at the moment of 'detribalization'.

In the above case the discourse of national identity, of assimilation and 'Australian' culture is undermined by Waipuldanya's minority discourse which shows the cracks in such totalizing discourses. The self-identity of the tribal-Aboriginal that Waipuldanya emphasizes runs counter to the totalizing one, and thus offers us a new perspective on the postcolonial state.

Minority discourse, therefore, disturbs the grand narrative of the nation. Indeed, we see minority discourse occurring in far more visible ways in *cultural and ethnic nationalisms* in various nation-states today: the Igbo attempt to break away from Nigeria, the Tamil-Sinhala conflict in Sri Lanka since the 1980s, the creation of Inuit self-governing homeland in Canada in 1992 and the Basques in Spain are all instances of ethnic nationalisms that seek self-determination. Religious nationalisms, such as the one that created Pakistan in 1947, the Iranian revolution, the Taliban in Afghanistan and the rise of the Hindu right wing in India are also attempts at altering national community and identity – but these are seen as threats to civic nations (which seek to be secular). Extending the anti-colonial struggle – which was, it is worth reiterating, rooted in a cultural nationalism – to postcolonial contexts, ethnic nationalisms disturb the idea of the nation in significant ways.

Colonialism, when it 'granted' independence, carved out nation-states and their boundaries with little attention to the ethnic identities of the people living there. Ethnicity is a *form of collective identity based on shared cultural beliefs, practices and customs*. In the case of ethnic nationalisms, various ethnic groups demand greater share of the state resources. This is where national projects clash with ethnicities, and often to catastrophic consequences. Studies of Sudan and Darfur, for instance, have shown how the atrocities of the *janjawid* built on the rhetoric of works like the anonymously authored *Black Book* which chronicled the wrongs perpetrated on specific tribes and ethnic groups (Daly 2007). In Nigeria ethno-regional identities (Igbo, Hausa-Fulani and Yoruba) are overlaid with religious and socio-economic differences that have resulted in the crisis since 2000. The

Serb 'ethnic cleansing' of Croats and Muslims in the Balkan area can also be treated as a horrific example of ethno-nationalism. In 1994 over 500,000 of the minority Tutsis had been killed by the majority Hutus in just over 100days of terror in Rwanda. The Sindhi community in the subcontinent has a distinct ethnic identity, but does not have a nation. Indians in Malaysia, in the recent past, have had conflicts with the nation-state. In the 1970s, under Idi Amin, Indians were expelled from Uganda. Thus ethnicity is very often *not* coterminous with nation-states. While nation identity often relies on territorial attachments, ethnic identities extend beyond borders. Thus Tamils in Canada and European nations supported the LTTE in Sri Lanka just as the Sikhs in these nations were funding the Sikh separatist movement in India in the 1980s. While ethnicity can provide the springboard for nationalism, it could also be directed at separatism.

Finally, nationalisms and ethnic-nationalisms face their biggest challenge in the form of globalization. In the face of dissolving national boundary, increased displacement and diasporic cultures, the dominance of transnational institutions and linkages (whether exploitative, as Hardt and Negri suggest in *Empire*, 2000, or for other causes, such as Amnesty or Greenpeace), global flows of capital and peoples, what we see, ironically, is the heightened emphasis on *cultural rootedness*. Displaced communities 'connect' with their roots (see Franklin 2004) with a fervour that is only explainable in terms of ethnic nationalisms. Studies have shown that diasporic Indians, for example, are far more entrenched in their 'Indian culture' than their relatives and friends living in India. Further, many of these diasporic Indians seek a more 'hardline' approach to customs and traditions (Lal 2003, Varghese 2003).

* * *

The nation is clearly at the forefront of postcolonial thought. The debates and disputes over what constitutes a nation's 'authentic' culture, the tensions over new forms of colonialisms and the very evident internal colonialism whereby some groups are marginalized figure prominently as themes in postcolonial writings from Africa, Asia, the Caribbean and South America.

CHAPTER FOUR

GENDER AND SEXUALITY

What is it about our menfolk? They belittle our coping skills, mock our decision-making abilities, jibe at our emotional frailty, but when crisis time comes, they just fall apart.

(Minhas 2007, p. 42)

Nations and nationalism are gendered, in anti-colonial struggles as well as postcolonial nation states. Notions of tradition, value and prestige within nationalist discourses very often fold into debates about the woman, seen as the placeholder for all these – as evidenced by the controversies over women's dress codes and behaviour (in India, Afghanistan and African countries) in postcolonial nations. The home, community and tradition become sites of identity, and the woman is the key figure here, as exemplified in the works of Wole Soyinka, Chinua Achebe, Flora Nwapa, Ama Ata Aidoo, Gloria Anzaldua, Salman Rushdie and other postcolonial writers. The very idea of 'nation-as-family' in postcolonialism is contingent upon particular roles for men and women. The Pakistani writer Shandana Minhas seems to indicate that these stereotypes of masculinity, femininity and national identity are all equally flawed and mythic, as the epigraph to this chapter shows.

In this chapter I address the theme of gender and sexuality, with attendant discussions of postcolonial feminism and postcolonial queer writing.

Feminist trends in postcolonialism have interrogated the assumptions behind such gendered ideas of the nation, as it investigates the role played by patriarchy in the construction of the nation *and* the woman. Women writers from Asia, Africa and South America have foregrounded the gendered nature of the nation, the patriarchal conditions of the family and the question of sovereignty over their bodies. Postcolonial women's writings involve a critique of

- colonialism
- the nationalist 'use' of women in the anti-colonial struggle
- the status of women in the postcolonial nation-state
- the crisis of 'development' and the differential effects on men and women
- religious fundamentalisms and
- the continuing patriarchal control over women.

In terms of their politics and contexts, postcolonial feminism is concerned with real *material* conditions of Third World women's lives:

- 'Third World' sweat-shops and women's labour,
- global sex tourism,
- effects of environmental hazards and accidents,
- medicine and public health,
- militarization and the effects of war (including rape camps, most recently at Darfur, Sudan and earlier in Bosnia, Serbia and Rwanda),
- education.

In Ama Ata Aidoo's *Our Sister Killjoy* (1988 [1977]), Sissie is unable to respond to her European friend Maria, yet also distances herself from the African community in England. Sissie seeks to escape *both her gender and her racial identities* – to assert her *individual* identity/agency in the process. Novelists Assia Djebar, Taslima Nasreen and Anita Desai who question the role of the patriarchal family, the possibilities of an egalitarian society, and the use of religious doctrine in oppressing women. Postcolonial women writers see the woman as being doubly colonized – by the European races and by their own men.

Gender themes in postcolonial writing include issues such as the following:

i. Identity – sexual, ethnic, national, socio-political, cultural
ii. The intersection of the discourses of racism, imperialism and sexism
iii. Marriage, sexuality, desire and the body
iv. The link between fundamentalism and patriarchy

v. The role of 'mothers', and the intimate linkage between motherhood and motherland

vi. Women and spirituality in postcolonial societies.

From within the gender-sexuality paradigm of postcolonialism,
postcolonial queer literature calls into question the kinds of identities
demanded, recognized and imposed by families. Their concern over
the assumption of heterosexuality and heterosexual relationships as
the norm within families and society is often thematized as the quest
for alternative forms of (perhaps stigmatized) relationships. Queer
sexuality has a problematic relation with postcolonial societies and
culture, exemplified in the work of Suniti Namjoshi, Shyam Selvadurai,
Mahesh Dattani and Cherrie Moraga. Associative links between
ethnicity and sexuality have also been explored by South Asian and
Southeast Asian diasporic writers of the postcolonial period. The
experience of gender and sexual preferences are different for different
ethnic groups (Takagi 1996). Even within marginalized groups (like
Blacks or Asians in the USA), heterosexuality is retained as a norm,
and queer seen as deviations. Moving out of a particular national/
cultural/ethnic group or territory is often coterminous with sexual
freedom. The works of Hanif Kureishi (of Pakistani origins) demonstrate how being queer brown/black results in a double colonization.

GENDER AND THE EMPIRE

Women were doubly colonized – by colonialism and by patriarchy
(Petersen and Rutherford 1986, p. 9). Postcolonial feminist readings
began by examining canonical European literatures for their
complicity in the imperial project.

The empire was always, primarily, a *masculine* adventure (Hyam
1990, Dawson 1994, Phillips 1997). Discovery, exploration, conquest
and rule were acts and symbols of the European *male's* dominance of
the world. This dominance extended to both, landscape and women,
their own as well as native. Sexualized themes in the literature of
empire include such well-known ones as

• the exploration of the Arab harem
• the need to safeguard the white woman from the libidinous, hypersexual native man
• the 'protection' of the native woman by the ultra-macho
European male and

- the instrumental use of the European women by the European male in the imperial project as guardians of European morals, traditions and principles.

The native woman is an important and persistent figure in European representations of the colony. Male travellers into the Orient treated the space itself as feminine. The numerous examples and descriptions of the mysterious, veiled, seductive Oriental women in eighteenth and nineteenth century travelogues converted the entire land into feminine, waiting for masculine exploration and conquest (Yeğenoğlu 1998).

European women did contribute to the imperial project, where they saw themselves as the repository of their culture's morals and values. Thus Evelyn Cecil writes in 1902: 'It is women of high moral character possessed of common sense and a sound constitution who can build up our Empire' (Cecil 1902, p. 683). Such women had to be protected, and events like the 1857 'Mutiny' in India (where the soldiers of the English East India Company rose in rebellion against the officers, banded together and waged battles across most of northern India) and the Morant Bay uprising in Jamaica (1865) became iconic of the danger faced by this species of empire builders. Stories of Englishwomen being kidnapped, raped and massacred circulated through Britain during this time, and reinforced the stereotypes of the hypersexual-brutal native and the innocent-virtuous Englishwoman (Gregg 1897, Semmel 1962, Lorimer 1972, Brantlinger 1988, Nayar 2007b). Philip Alexander Bruce wrote of the Africans' 'return' to savagery thus:

> There is something strangely alluring and seductive to them in the appearance of a white woman; they are aroused and stimulated by its foreignness to their experience of sexual pleasure, and it moves them to gratify their lust at any cost and in spite of every obstacle. This proneness of the negro is so well understood that the white women of every class, from the highest to the lowest are afraid to venture any distance alone, or even wander unprotected in the immediate vicinity of their homes. (quoted in Ware, p. 206)

The woman becomes the boundary-marker of colonial/European purity here in this gendered discourse of native violence.

The men of the empire believed that, for the empire to retain its aura, their women should appear only in certain kinds of roles: the

Memsahib, the judge's wife, the teacher. Working class English-women, for instance, were not really welcome because they lowered the glamour of the empire. This is made explicit in a Minute of 1902 in the context of European bar-girls in India:

> Whether the barmaids do or do not for the most part serve European customers, yet there is nothing to prevent natives from frequenting the bars; very often they do so; the girls cannot refuse to serve them; the spectacle of the service is open to the eyes of natives equally with Europeans, and occasionally as in Rangoon, incidents occur which are profoundly degrading to the prestige of the ruling race . . .
>
> But what I ask is the need for them in Calcutta at all? Why bring them out from home, whether it be to ruin, to concubinage, or to marriage? Why place them behind Calcutta bars to tempt in the young English clerks, and persuade the latter to spend their sub-stance in drinking and frivolity, if not worse? Why make public spectacle of English girls engaged in duties which must carry with them some sense of humiliation to the native eye, and which must suggest the ideas of immorality, ever where the reality does not exist? (quoted in Ballhatchet 1980, pp. 139–40)

The English women back 'home' may not have been particularly proud of their Anglo-Indian sisters, and a novelist-commentator deplored this attitude of English women towards their colonial sisters:

> English women are disposed to pass judgment on their Anglo-Indian sisters . . . From pedestals of sober respectability and ener-getic industry they denounce as idle, frivolous and luxury-loving, those other women of whose trials and temptations they know little or nothing. (Maud Diver quoted in Trollope 1983, p. 125)

Postcolonial feminism sees European women as caught in a double bind within colonial structures and ideologies, as seeking answers to two questions:

- Should they, by virtue of their *racial* identity, support their men in the imperial cause?
- Should they, by virtue of their *gender* identity, support the native women?

Symptomatic is Annette Ackroyd's protest against the Ilbert Bill – which allowed native judges to try Englishmen and women – in India:

> I speak the feeling of all Englishwomen in India when I say that we regard the proposal to subject us to the jurisdiction of native judges as an insult.
>
> It is not pride of race which dictates this feeling – it is the pride of womanhood. This is a form of respect which we are not prepared to abrogate. (Beveridge 1947, p. 220)

In the heyday of Victorian feminism, race complicated the English-woman's relations with Englishmen in the colonies (on Victorian feminism see Levin 1987). Many women travellers in the colonial period therefore found it difficult, given their feminism, to internalize, masculinized ideologies of imperial conquest (Spivak 1985, Suleri 1992, Jayawardene 1995). Instead, their views and engagements with non-European cultures were of an entirely different order.

European women in the colonial context

- fought their gendered (proto-feminist) battles, seeing the colony as a space where their rights and identities could be gained,
- rejected masculinist appropriations and engagements with native cultures,
- some were complicit with imperial projects of reform (especially in the nineteenth century),
- built connections with native women, often excluding men (both native and European) from this 'sisterhood',
- even encouraged native women in the anti-colonial struggle.

Clearly, the European woman was embedded in complex negotiations of her gender identity within the imperial context. Early European feminists like Florence Nightingale, Josephine Butler and Mary Carpenter were seeking a space for themselves *within* the masculinized space of the empire. Thus these white women used the imperial project to further their own feminist agenda, even though they might have furthered the imperial enterprise. In such cases, gender relations (of the English women with Englishmen) took centre-stage over race, and the white woman came to see/represent herself as a morally superior creature with the agenda of the 'white *woman's* burden' of helping the 'poor' native woman. This race differential was also, of course, the justification for different evaluations of the white and native woman, a differential that is most frightening expressed in the statement of the Lieutenant-Governor of New Guinea in 1925:

Doubtless there are native women who set the highest value on their chastity, but they are the exception and the rape of an ordinary native woman does not present any element of comparison with the rape on a respectable white woman, even where the offence upon the latter is committed by one of her own race and colour. (quoted in Ware 1992, p. 35)

GENDERED NATIONS, GENDERING NATIONALISM

Partha Chatterjee in *The Nation and Its Fragments* (see Chapters 6, 'The Nation and its Women' and Chapter 7, 'Women and the Nation') has argued that nationalist ideologies during India's anti-colonial struggle resolved the tension of nationalism and colonialism by separating the spheres of native culture and life. The public realm was colonized, but the inner domain of the domestic was kept 'pure'. While the public realm sought to incorporate the material benefits and changes from the colonial, the nationalists also sought to keep the 'spiritual' or domestic realm pure from any such contamination. In other words, the preservation of a 'national culture', in the Indian context, was the woman's responsibility. In a related critique, Anne McClintock (1995) has argued that the woman becomes a 'boundary marker' for cultures. Colonial conquest relies upon a conquest of the native woman, and concomitantly, for the natives, the 'preservation' of the purity of their women becomes a metaphor for the preservation of their culture itself. Women who appropriated Western modes – of dress, manners – were therefore ridiculed in the nineteenth century by Bengali writings of Michael Madhusudan Dutt, Dinabandhu Mitra and others for having abandoned their tradition. What Partha Chatterjee shows in a later essay (2001 [1990]) is the *engendering of postcolonial national identity*. Gender, summarizes Elleke Boehmer, has been 'intrinsic to national imagining' (2005, p. 5. Also Nasta 1992). Joane Nagel has argued that state power, citizenship, nationalism, militarism, revolution, political violence, dictatorship, and democracy are essentially 'masculinist projects, involving masculine institutions, masculine processes and masculine activities' (2005, p. 111).

In India, Indira Gandhi, the country's first woman Prime Minister, rode to power and retained it with an interesting conflation of 'Mother India' and herself. When defeated in the general elections after having controversially declared a state of 'national Emergency', she then functioned as a victim, a woman who sought the nation's forgiveness for her *son's* excesses during the period. Indira Gandhi drew upon cultural icons from the Hindu epic, *The Ramayana*, the tradition of the mother-goddess and the concept of female energy and power (*shakti*) while also speaking of her duties towards her 'family', the entire nation. Indira Gandhi therefore retained the cultural iconography of Indian womanhood – of daughter, mother – while nudging it into the realm of nationalism and national responsibility (Mishra 1989, Silva 2004). 'Your burdens', she said, 'are relatively light because your families are limited and viable. But my burden is heavy because crores of my family members are poverty-stricken and I have to look after them' (quoted in Silva 2004, p. 54). Salman Rushdie's portrayal of the Widow as the controlling power in *Midnight's Children* was a direct referencing of Indira Gandhi, who was a 'political widow' (as Silva terms her). Further, explicitly linking Indira Gandhi's repeated use of the cliché of 'Mother India', Saleem Sinai's mourns his – and, by extension, the nation's – lot:

> Women have made me; and also unmade. From Reverend Mother to the Widow, and even beyond, I have been at the mercy of the so-called (erroneously, in my opinion!), gentler sex. It is, perhaps, a matter of connection: is not Mother India, Bharatmata, commonly thought of as female? And, as you know, there's no escape from her. (1982, p. 404)

In Nayantara Sahgal's political novel *Rich Like Us,* any dissent is quelled by 'Madam' (Madam being a code for Indira Gandhi). What is significant about Sahgal's novel is that, on the one hand there is the demagogic, powerful and tyrannical woman figure of the 'Madam', and on the other there are the beggar's wife and the village women who are raped and beaten (1987, pp. 246–7). In novels like Rohinton Mistry's *A Fine Balance* (1995), the state of the country under the 'mother-figure' of Indira Gandhi is portrayed as oppressive, cruel and favouring the ruling elite. Such readings of women political figures map the national, cultural and political landscapes of postcolonial nations in terms of their appropriation of not only feminine *tropes* – 'Mother India' or Sita from the *Ramayana* – but also social structures specific to those cultures – of the nation as *family* (for nation as family see, along with Mishra 1989, Schultheis 2004).

Postcolonial theories and debates around gender have interrogated this conflation of landscape, national identity and the woman in literary and cultural representations (see section on postcolonial feminism below). Nations are therefore gendered because women

- become iconic of the 'motherland',
- carry the burden of being symbols of the nation's purity,
- are represented as the reservoirs of tradition,
- are the first to be circumscribed by fundamentalists under the pretext of guarding 'tradition',
- become the primary victims of war and conflict (internal as well as external).

In the remainder of this section I explore feminist nationalisms.

Feminist Nationalism

The work of scholars like Nira Yuval-Davis and Floya Anthias (1989) offers a major feminist reappraisal of nationalism. Women, they argue, somehow are retained for their reproductive functions: they reproduce not only families but also ethnicities and identities (Yuval-Davis 2002 [1997]). In Third World nations, as Sri Lankan critic Kumari Jayawardene has demonstrated (1986), feminist ideas emerged from *within* native traditions. Jayawardene's key contribution was to show how *women's loyalty to and participation in national liberation and revolutionary struggles did not preclude their struggle for equality and rights within their own cultures.*

The key 'problems' of gendered nations as feminist postcolonialism sees it are as follows:

- Nationalism becomes associated with masculinity.
- Anti-colonial and post-independent societies both take recourse to conservative views of women.

- The reliance on the nation-as-family metaphor consigns the woman to specific roles, even in post-independent nations.
- Nationalism is always projected as something achievable within the ambit of 'traditional' values and systems of thinking – even if those values and beliefs are anti-women.
- Legal systems, in particular, in postcolonial societies draw upon these same values – with the result the law seldom favours the woman.
- Rising fundamentalisms in postcolonial nations also target women, relying on moral policing and a reiteration of older beliefs in order to limit the 'modernization' of women.

This linkage between nationalism and patriarchy is visible in various Asian and African cultures.

In Rabindranath Tagore's classic novel, *The Home and the World* (1985 [1915]), published during India's anti-colonial struggle, Bimala, the woman protagonist is shown making the shift from private to public. Tagore of course uses the traditional trope of the nation as the Hindu mother-goddess, *Shakti*, here (and thus excludes Muslims from seeing the nation the same way, as Ray points out, p. 91). Bimala is seeking to create an identity for herself. She does so by becoming 'modernized'. A conversation between husband and wife gestures at the private-feminine and public-masculine divide the novel sets up. Nikhil has just asked Bimala to come out of *purdah*:

'What do I want with the outside world?'
'The outside world may want you,' he replied.
'If the outside world has got on so long without me, it may go on for some time longer. It need not pine to death for want of me.'
(1985, pp. 17–18)

Bimala slowly shifts away from her previous duty-bound roles of the 'good' wife and daughter. Her attraction to Sandip eventually results in her keener interest in politics and 'national' questions. But when the novel ends she has discovered that Sandip has shown her an 'evil' path when he leads her into public life and national questions. She mourns: 'Things that were well-ordered have become jumbled up' (p. 254). And wonders in anguish: 'what rigour of penance is there which can serve to bring me once more, as a bride adorned for her husband, to my place upon that same bridal seat?' (p. 255). So is

Tagore's implication that the 'true' world of the native woman her *home* alone, as Sangeeta Ray's astute reading suggests (p. 120).

In Ghanaian novelist Ama Ata Aidoo's *Changes,* the wife, Esi Sekyi, is more educated than the husband, Oko. Her job threatens him, and his confidence begins to collapse. He then accuses her of not being an African woman at all. In an effort to reinforce what he sees as the true relationship, he rapes her, and Esi Sekyi leaves him. Her subsequent polygamous marriage to Ali – under the hope that this arrangement would give her more freedom – also leaves her unhappy. When the novel ends she is still alone. *Changes* criticizes a Ghanaian society that is unwilling to see its women contribute to the social and economic realm. It is a postcolonial society that sees nation-hood and the social order predicated upon the circumscription of the woman within domesticity.

In a fascinating study of Afghanistan, Valentine Moghadam has shown how a nationalist project was invariably *masculinized.* Moghadam notes the contradiction at work here:

> Although the Islamist movement was explicitly antifeminist, it received more international support (even from many European feminists) than did the modernizing government, because the mujahideen were perceived as attempting to liberate their country from Soviet domination. (1997, p. 75)

Moghadam goes on to show how tribal feudalism reliant on patriarchal systems of thought ensured that the modernization – especially in the fields of education and political culture – did not occur. National identity, subsumed under an Islamist identity refused to acknowledge the woman's role in nation-building except as a passive adjunct to the male. Moghadam therefore proposes that 'movements for national liberation must be judged on their social programs, especially on women's rights' (p. 97). Moghadam's shift toward a feminist nationalism in the postcolonial context is an interesting one. She is proposing that unless education, cultural, economic and reproductive rights are guaranteed for the women there cannot be a proper 'national' programme. Moghadam notes how nationalism has, in many Islamic societies – Algeria, Egypt, Tunisia, Turkey, Malaysia and Pakistan – explicitly aligned national development with *women's* liberation. As she puts it, 'they [feminists] have taken strong exception to forms of nationalism that link cultural and national to an exclusively domestic role for women or to certain forms of mandatory dress' (p. 97). Postcolonial women must remember their dual exploitation: of their racial as well as gender identities, as Grace Nichols does in 'One Continent/To Another':

> Child of the middle passage womb
> Push
> Daughter of a vengeful Chi
> She came
> Into the new world
> Birth aching her pain
> From one continent to another.

Nichols shows how the woman links two continents and cultures in her violated body. But Nichols is also careful to see the woman's body as a source of hope:

> But being born a woman
> She moved again
> Knew it was the Black Beginning. (1996, pp. 582–3)

After Algerian independence the women were driven back into their homes as all the promises of the national liberation were forgotten (Helie-Lucas 1993, Lazreg 1994). In the case of South Africa, as Zengie Mangaliso argues (1997), women's struggles in resistance movements initially derived from issues that were directly about their lives *as* women.[1] But for nation-building to take place effectively in the post-independence period women must be a part of that process. Writing in the immediate aftermath of the end of apartheid, Mangaliso notes that the African National Congress's policy guidelines explicitly reference gender equality in private and public spheres and encourage women's participation in socioeconomic national development (p. 139). Nationalist agendas of legal reform and social welfare work adversely on women because women have *not* been a part of the decision-making process (Rajeswari Sunder Rajan, 2003). In line with such thinking in the political domain, recent feminist work on citizenship (Voet 1998, p. 127) has often proposed alternatives to traditional models of political citizenship such as,

• special rights collective for women (called women's forum side of woman-centred feminism),

- special rights for carers and seeking a different morality in political thought – an ethics of care and compassion (called women's morality side of woman-centered feminism).

This might involve, argues Voet, redefining and reconfiguring political practices so that women can participate in them. As she puts it,

> politics should not only welcome women on the condition that they ignore their femaleness . . . on the contrary, citizenship . . . would also mean that feminism should no longer be relegated to women's spare time. (p. 141)

In Central America, the revolutionary movements in Nicaragua, El Salvador and Guatemala, women did not reach the top ranks in their organizations. However, even their minimal participation opened up the route into feminism. In other words, national liberation and revolutionary movements enabled the rise and spread of a feminist consciousness, even if does not result in the transformation of gender ideology and culture. But the struggle for democracy in many Asian, Central American and African nation-states in the postcolonial era is inextricably tied in to the transformation of civil society – and this means ensuring greater access of women to decision-making and participation (Chinchilla 1997). Chicana feminism too, Alma Garcia argues (1997), treated nationalism as linked to an internal, gender-based colonialism. Thus while Chicanos themselves were internally colonized, women were further marginalized within these. Hence Chicana feminism arose as an offshoot of Chicana cultural nationalism, but *rejected* its machismo cult. In other cases, women's interests in the postcolonial society are often represented by highly educated middle class women. In India the category of 'woman' itself, as a result of this skewed representational politics, becomes coded as 'middle class' and 'Hindu', automatically marginalizing women of other faiths, castes, classes and cultures (Tharu and Niranjana 1994).

Feminist nationalism in the postcolonial context thus seeks

- the rejection of masculinist models of the nation;
- the rejection of traditional patriarchal ideas, drawing upon myths, religious beliefs and legends, about women and politics;

- a redefinition of the public sphere as one that can accommodate – and indeed encourage – the participation of women in decision-making processes;
- an integration of the domestic as an element of 'larger' ideas of cosmopolitanism (as demonstrated in the work of Pollock et al. 2000) and the political;
- a reconfiguring of the political domain where the women find it possible to participate – in terms of time, access and safety.

From this reconfiguring of the political space of the nation in feminist terms, postcolonial thought generates a particular form of 'postcolonial feminism', the subject of the next section.

POSTCOLONIAL FEMINISMS

Postcolonial feminisms emphasize location and cultural difference among women, especially in the racial nature of this difference. It notes how spirituality, language and experiences of age, sexuality or motherhood are context-specific: for the woman in rural India to tribal women in the Congo to Sonia Sotomayor being appointed the first Hispanic justice in the US Supreme Court (2009). Postcolonial feminism is concerned with

- the homogenization of cultural difference among women into a universal category – which they believe is what mainstream (white) feminism does,
- the erasure of differences in lived experience for Asian, South American and African women in the name of this universal category,
- the assumption that the Western model of the feminine or feminism is the standard one and therefore applicable in terms of its politics to the Aboriginal woman in Australia and the Asian American academic in the First World,
- the rejection of alternate modes of life – such as spirituality – within 'modern' or 'secular' Western feminism.

In her now-cult essay Chandra Talpade Mohanty (2003 [1984]) argued that the entire feminist discourse about 'Third World Women' homogenized women from Asia, Africa and South American into a single, coherent category. This, argued Mohanty, resulted in the homogenization of the rest of the world's women as 'one' woman.

The category 'women' implies a coherent and undifferentiated group where the woman's class, ethnic or racial identity and experiences are ignored. Particularities such as the Islamic woman's quest for equality within the law or for the Indian woman's for equal wages cannot be converted into generalizations. There is no 'average Third World woman', argues Mohanty. Mainstream white feminism posits a linear progression: from the primitive, vulnerable and ignorant 'Third World' woman to the modern, knowledgeable and empowered Western/white woman. In 'US Third World feminism' women of colour could stand in opposition to the prevalent white feminism (Sandoval 1991).

'Islamic feminism', making its appearance from the early 1990s, is an example of this oppositional and culture-specific postcolonial feminist thought. The term refers to the attempt at *legal* reforms of the Islamic nations. This involves a very clear material-political agenda: greater rights for Muslim women *within the ambit of Islam*. Unlike mainstream Western feminism and its dominant Marxist philosophies, this one does *not* seek to abandon its religious dimension: only demanding a more *gender-sensitive interpretation of Islamic laws* (Mojab 2001).

Najat Khayyat's 'Had I been Male' (1998, pp. 19–22) explores the commodification of the Arab woman. In Badriyyah al-Bashir's 'School Diaries' (pp. 23–7) all the girls live in perpetual fright of their brothers and other men in their families. In Sharifah ash-Shamlan's 'Zainab' (1998, pp. 39–41), a woman is condemned as a sinner, and is perhaps murdered by members of her family. Imtiaz Dharker's controversial volume, *Purdah* (1989) demonstrated how the veil becomes symptomatic of a social condition and the resultant resistance of the Muslim woman in India. Asar Nafisi's best-selling *Reading Lolita in Tehran* (2003) shows a minor rebellion when women create a community of readers. Marjanie Satrapi's graphic memoir, *Persepolis*, explores the life of the woman in post-revolution Tehran, and the quest for greater freedom (negotiating between Islamic modernization and the Western model).

African feminisms arose as a result of their meager presence in the discourses of Western feminism. Several versions of African feminism circulate now. 'Negofeminism', a term coined by Obioma Nnaemeka, is 'the feminism of negotiation, accommodation and compromise; no ego feminism' (1998, p. 371). 'Motherism' (see below) is the feminism built upon the experience of shared mothering, the collective childrearing system that African communities have had for centuries. Thus postcolonial feminisms have evolved out of specific contexts in Asia, Africa and the diasporic cultures of Black Britain or Asian American communities. This *lived experience* of the Asian, Arab or African woman involves a deep engagement with spirituality and religious beliefs, as seen in the case of Islamic feminism. Feminism, as often deployed in the white mainstream one, has chosen to ignore spirituality (one reason for this could be its reliance on Marxism). But for the Asian or African woman, her battles against patriarchy often use religion and spirituality. The spiritual, in other words, can be a means of self-empowerment too. Alice Walker therefore gives primacy of place to the Spirit: '[A womanist] loves the Spirit. Loves love and food and roundness. Loves struggle . . . Loves herself. Regardless' (1983, p. xii). The 'Amman' goddesses from Hinduism adapted by regions in South Africa, can become role models for women, argues Alleyn Diesel (2002). In Suniti Namjoshi's *The Mothers of Maya Diip* the Matriarch visits a temple which only has the goddess:

> The goddess was everywhere, depicted among her friends, her lovers, her warriors, her servants, her enemies and her babies. And she was there in all her aspects: grim, giddy, austere, tender and maternal, languid and luxurious, asleep and waking, austere and amorous, warlike and proud . . . This was stone made flesh. She [Jyanvi] was overwhelmed. (1989, p. 56)

Much of Namjoshi's fiction contains quasi-mystic and spiritual elements that foreground the role of the mother-spirit as a powerful force to aid women.

The critic Jaimes Guerrero (2003) conceptualizes a 'native woman-ism', especially among indigenous peoples and Kristina Groover (1999) argues that native uses of spirituality within feminism turn to the *community* rather than the individual. While Western (white) feminism is all about individual enterprise and empowerment, the postcolonial feminist works towards the empowerment of a *community*. Postcolonial feminism situates the woman's experience within both the community and the environment.

The community is an important theme common to much African writing: mothering. African and Caribbean writing often celebrates Black womanhood in a move toward a specifically African feminism.

The 'Nanny' in African and Caribbean writing is a mother-figure, a person who nurtures and protects, possessed of secret knowledge and special powers (such as healing). Postcolonial feminism rooted in the African cultures of Sudan, Nigeria and Zimbabwe has even resulted in a strand of thought termed *motherism*. Motherism is an attempt to re-work two kinds of representation of women: the image of 'Mother Africa' and images of African femaleness. Motherism seeks to foreground the idea of women as essentially mothers. Catherine Obianuju Acholonu (1995) argues that the mother, the spiritual heart of the African family, is rooted in the earth, and therefore suggests an almost elemental connection between woman and earth. One should not forget, she argues, 'her [Africa's] quintessential position as the Mother Continent of humanity' (quoted in Godono, http://www. thecore.nus.edu.sg/post/africa/godona1.html). Ifi Amadiume, developing this motherist model of African feminism argues that we need to shift to the 'motherhood paradigm' to allow for 'a shift of focus from man at the centre and in control, to the primacy of the role of the mother/sister in the economic, social, political and religious institutions' (1997, p. 152). Oyèrónké Oyewumi claims that motherhood binds women together in a collective experience of childbirth and nurture. Eventually this means a nurture of the community itself, and hence the significance of mothering (2000 pp. 1093–8). And this collective experience is crucial to understanding this particular strand of postcolonial feminism.

Alice Walker (1983), Angela Davis (2002 [1971]) and others have all praised the women who *collectively* raised them (these other women were known as 'other mother', 'little mother', 'auntie' or 'second mother'). Children in the African context are raised by a *group* of adults and not necessarily by parents alone. The African American theorist bell hooks writes:

> Childbearing is a responsibility that can be shared with other childrearers, with people who do not have children. This form of parenting is revolutionary in this society [African] because it takes places in opposition to the idea that parents, especially mothers, should be the only childrearers. (1984, quoted in Forna 2000, p. 367)

The sharing of child-rearing duties means that, in effect, the women are *not* dependent on the men/fathers – and this marks a major shift in gender power relations. Unfortunately, as contemporary critics note (Forna 2000), this brand of feminism built on the collective job of motherhood has been ignored by white feminism because of its insistence on autonomous individuals.

In the novels of Flora Nwapa, Bessie Head, Buchi Emecheta and others, the longing for a child by the protagonists becomes a paradigm of feminine desire itself. Writing becomes a fulfillment of desire, and therefore a mode of producing their own subjectivity and identity itself. In an interview Nwapa made the link between creativity and mothering as she recalled her own childhood:

> I happened to have known this particular woman. Efuru [the eponymous heroine of Nwapa's novel] is so many women in one. I loved listening to stories. My mother would make clothes and . . . many women came while she sewed. I think it must have been from there that I got the idea of how these women behave. (quoted in Innes 1992, p. 204)

Nwapa's statement captures several of the themes of women's writing: motherhood, language, communication, lineage, community and, of course, gender. In Bessie Head's *A Question of Power* (1974) it is Elizabeth's mother-role that enables her to regain a measure of sanity.

WOMEN, THE BODY AND POSTCOLONIALISM

It is we sinful women
While those who sell the harvests of our bodies
become exalted
become distinguished
become the just princes of the material world.
                    —Kishwar Naheed (quoted in Suleri 1992, p. 345)

A short inventory of the themes encapsulated under the rubric 'Women, the Body and Postcolonialism' would include

- The maternalization of the national/nation's 'body',
- Tradition as *embodied* in the woman (the woman's body as the site of cultural meanings and the site of battles between 'modernity' and 'tradition'),
- The autonomy and agency of the woman's body (including sexuality and its configurations).

The Maternalization of the National/Nation's 'Body'

The nation as 'motherland', as noted above in the section on gendered nations and nationalism, conflates the body of the nation with the maternal body: all-sacrificing, nurturing, fertile, the space of safety and home but also as something under threat, needing protection and to be revered. This maternalization of the nation has several antecedents in the anti-colonial struggle when the rhetoric of nationalist movements often took recourse to the image of the homeland as 'mother'.[2] It is the persistence of this 'maternalization' principle in the post-independence era that postcolonial women authors like Mariama Bâ interrogate:

> The woman writer in Africa has a special task . . . to present the position of women in Africa in all its aspects. There is still so much injustice . . . In the family, in the institutions, in society, in the street, in political organisations, discriminations reigns supreme . . . Like men, we must use literature as a non-violent but effective weapon. We no longer accept the nostalgic praise to the African Mother, who, in his anxiety, man confuses with Mother Africa. Within African literature, room must be made for women . . . room we will fight for with all our might. (in Schipper 1984, pp. 46–7)

A nineteenth century Urdu poet from the Indian subcontinent, Akbar Allahabadi wrote:

> When yesterday I saw some women without purdah
> Oh, Akbar I sank into the ground for loss of national honour
> (quoted in Saigol 1999, p. 117)

Kwame Nkrumah declared that the 'women of Africa have already shown themselves to be of paramount importance in the revolutionary struggle' (quoted in Young 2001, p. 363). Many women accepted this assigned role. Marjani Satrapi's *Persepolis* (2003, 2004) shows women protesting draconian laws in the days of the Iranian revolution. Nefissa in EL Saadawi's *The Innocence of the Devil* is physically affected by the very word 'nation':

> She shivered as though with fever. The word *country* expressed for her a deep love . . . Her heart sagged with the weight of the love

she had for it . . . Her heart burned passionately with the love she had for the word *country*. (1994, p. 45, emphasis in original)

In Manju Kapur's *Difficult Daughters* (1998), set in the days of the Indian freedom struggle Virmati is educated by her husband Harish, and soon wishes to assert herself at the national level: 'I fret about my petty, domestic matters, at a time when the nation is on trial. I too must take a stand' (p. 239). Virmati is demanding a more public role for herself.

Partition literature – writings that deal with the partition of the subcontinent into India and Pakistan – as critics like Sangeeta Ray have shown (2000), places women in 'metaphoric or symbolic roles in the nationalist scenario' (p. 135). Women are raped in the course of the violence that marked the Partition, and such 'fallen' women, as Bapsi Sidhwa shows in her Partition novel *Cracking India* (1991) were subsequently denied a role or identity in the newly formed nations.

Tradition, Culture and Gendered Embodiment

Postcolonial nations built upon this set of binaries too, and argued that the woman is the guardian of tradition and spirituality and hence must assume responsibility for these. This became a means of regulating the woman. We see an illustration of how the postcolonial state extended this theme of retaining the woman's domain that Chatterjee examines in Cherríe Moraga's *The Hungry Woman* (2001), a futuristic play about the Chicano/a 'nation' of Aztlán, Moraga's characters Savannah and Mama Sal exchange this dialogue:

Mama-Sal: We were contento for awhile –
Savannah: Sort of. Until the revolutionaries told the women, put down your guns and pick up your babies . . .
And into the kitchen! (p. 24)

Once the anti-colonial struggle is over, Moraga suggests, the woman is sent away into the kitchen, her movements, actions and role all defined for her by the newly independent but continuingly patriarchal nation. Beatrice in Achebe's *Anthills of the Savannah* tells Chris: 'the story of this country, as far as you are concerned, is the story of the three of you [men]' (1988, p. 66). In an innovative and important reading in postcolonial feminism, Ketu Katrak (1992) argues that Gandhi's appropriated images of the passive feminine for his passive resistance programme. This, Katrak suggests, created a scheme of representation where the passive feminine became a model of ideal 'womanly' virtue and qualities. In short, Gandhi's political strategy might have been useful against the colonial power, but it ended up reinforcing the very myths and images that patriarchy thrived on.

In the post-independence era the woman's body becomes the space of struggle for a culture. What I mean by 'space of struggle' is that the woman's body is often located as a site where meanings are fought over: the protection of the woman *is taken to mean* the protection of the country's cultural heritage, the 'immorality' of the woman's body *is taken to mean* the dissipation of the culture. Indian author C. S. Lakshmi puts it this way:

> The 'notion' of an unbroken tradition is constant and attempts are made to write this notion of tradition on the body of the woman to dictate its movement, needs, aspirations and spheres of existence even while the body is moving along time, space and history. (1999, p. 55)

The woman *stands for* the national territory and values, suggests Elleke Boehmer (2005, p. 29). Debates over the appropriate dress codes for women, women's education, the right to divorce and property in postcolonial societies indicate that the woman and her body remain the imagined, constructed centrepiece of a culture.

Claims of women as the 'guardians of tradition' result in greater policing of the woman's *body*. 'Tradition' is often invoked when the woman seeks to make changes in her status and role. In other words the 'modernizing' of the woman – whether in her dress, choice of career or education – is often taken to mean a loss of traditional values. This is the reason why the body is at the centre of the lived experience for women in postcolonialism.

Critiquing 'white', mainstream feminism, postcolonial feminist writers (Mohanty 1991, Suleri 1992, Katrak 2006) call for a close examination of the way the condition of women postcolonial societies require a different version of feminism. This feminism might have to be located in the lived experiences of

- oppressive or indifferent laws
- the horrifying material conditions of poverty, poor health services, safety and education

- rape warfare
- economic dependence
- patriarchal control over their bodies.

The woman's sexuality remains a taboo subject in/for public discourse in several postcolonial nations, for instance. Their exploited bodies become insignificant in the face of 'larger' political issues, almost as though what happens to their bodies is not political. Pakistani poet Kishwar Naheed's poem cited as the epigraph to this section gestures at this social indifference to the woman's body which remains a sexual toy for the patriarchal set up to play with.

What is interesting is that numerous women writers have, since the 1990s, begun to recognize and speak out against this patriarchal construction of the nation. Thus Nayantara Sahgal finds the unconditional acceptance of Hinduism problematic because it constructs a particular, limited image of the woman. She writes:

I have to ask, as I did in my novel *Rich Like Us*, whether Hinduism inclines a whole society to the status quo? Does it put out the fires of rebellion? Does it incline women to vicitimization, to individual and mass acts of horrifying self-sacrifice [Sati]? (Sahgal, 'The Schizophrenic Imagination', 1992)

Women writers suggest an abandonment of these stereotypes, and we see numerous postcolonial authors calling into question traditional myths about women.

The Autonomy of the Woman's Body

The Muslim poet, Imtiaz Dharker consciously links militarism with patriarchy in her poem 'Battle-Line':

All you see is bodies
Crumpled carelessly, and thrown
Away.
The arms and legs are never arranged
Heroically.

She then compares the battle field to the scene of lovemaking:

It's the same with lovers
After the battle-lines are drawn:
Combatants thrown
into something they have not
had time to understand. (1988, pp. 46–9)

Firdaus in Nawaad El Saadawi's *Woman at Point Zero* eventually decides that she will take control over her sexuality and her body and begins to prostitute herself. Firdaus is now in charge of her sexuality and declares to a prospective customer: 'There are plenty of men and I want to choose with whom to go' (p. 68). The unmarried Lucia in Dangarembga's *Nervous Conditions* eventually retains autonomy over her body, much to the admiration of the other men and women. (In sharp contrast, the educated Maiguru continues to efface herself so that the family remains intact.) In each of these cases the question of the body is in fact a question of ownership. Postcolonial women authors seek to demonstrate how the autonomy of the woman can be achieved primarily through an autonomy over her own body.

This autonomy is essentially a question of agency. 'Agency' is the capacity of an individual to determine the course of her/his life, and to make the choices to determine this course. In other words, agency is contingent upon *social* conditions in which the capacity and choice could be asserted and acted upon. As Mariama Bâ warns us the 'nostalgic praise to the African Mother' does not serve the African woman – what is needed is more than just a sentimental view of the woman or the nation. What postcolonial feminism argues is: the woman in the postcolonial nation is unable to exert agency because the patriarchal social conditions do not allow her any choice. Her roles, functions and futures are predetermined for her.

Many women authors turn this oppressive condition into social satire, suggesting that the men are worried about their women's capacities. Arab writer Nawaad El Saadawi writes in a particularly savage passage in her novel *The Hidden Face of Eve*:

Segregation and the veil were not meant to ensure the protection of women, but essentially that of men. And the Arab woman was not imprisoned in the home to safeguard her body, her honour and her morals, but rather to keep intact the honour and morals of men . . . The tyranny exerted by men over women indicates that they had taken the measure of the female's innate strength, and needed heavy fortifications to protect themselves against it. (1980, pp. 99–100)

If some authors turn to satire, a few use disease, the body's ailments and the art/practice of writing as metaphors for the postcolonial woman's conditions. Diseased, broken, tortured and mentally afflicted bodies are almost a staple in postcolonial women's fiction. India's Kamala Das explored the madness of women's oppressed, frustrated and exploited bodies in her *My Story*. Jean Rhys' *Wide Sargasso Sea* (1982 [1966) and Tsitsi Dangarembga's *Nervous Conditions* (1988) used madness as well as bodily ailments to signify gendered social injustice. Assia Djebar the Maghrebian author in the prefatory remarks to her collection *Women of Algiers in their Apartment* wrote of the 'words of the veiled body, language that in turn has taken the veil for so long' (1992, p. 1). Language, the body, the right and space to speak all come together in postcolonial women's obsession with 'writing the body'. Kamala Das' *My Story* suggests writing and creativity as a solution to bodily and mental problems. Her protagonist, driven to mental breakdown because of her tension between idealized love and bodily needs, takes to writing as a means of fighting insanity. We are then told some horrific truths about her libido: she had been the victim of child abuse. It is when she puts this down in writing – an instance of the linkage between creativity, mental health and the body – that she is able to deal with the nightmares of her past.

Postcolonial women authors are, however, alert to the fact that writing the body attracts criticism, and even the dissolution of their bodies at the hands of patriarchy. Pakistani author Tehmina Durrani in *My Feudal Lord* examines the power the feudal Muslim family and its men have over the woman's body. In Ama Ata Aidoo's *Anowa* the protagonist (Anowa) is prevented from being betrothed as a priestess by her mother. This breaks the tradition. When Anowa is found to be barren, this 'problem' is attributed to her breaking of the tradition. Here childbirth, tradition and the woman's body are all 'subjects': to be commanded by the patriarchal society.

Family, Patriarchy and the Social Order

The idealized family of the Asian and African cultures comes in for considerable criticism from postcolonial women authors. As noted above, the anti-colonial struggles appropriated the woman for symbolic purposes as the epitome and essence of their cultures. Post-independent nation-states continued this theme, and demanded of their women chastity, virtue and an uncompromising subservience to the cause of the family. The family, therefore, becomes the target of sustained interrogation by women writers across the Third World.

In order to understand the significance of the questioning of the family 'norm', one must first look at how male postcolonial authors have presented women. Chinua Achebe, the doyen of postcolonial writers, idealizes the quiet, docile Ibo woman. Kirsten Holts Petersen writes:

His [Achebe's] traditional women are happy, harmonious members of the community, even when they are repeatedly beaten and barred from any say in the communal decision-making process and constantly reviled in sayings and proverbs. (1999, p. 253)

In India, the family remains the cornerstone of the cultural arch. Ngũgĩ wa Thiong'o's *Decolonising the Mind* (1986), does not mention a single woman author even as he proposes an *expanded* curriculum. Is there a 'great tradition' of male writers that the postcolonial critic wants enshrined?

Anita Desai's fiction is full of women characters who sacrifice their happiness and even their health to serve the greater cause of the family. In Dangarembga's *Nervous Conditions* Tambu says of the uneven nature of the family's power relations: 'the needs and sensibilities of the women in my family were not considered a priority, or even legitimate' (p. 12).

Postcolonial women writers foreground the subject-position of women in the legal, economic, familial and narrative domains. What this means is simply that patriarchy ensures a secondary status for them in all these domains since the laws, policies, relationships and aesthetic principles are all determined by males. Thus women

- do not possess equal rights over property,
- do not participate in decision-making processes of development,

- do not have the opportunity to construct or reject their relation-ships (which are predetermined for them),
- do not find space in literary traditions except as creators of 'domestic' and therefore minor literary artifacts.

In the literary domain, for instance, one of postcolonial (as well as mainstream white) feminist projects has been the retrieval of women's literary and other texts. Studies of canon-formation in postcolonial societies (Tharu and Lalita 1993; de Mel and Samarakkody 2002) have shown how the canon has been exclusionary and marginalized women's writing. The retrieval of thus-far ignored texts has resulted in the increasing awareness of the women's role in the construction of social, community, national identities, their oppression at the hands of not just colonialism, but also patriarchy in native cultures, and their strategies at escaping/negotiating the power relations between genders.

Gayatri Spivak's now famous question, 'Can the Subaltern Speak?' (1988), was a question about the woman's agency. Spivak was critiquing the poststructuralist and Foucauldian argument that identities and subjectivities are constructed within discourse. These forms of thought, she argues, however treated the intellectual's discourse as one that provides and generates transparent access to the voices of the oppressed. Spivak argues that

i. any attempt to regain the 'subaltern consciousness' or/and
ii. to assume the oppressed victim has an independent and sovereign subject

are risky situations in critical practice. The very idea that the subaltern consciousness can be captured is driven by an old colonial notion: that *the Westerner is able to comprehend the native*. Shifting the focus to gender, Spivak argues that the woman is even more of a subaltern, oppressed by both her race and gender identities. Spivak argues that the quest for discovering the gendered subaltern's consciousness is to replicate the colonial context: the native cannot speak for or represent herself, and hence this task of representing the native must fall to the white man. Everyone speaks for the subaltern, and the subaltern retreats further into silence. What Spivak is calling for is a close attention to *the practices of representation*, the ethics of narration, image-making and meaning-generation.

QUEERING POSTCOLONIALISM

Postcolonial studies shares with gay and lesbian studies an interest in the contestation of systems of domination. Power relations and social systems determine that some kinds of sexual preferences (heterosexuality) are dominant, and represented as such in popular culture, critical work and history. Just as postcolonial studies is interested in systems of representation that use race as a critical site of difference, domination and inequality, queer studies focuses on sexuality as the terrain where such a domination takes place. More significantly in the 1990s the shift has been towards an intersection of queer and postcolonial studies. Asian queer males and Chicano/a lesbians become the focus of queer postcolonial studies when the two categories of race and sexuality conflate in critical discourse.

In *The Mothers of Maya Diip* (1989) Suniti Namjoshi offers us a fable where lesbians and mothers are in power. In her *Building Babel* (1996), she constructs a society run entirely by women, where men are 'immigrants' to be trained as a workforce. Since the 1980s such writings that problematize postcoloniality's heteronormative condition – where heterosexuality is deemed to be the norm – have emerged from numerous Asian authors. Closely aligning their ethnicity with their homosexuality, Suniti Namjoshi, Raj Rao (India), Shyam Selvadurai (Sri Lanka), Cherríe Moraga (Chicano/a) have broken new ground within the postcolonial canon.

Traditional European stereotypes of the African or Indian male or the Asian woman have focused on their 'excessive' or 'deviant' sexuality. Indeed, the stereotype has been powerful enough to construct an entire industry: of Third World sex tourism involving the Southeast Asian countries. Shyam Selvadurai's *Funny Boy* (1994) wryly observes the Westerner's stereotyping of Eastern sexuality and its consequences when Arjie's father says: 'It's not just our luscious beaches that keeps the tourist industry going. We've other natural resources as well' (pp. 166–7). Selvadurai is hinting at an exploitative link between race and sexuality in the context of global tourism – a theme that goes further back, into the colonial era.

Imperialism also had a problematic relationship with other forms of sexuality. The Fielding-Aziz relationship in Forster's *A Passage to India* suggests a homoerotic relationship. In Paul Scott's Raj Quartet (set in the last days of the Raj) Ronald Merrick, the homosexual English officer, abuses the Indian Hari Kumar. Homosexuality was deemed an 'aberration' that blunted the masculine edge of the empire.

Specific notions and views of masculinity and femininity informed colonial interaction with natives. When the British, for example, depicted the 'effeminate' Bengali in India, they were positing the imperialist as a masculine Other in contrast. Iconic figures like Richard Burton and TE Lawrence have been revealed as homosexuals whose role in imperial dominance was actually a complex negotiation between a masculine dynamic (imperialism) and their own 'unacceptable' sexualities.

Contemporary postcolonial studies, drawing upon black feminist and queer theory, argues that being a *white* lesbian or gay is remarkably different from being an *Asian* queer in an American metropolis. That is, the experience of sexuality and sexual preferences are different for different ethnic groups and even within marginalized groups (like Blacks or Asians in the USA), heterosexuality is retained as a norm, and to be queer is to be deviant. The 'queering' of postcolonialism is essentially a debate around the following themes and issues:

Postcolonial queer writing presents the following themes

- the link between race, ethnicity and sexual identities
- the structures of kinship and families
- diasporic queer identities in the age of globalization.

Writing Postcolonial, Writing Queer

Postcolonial queer writers as varied as Shyam Selvadurai and Suniti Namjoshi explore the following themes in their work:

- The assumption of heterosexual relationships as the norm and queer ones as 'deviant',
- The construction of nations as 'families' which legitimises the heterosexual family as norm,
- The construction of particular cultural identities within the 'nation' that does not account for queer culture, or even the queer elements within a culture,
- The forging of alliances between gays and lesbians of different racial and ethnic identities in campaigns against AIDS, Gay Rights, etc.

When Ismat Chughtai published her short story, 'The Quilt' in Urdu in 1942 in which a 10-year-old-girl narrates the sexual relationship between an aristocratic woman and her servant girl, she was taken to court on charges of obscenity. A few decades later Kamala Das published *My Story* (1996 [1976), initially marketed as an autobiography and then later as a novel, she acquired unparalleled notoriety. The Indian subcontinent, with its history of queer and transvestite representations in its epics (Vanita and Kidwai 2000, Vanita 2002), was not prepared for this assault on its 'sensibility' and heteronormative family ideals. It is only in the 1990s that Hoshang Merchant, Raj Rao (poetry) and Mahesh Dattani (drama) with diasporic authors like Suniti Namjoshi (poetry and fiction), Shobha De and Manju Kapur (fiction), Agha Shahid Ali (poetry) and theorists (Martin Manalansan IV 1993, Gopinath 1996, 2002) began to put together a body of work that acquired not only national recognition but a fair amount of international status. The postcolonial had, in the work and worlds of these authors, just broken 'out' of the sexual codes imposed upon writing.

Postcolonial queer writing is a political project that seeks more than literary expression: it seeks a common platform with larger, global gay/queer movements. While this is not to reduce postcolonial queer writing to political propaganda literature, it cannot be denied that the political does constitute a major agenda for Hanif Kureishi, Suniti Namjoshi, Gayatri Reddy, Ruth Vanita, Andrew Koh, Martin Manalansan IV, Cherríe Moraga and other critics/writers. Gloria Anzaldúa makes this political project of creative work explicit:

As a *mestiza* I have no country, my homeland cast me out; yet all countries are mine because I am every woman's sister or potential lover. (As a lesbian I have no race, my own people disclaim me; but I am all races because there is the queer of me in all races.) (1994, pp. 102–3)

What has to be kept in mind is that representations of queer sexuality or relationships in literature or cinema is linked, *more than any other category of the postcolonial, to social and cultural contexts*: of development and under-development, debates about modernity and tradition (I write at the time when a huge debate has been opened up in India in the wake of the High Court having decriminalized homosexuality, July 2009), AIDS activism and legal measures. It is therefore quite accurate that in a review of India's first queer anthology, Hoshang Merchant's *Yaarana*, the reviewer complained about the volume's complete lack of reference to Gay Rights, the Gay Movement and political issues (Vikram 2000).

In most cases, authors from the Asian cultures locate their sexualities within contexts of the family, tradition and local cultures. Postcolonial queer literature often calls into question that kinds of identities demanded, recognized and imposed by families. Their concern over the assumption of heterosexuality and heterosexual relationships as the norm within families and society is often thematized as the quest for alternative forms of relationships. In Mahesh Dattani's *On a Muggy Night in Bombay* (2000 [1998]) he critiques gays who succumb to social pressures and accept the stereotypes of the 'ideal' heterosexual family. Prakash, who is gay, has decided to go 'straight' and is all set to marry Kiran, the sister of his former lover, Kamlesh. Kamlesh is now caught between revealing the truth about Prakash to his sister, and his own affection for Prakash. Dattani's play is an attack on the notion that only heterosexual families are 'proper'. Given that he is writing this in the context of India, where the family continues to be (inexplicably?) revered, the play becomes an indictment of social hypocrisy (but also, at the time of the play, legal repression of alternate sexualities) where the gay not only does not reveal his preferences but opts for the socially respectable 'role' predetermined for him. Queer families, as theorists have argued (Butler 2002), present a challenge to the nuclear family unit. The variations within queer families – gays bringing up children, lesbians not wanting children, non-monogamy – counter the established the ideal (and notions) of a heterosexual family, as the life and writings of Cherrie Moraga shows us. This context-specific nature of all postcolonial queer writing is what makes for its political edge. This is also the reason why lesbian separatist fantasies in the work of Suniti Namjoshi (cited above) attain such importance – to envisage a country/culture where queer families dominate is surely a political act of great power.

What I propose is that the work of Hanif Kureishi, Namjoshi and other writers undertake nothing less than a subversion of the *postcolonial's heteronormative paradigm* by calling into question the cultural contexts in which certain kinds of writing have been thus far impossible. It is within these authors that one finds the most exemplary efforts at pushing the frontiers of postcolonial writing. Postcolonial writing, which has essentially been fixated about race and ethnicity has, in the work of these authors added sexuality as an analytical, political and theoretical category.

The Postcolonial Queer Diaspora

The romance between Omar, a young British-born Pakistani and Johnny, a working-class Englishman in Hanif Kureishi's *My Beautiful Laundrette* (1986), adds another layer of complexity to the race-sexuality theme: that of class. But it also indicates a new component of diaspora culture – that of the queer diasporic immigrant from Third World nations in First World cities. Hanif Kureishi, Shyam Selvadurai and Leela Gandhi are non-European writers settled in First World nations whose work offers one more dimension to postcolonialism: that of alternate sexualities.

Postcolonial authors, especially of the immigrant variety, see their own cultures as intolerant of alternate sexualities. Migration to First World cultures therefore seems a way out. Hanif Kureishi, of Pakistani descent makes this point explicit in an interview:

> using your sexuality as a way of moving away from your family. Indian and Pakistani families can be claustrophobic. They never want you to leave. (2001, p. 6)

The point Kureishi makes is that in the context of his own 'native' culture, his sexuality marginalizes him. Amitava Kumar therefore speaks of Hanif Kureishi's writing as representing a 'whole new world of migration and sexual freedom' (2001, p. 117). This indicates a new axis: of race and sexuality but within the context of migrant cultures, a *raced queer diaspora*.

However, such an escape is not possible for many gay and lesbian individuals. The black gay or the Asian lesbian is 'outside' even within the black or Asian identity. That is, it is assumed that hetero-sexuality is the norm among all ethnic and racial groups, even when these are immigrants in the First World. To be black and lesbian is, therefore, to be doubly marginalized. The Chicano author Cherríe Moraga put it this way: 'I have always experienced my lesbianism as radically different from most white gays and lesbians' (1997, p. 18).

'Border writers' like John Rechy (*City of Night*, 1963) and Alicia Gaspar de Alba (*Sor Juana's Second Dream* 1999) queer the borders of First World USA and Third World Mexico even as their queer characters disturb the borders between 'acceptable' (heterosexual) and 'deviant' (homosexual) sexualities. Constituting a whole new dynamic of race, sexuality and nation-state borders, queer writing from the borderlands is the deliberate blurring of identities.

More recent work has focused on identities of intersex and transgender individuals. 'Transgender' as a term is increasingly used to refer to pre- and postoperative transsexuals: transvestites, drag queens, cross dressers, gays and lesbians, bisexuals and straights who exhibit behaviour that may be seen as 'transgressing' socially assigned gender roles (Raymond 1994). Gayatri Reddy's excellent work (2006) on the 'third sex' (known as '*hijras*') in India notes how, in a postcolonial society where identity politics reign supreme, sexual difference is only *one* axis of identity. Reddy proposes that sexual politics and gender performativity are inadequate when it comes to understanding third sex identification. She proposes that third sex identities are constructed as more than sexual identities but rather through several morally evaluated differences such as 'respect' and 'honor'. These notions extend far beyond the category of sex/gender and include other domains like religion, kinship and class (2006, p. 43).

Global gay movements are being increasingly forced to take cognizance of what Katie King terms 'local homosexualities' (2001). King warns against the appropriation of queer discourses and studies as one more element within global capitalism – what she terms 'the imperializations of Gay Liberation as a global movement – which would erase the liberatory potential needed for 'local homosexualities' (p. 512). This means, in short, one needs to be cautious when speaking of queer globalizations or global movements because there is every chance that such a move will ignore crucial cultural differences in the construction, history and experience of homosexuality, especially in the Third World. That is, one cannot easily make 'queer' the *only* dominant mode of critical analysis because the Asian, South American or Native American experience of being gay is radically different from that of the Caucasian male in Europe or the USA. What is needed is a careful postcolonializing of queer theory with attention to specific historical circumstances (of race, ethnicity, community, cultural location) which determine an individual's experience of homosexuality.

* * *

Postcolonialism, as the above discussion demonstrates, has much to offer feminist theory and praxis. Adding race to the critical category of gender helps feminist studies to become more inclusive, and look at the conditions, needs and politics of Third World women. In similar fashion, adding sexuality to the critical mix enables an expansion of categories to include gays, lesbians and transsexuals. If the task and aim of postcolonial thinking has been essentially about social justice, inclusiveness and agency, then postcolonial feminism and queer studies is a step in the right direction, for it offers to queers, Third World women and First World underprivileged women a common foundation – oppression and injustice – to build a platform on.

CHAPTER FIVE

SPACE AND PLACE

We have put the wild above us.
—*(Les Murray* 'Cumulus', *1992, p. 4)*

Colonialism was about territory, and it is territory that continues to inform postcolonial politics. This chapter moves from the colonial appropriation, literal, cultural and even metaphoric, of territory and the national sentiment towards lands and territory. Moving from 'territory' as land to 'territory' as social, cultural and political spaces it then explores particular social formations – subalterns – that have existed at the peripheries of the nation.

COLONIAL SPACES

In Jeanette Armstrong's 'This is a Story' (1996) white settlers build dams over the rivers in Canada preventing salmon migration and soon the natives find themselves deprived of their fishing and food. Kyoti's (a version of the coyote figure) view of the dam is: 'It didn't look good . . . something was worrisome about it' (p. 429). Kyoti finds that the native People have all gone away and everywhere there are the 'Swallow people' (whites). Nobody offers Kyoti any food because there has been no salmon in the river. The natives also start eating the white man's food – a metaphor for the assimilation of the colonizer's culture – and Kyoti warns them that it will make them sick. Kyoti then concludes:

> [The] Swallows were still a Monster people. They were pretty
> tricky making themselves act like they were people but all the

while, underneath, being really selfish Monsters that destroy
People and things like rivers and mountains. (1996, pp. 431–2)

Here the colonization of land, space, people and culture proceed
apace, indeed one form of colonization becomes another. There is
of course a binary put in place: the white man is the destroyer and
the Native American is the ecological native (a stereotype we see
frequently in the works of Native American authors like Paula Gunn
Allen. Allen in her *The Woman Who Owned the Shadows* (1983), has
a description of California where 'death hung like dirty air over the
land where once had walked the peaceful ones.' She goes on to list
the death of animals, birds, reptiles, insects, plants and herbs and
people, p. 73).

Colonialism mapped non-European spaces into segments for
better understanding and control. In John Keats' 'On First Looking
into Chapman's Homer' he refers to the explorer Cortez. In the
nineteenth century the explorers Mungo Park, David Livingstone
and others penetrated interior Africa and drew maps for other
later travellers, missionaries and colonial businessmen. In India the
Trigonometrical Survey of the last decades of the eighteenth century
mapped the subcontinent into knowable grids. As I have discussed
in Chapter 2, the enumerative and survey 'modalities' were central to
the conquest of non-European spaces by Europeans. A passage from
Memoir of a Map of Hindoostan (1788) gives a sense of the survey
modality:

A very extensive tract of woody and mountainous country [the
Berar-Golconda-Orissa's mountain regions] . . . We may fairly
suppose that to be a country void of the goods in general esteem
among mankind, that does not tempt either their avarice, or
ambition. Although surrounded by people who are in a high
degree of civilization, and who abound in useful manufactures,
we are told that the few who have appeared in the circars, use no
covering but a wisp of straw. We know not, with any degree
of certainty, how far this wild country extends within the great
ridge of mountains, between the parallels of 17^0 and 20^0, but the
first civilized people that we hear of beyond them, are the Berar
Mahrattas. (Rennell 1788, pp. 168–9)

In some cases, of course, the explorer and proto-colonial found the land 'empty', a blank slate on which the European could (i) 'discover' newness and (ii) inscribe his own culture. Thus TL Mitchell 'discovering' Australia could state with complete conviction:

> This territory, still for the most part in a state of nature, presents a fair blank sheet, for any geographical arrangement, whether of county divisions – lines of communication – or sites of towns. (quoted in Ryan 1994, p. 127)

Simon Ryan argues:

> not only is previous Aboriginal occupation and ownership . . . ignored, but the land itself is inserted into a particular narrativization of history . . . the cartographic inscriptions . . . organize and license the appropriation and exploitation of the land. (p. 127)

The map was an example of the 'imperial gaze'. This was the gaze of knowledge-seeking but also one which ordered what was being seen into particular modes. In other words, the European traveller or missionary did not use a neutral or objective gaze. In fact, 'seeing' was an activity that proceeded from European ways of knowing and perception, informed by European ideas and opinions. In European perceptions *the pagan, non-white, non-Christian Aboriginal could not be treated as a propertied class/individual.*

The conquest of non-European space by the European meant:

- Discovery
- Exploration
- Study (cartography)
- Construction

In Daniel Defoe's cult novel, *Robinson Crusoe* (2007 [1719]), often treated as a prototypical text about colonialism, the European Crusoe reflects on his dominion:

> My Island was now peopled, and I thought my self very rich in Subjects; and it was a merry Reflection which I frequently made, How like a King I look'd. First of all, the whole Country was my

own mere Property; so that I had an undoubted Right of Dominion. *Secondly*, My People were perfectly subjected: I was absolute Lord and Law-giver; they all owed their Lives to me, and were ready to lay down their Lives, if there had been Occasion of it, for me. (2007, p. 203)

Crusoe *imagines* himself governor, ruler, authority and sole power. As the years progress, his sense of power and control increase. At the end of the first year he thinks:

that this was all my own, that I was king and lord of all this country indefeasibly, and had a right of possession; and if I could convey it, I might have an inheritance, as completely as any Lord of a Manor in England. (p. 85)

After the eleventh year he thinks:

Lord of the whole Manor; or, if I pleased, I might call myself King, or Emperor over the whole country which I had possession of. There were no rivals. I had no competitor, none to dispute sovereignty or command with me. (p. 109)

The sovereignty of the European individual is characterized, in Defoe's novel, as the sovereign control of non-European spaces and its native inhabitants. Crusoe's mastery over Friday somehow reminds us of the master-slave relationship. It is significant that the first words he teaches Friday (in Chapter 23) is 'master' and teaches him that 'master' is his name! Friday, suggests Defoe, is the slave to Crusoe. Like nature and the animals, everything on the island is enslaved to Crusoe. The entire novel is about the subjugation of *space* – the territorial-physical one, but also the cultural-social one. As Crusoe's sovereignty and dominion are established over the land, he also asserts control over the native inhabitant, Friday.

The vision of the *terra nullius* was also gendered. The land was the space of masculine desire – it was a female body meant to be desired, conquered and controlled by the heroic male explorer. H. Rider Haggard's notorious depictions of Africa as a woman in *She* (1886–1887) and *King Solomon's Mines* (2005 [1885]) is a case that comes to mind here. Here is Haggard's notorious feminization of the African landscape in *King Solomon's Mines*:

> There, not more than forty or fifty miles from us, glittering like silver in the early rays of the morning sun, soared Sheba's Breasts; and stretching away for hundreds of miles on either side of them ran the great Suliman Berg . . . Straight before us, rose two enormous mountains . . . These mountains placed thus, like the pillars of a gigantic gateway, are shaped after the fashion of a woman's breasts, and at times the mists and shadows beneath them take the form of a recumbent woman, veiled mysteriously in sleep. Their bases swell gently from the plain, looking at that distance perfectly round and smooth; and upon the top of each is a vast hillock covered with snow, exactly corresponding to the nipple on the female breast. The stretch of cliff that connects them appears to be some thousands of feet in height, and perfectly precipitous, and on each flank of them, so far as the eye can reach, extent similar lines of cliff, broken only here and there by flat table-topped mountains, something like the world-famed one at Cape Town; a formation, by the way, that is very common in Africa. (p. 36)

But not *all* Europeans saw the colony in the same way. Women, for example, had a more complex view (Ghose 1998). When these women, subjects of patriarchy in their European homes and societies, travelled out to the colonies it was their *race* that enabled them to acquire a degree of power. They were no more complete 'subjects' on account of their gender – they were also colonizers because of their race. Thus *women came to occupy a dominant position over non-European men and women in the colony, even though they might have been secondary citizens back in their own home countries.*

Thus Mary Kingsley travelling in West Africa was not travelling only as a *white* woman. Unlike the male European who always saw himself as *representative* of a nation, race and culture, Kingsley is concerned mainly with her own individual responses in *Travels in West Africa* (1897):

> To my taste there is nothing so fascinating as spending a night out in an African forest, or plantation . . . It is like being shut up in

a library whose books you cannot read, all the while tormented, terrified, and bored. (p. 102)

What is interesting about Kingsley is that she expressed her feeling of 'being at home' in Africa: 'I am more comfortable there than in England' (p. 347). Kingsley sought to establish a subjective authority of herself as an individual traveller. Her narrative therefore is full of a sense of personal identification with the land:

Do not imagine it gave rise in what I am pleased to call my mind, to those complicated, personal reflections natural beauty seems to bring out in other people's minds. It never works that way with me; I just lose all sense of human individuality, all memory of human life, with its grief and worry and doubt, and become part of the atmosphere. If I have a heaven, that will be mine. (p. 177)

Postcolonial Reclamations

As noted above, colonialism was marked by a discourse of territorial discovery, exploration and conquest. Joseph Conrad's *Heart of Darkness* (1902) with its story of the European's presence in and penetration of this space becomes a paradigmatic text in the spatial theme of colonial writing. Other colonials focused on the native space as ruined, as only bearing depleted reminders of a glorious past. Practically every single European traveller to India in the eighteenth and nineteenth centuries described Indian ruins. Thus Maria Graham visiting Calicut in India she 'finds no trace of its former grandeur and beauty', reports a review (*Quarterly Review* 8 2000 [1812], p. 416). William Petrie's evidence before the Secret Committee: '[Tanjore, in South India] one of the most flourishing, best cultivated, populous districts in Hindostan . . . but its decline has been so rapid . . . it would now be difficult to trace the remains of its former opulence' (House of Commons, *Fourth Report of the Committee of Secrecy*, 1782, p. 705). George Forster writes:

a vast mass of ruins interspersed through a wide space, marks the ancient extent and grandeur of Kinnouge [Kanauj], though few distinct vestiges now exist. (I, p. 92)

And later:

> The country from Najeb Ghur to this frontier is chiefly a waste . . .
> The inhabitants say, that in the time of Najeb-ud-Dowlah, the
> land now overgrown with wood, was a cultivated plain; but such
> is the precarious state of the native territories of Hindostan,
> from the inert disposition which, with little deviation, pervades the
> body of the people . . . we are not to wonder at the ruinous state
> into which many of the most valuable provinces of Hindostan have
> fallen. (I, p. 93)

George Thomas and Jemima Kindersley also report several ruined
towns (G. Thomas, pp. 13, 65; Kindersley pp. 74–5, 91, 106). As
I have argued elsewhere (Nayar 2002), the ruin enables the colonial to
inscribe whatever she/he chooses on to the Indian landscape, and
thus asserts a kind of narrative authority over the territory.

Several postcolonial writers seek to call into question not only
these clichéd 'European expansion' and 'European discovery'
themes, but also seek to rewrite it, to reclaim a measure of control
over space. In V. S. Naipaul's *An Enigma of Arrival*, it is the native
who travels. 'Travelling' here also serves Naipaul as a spatial
metaphor for the journeys of his writing career. What he does in
this part-autobiography, part-novel, part-travelogue is to call into
question the myths of Edenic spaces. Naipaul reverses the standard
Christian, imperial trope of the English garden when he shows
how the Wiltshire countryside is in a state of decay. The Eden is a
ruin, and is symptomatic of a collapse of English social order and
civilization itself. Reversing also the stereotype of the Westerner's
right to name (Crusoe designating the native 'Friday', the colonial
naming of places in Africa and Asia), Naipaul finds himself unfa-
miliar with the nomenclature: fields are 'wet meadows' and hills
are 'downs'. Here is a postcolonial also embarking on a voyage of
discovery – only, what he 'discovers' is the ruins of imperial Britain.
The settings are tragically comic: 'Jack was living in the middle
of junk, among the ruins of nearly a century' (1987, p. 19). Naipaul
suggests the ruins of a great civilization. The cottage – emblematic
of English culture and history – is situated in the midst of 'junk',
thereby suggesting decay.

NATION, SPACE AND BELONGING

In Nadine Godimer's short story, 'Six Feet of the Country' (1996 [1993]), an anonymous illegal immigrant, the brother of one of the farm hands crosses into South Africa and into the narrator's farm looking for work. He contracts pneumonia and dies. The narrator is informed about the incident only after the death. The narrator makes arrangements with the health authorities to retrieve the body because the dead man's relations want a proper ceremony (for which the dead man's aged father comes all the way from Rhodesia). The blacks all pool together the 20 pounds needed for the ceremonies. During the funeral procession the old man claims his son (in the coffin) could not have been so heavy. They discover that the health authorities had sent the wrong body, while the original remains untraceable. The story's evocative power is the anonymity of both life and death. The 'real' body remains buried somewhere by the health authorities. The relations are denied that chance to perform their rituals for their departed one. On the other hand, another black man's boy gets the burial. The switching of identities – one black body for another – inscribes the black into the space of the apartheid nation's space: burial in 'six feet of the country' is the same for any black. It is simply, for the authorities, six feet of earth minus the rituals that are designed for every 'body'.

Three questions indicate the complexity of the national-space problem:

- Who belongs to the space of the nation?
- Conversely, to whom does the sovereign space of the nation belong?
- How is belonging demonstrated?

These questions have informed numerous postcolonial works. The 'space' of the nation here is more than just geographical-spatial territory, as Godimer's story demonstrates. 'Space' is always cultural space, the space of the home, the homely and the secure.

Postcolonial writers demonstrate their affiliation (or disjunction) with any nation-space through a process of cultural belonging where markers of authenticity, rootedness, realist accounts of their cultural practices – what I term 'ethnofictions' later in this section – underscore their location, even when they are not physically rooted in 'their' home/

land. The theme of space and belonging in postcolonial literatures could be organized around the following themes:

- Space, Identity and Belonging
- Home/lands and Cultural Belonging

Space, Identity and Belonging

If Godimer's story demonstrates the absence of belonging then other postcolonials show how 'belonging' itself is a fraught condition, for to 'belong' is to be embedded. It is a theme that figures in postcolonial literatures as a theme of *identity* and *citizenship*.

Take, for instance, Salman Rushdie's description of the migrant identity in his novel, *Shame*:

> What is the best thing about migrant peoples . . .? I think it is their hopefulness . . . And what's the worst thing? It's the emptiness of one's baggage. We've come unstuck from more than land. We've floated upwards from history, from memory, from Time. (p. 91)

Rushdie celebrates a non-belonging.[1] The free-floating migrant has little attachment to space or history and is therefore free to belong everywhere and nowhere. Sara Upstone in her recent work has argued that Rushdie moves away from a 'solid nation' (2009, p. 27) marking a break with a specific conception of the nation-state (but not, perhaps, concepts of nationality). Rushdie himself argues that a 'frontierless nation is not a fantasy', and that in postcolonial authors 'if writing turns repeatedly towards the nation, it just as repeatedly turns away' (2002, p. 67). Are there, then, ways of belonging that are not bound to the 'nation' but which do retain a *nationality*? As Upstone argues in the case of Wilson Harris' fiction, after colonialism the scale of the nation (linked to specific social elites and classes) is replaced by smaller scales and so the specificity of the nation-state as the location of identity-formation is denied (p. 43). Upstone is arguing for other ways of cultural belonging, where the nation does not remain the central space of belonging (as we shall see in the case of the postcolonial cosmopolitan in the next chapter, multiple spaces of belonging are possible).

Rushdie is the cartographer of spaces where there are many kinds of belonging, of postcolonial cities which took in all kinds of people, became 'home' to variety, diversity and chaos and celebrated it. Here is Rushdie's description of Bombay/Mumbai in *The Moor's Last Sigh*:

> Bombay was central, had been so from the moment of its creation: the bastard child of a Portuguese-English wedding, and yet the most Indian of Indian cities. In Bombay all Indias met and merged. In Bombay, too, all-India met what-was-not-India, what came across the black water to flow into our veins . . . Bombay was central; all rivers flowed into its human sea. It was an ocean of stories; we were all its narrators, and everybody talked at once . . .
>
> Bombay was not inoculated against the rest of the country, and what happened elsewhere, the language business for example, spread into its streets. But on the way to Bombay the rivers of blood were usually diluted, other rivers poured into them, so that by the time they reached the city's streets the disfigurations were relatively slight . . . (p. 350)

Rushdie is demonstrating the plural nature of India's space (the city) as well as that of its cultures. The 'national' has often been conflated with the urban (as seen above in the case of Harris, in Upstone's argument), and this is precisely what is disturbed in some postcolonial novels. Thus Amitav Ghosh's *The Hungry Tide* (2004) demonstrates how the postcolonial urban collapses in the face of the raw reality of the untamed country of the Sundarbans. Urban Kanai does not 'belong' in the Sundarbans, whereas the illiterate Fokir – who would be the marginalized within the postcolonial nation – does. At a crucial point in the novel Kanai is left behind on one of the islands in the middle of the river and Kanai believes he sees a tiger. The horror and the experience transform him forever.

> Kanai's head filled suddenly with visions of the ways in which the tide country dealt out death. The tiger . . . killed you instantly, with a swipe of its forepaw . . . was'nt this why people who lived in close proximity with tigers so often regarded them as being something more than just an animal?
>
> He could not bring himself to look around the clearing . . . what was he thinking of? He could not recall the word . . . it was as if his mind, in its panic had emptied itself of language. (p. 353)

From the confident, indeed arrogant, city-man he becomes an uncertain and vulnerable one:

I had always prided myself on the breadth and comprehensiveness of my experience of the world . . . at Garjontola I learnt how little I know of myself and of the world. (p. 353)

He is literally 'out of place' and he tells Piya: 'I want you to see me – on my own ground, in the place where I live' (p. 335). Ghosh suggests how one's identity does not ever remain stable – when the space changes, the sense of belonging (or non-belonging) also changes.

As Kanai and Piya discover in *The Hungry Tide*, maps, which ought to help them feel at home and in control, become irrelevant in the space of the Sundarbans. Mapping and belonging is a major theme in postcolonial fiction, as Graham Huggan has noted (1989). If the colonial regime drew maps as a mode of imperial control over territory and peoples, the postcolonial condition has constantly questioned arbitrary divisions, belonging and borders. In extreme cases such as Rwanda and the Partition of India the cartographic imaginary has resulted in genocide and massacres. Refugee problems and secessionist, claims for self-affirmation in many postcolonial nations are also questions of cartography – and these find expression in much fiction and poetry. Ghosh's earlier novel, *The Shadow Lines* questioned the construction of borders and barriers on maps. The old grandmother asks if she would be able to see the 'border between India and East Pakistan from the plane', at least 'trenches . . . or soldiers, or guns pointing at each other' (151). Singaporean poet Edwin Thumboo speaks of the effort to

Evacuate the disagreeable
Bring the hill to valley, level the place and build
And generally cater for the people. (1993, pp. 53–4)

Edward Kumau Brathwaite wonders in *The Arrivants*:

How will new maps be drafted?
Who will suggest a new tentative frontier?
How will the sky dawn now? (1981 [1973], p. 184)

In Michael Ondaatje's *Running in the Family*, the protagonist is planning a journey to Sri Lanka. He spreads out the maps on the floor and searches for possible routes. He notes a feature of the place and geographical names:

Asia . . . the word sprawled. It had none of the clipped sound of Europe, America, Canada. The vowels took over, slept on the map with the S. (1982, p. 22)

In Somalian Nuruddin Farah's *Maps* he writes:

Someone else insisted that passengers be told where the "inexistent" border used to be – inexistent, because Somalis never admitted it . . . Non-Somalis, because they were total strangers or knew no better, looked at maps, where they found a curvy line, drawn to cut one Somali people from another. (Farah 1999, p. 132)

Indian poet Keki Daruwalla's map-maker wonders whether the world really needs any kind of map when much of human condition cannot be located in grid lines or paper. The map-maker therefore calls upon the people to 'map the undefined . . . the hedge between love and hate', to 'map the wrinkles on the ageing skin of love'. Lust cannot be mapped, not the 'heaving salt of desire that floods the creeks'. He concludes:

Forget maps and voyaging, study instead
The parched earth horoscope of a brown people. (Daruwalla 2006
    [2002], pp. 334–6)

The postcolonial anxiety over maps and borders suggests several interrelated themes:

- The colonial redrawing and reframing of borders and lands,
- The unsettling legacy of this colonial cartography,
- The impossibility of aligning a lived experience of cultural mixing with cartographic divisions (a theme we see with considerable poignancy in conversations about India and Pakistan),
- The anxiety over map-making as a means of redrawing populations, assigning property and rights of belonging.

Spaces therefore are spaces not only of geographical mapping but of *cultural, emotional belonging*, which has to be politically, socially, juridically legitimized. This legitimization and debates over 'who belongs' has been a theme in postcolonial literary and cultural debates. When Gyan Pandey asks 'Can a Muslim Be an Indian?' (1999), he is addressing the question of identity: who belongs to the (space of the) nation-state? As we shall see, this question has ramifications for subaltern spaces within the postcolonial nation-space. The debates about the American identity and patriotism of the Muslims in the USA after 9/11 – epitomized in the writings of Khaled Hossaini, for instance – and the black British authors are constant reminders of the link between space, identity and belonging.

Home/lands and Cultural Belonging

Belonging is a sentimental attachment to territory or space. As Benedict Anderson has forcefully argued (1991, rev. ed.), patriotism and nationalism are 'feelings' towards the nation-state and its peoples. A nation is the consequence of people imagining it into existence, of the feeling of unity and identity that discourses generate. Thus the nation is not always the 'concrete' physical entity. It is tenuously constructed and kept alive through imaginative and emotional acts. Identities rooted in space/territory have been the concern of Canadian and Australian literatures with their settler colonial history as they have been of India and Africa. (In fact, recognizing the significance of territory in the Canadian imagination, the journal *Studies in Canadian Literature* ran a special issue on 'Writing Canadian Space', 23, 1, 1998.)[2]

In Wilson Harris' *The Palace of the Peacock* maps become 'dreams' (1988, p. 24). Salman Rushdie speaks of the 'Indias of the mind' and 'imaginary homelands' (1991). When speaking of 'spaces', therefore we need to speak of cultural spaces that allow people to feel that they 'belong' to a nation. 'Home', 'country', 'national identity' are terms that suggest emotional, abstract and socio-cultural modes of defining the space-people linkage. It is this linkage that the present section explores.

If the nation serves as the space of 'home', then it also serves as a space of safety, comfort, security. It could be imaginary, imagined or utopian. These spaces become 'analogues of home', as Helen May

Dennis puts it in her spatialized reading of Native American literature (2007, p. 8). Thus for displaced peoples like Native Americans,
there is the yearning for the traditional home (as we shall see
in the section on subaltern spaces). In the case of women authors,
the space of the home constitutes a geography of intimacy and care,
a space where they have a measure of freedom. However, as we shall
see in the section on subaltern spaces, this space of the home is
also, often, a space of the loss of freedom and agency. The home/
land functions in most postcolonial works as a *space of cultural
belonging*. This sense of cultural (be)longing is most emphasized in
diasporic authors, where the distance from the spatial 'home/land'
seems to energize them to engage with their family, tradition and
culture (indeed, Lal 2003, Varghese 2003 have shown how diasporic
communities seem to be far more entrenched in conservative ideas of
'nation', 'tradition' and gender roles than those who continue to live
in Third World spaces).

In Amitav Ghosh's *The Shadow Lines*, Ila's grandmother believes
that Ila does not belong to England because 'Everyone who lives
there has earned his *right* to be there with blood: with their brother's
blood and their father's blood and their son's blood' (pp. 77–8,
emphasis added). What the grandmother is gesturing at here is the
right to belong to a particular nation-space. This belonging is about
traditions, family and sacrifice – in other words, belonging is never
automatic, it must be earned by the citizen.

A key argument about home/lands and belonging has been made
by Meenakshi Mukherjee in her essay, 'The Anxiety of Indianness'
(2000). Examining the tradition of Indian fiction in English,
Mukherjee argues that the Indian writer in English (as contrasted
with the Indian writers in regional languages), seeking to gain
attention from a predominantly Western readership, exhibits an
'anxiety of Indianness'. This anxiety manifests as the forced use
of 'Indian' myths, allegories of India and such exoticism. Where
the writer in regional languages uses local themes and has local
concerns rather than national, pan-Indian ones, the Indian writer
in English must always use India as a *metaphor*. The Indian novelist
in English must speak of the colonial legacies rather than local
matters. We see evidence of Mukherjee's argument in the fiction
of the 1990s. For example, in Upamanyu Chatterjee's *English, August*
(1988) – subtitled conspicuously, 'an Indian story' – the opening
chapters has references to 'a typical Indian story' (p. 3). Later the

novelist offers us a continuity between India's colonial period and the present:

> District administration in India is largely a British creation, like the railways and the English language, another complex and unwieldy bequest of the Raj. But Indianization is integral to the Indian story. Before 1947 the Collector was almost inaccessible to the people; now he keeps open house . . . In Madna, as in all of India, one's importance as an official could be gauged by how long one could keep a concert waiting. (p. 10)

In Vikram Chandra's *Love and Longing in Bombay* and Shashi Tharoor's *The Great Indian Novel*, the authors take recourse to the Hindu epics, the *Mahabharata* and the *Ramayana* for their characters and plot. The use of these epics somehow conveys an air of authenticity. In Rohinton Mistry's Booker-winner novel, *A Fine Balance* (1996), we see all the elements of an India that Western audiences want to know about: the exploitative caste system, the all-pervasive poverty, oppression, corruption, urban squalor and rural poverty. Many of these writers, argues Mukherjee following Tim Brennan, are 'Third World Cosmopolitans' (p. 178). They function as the authentic voices of the Third World in the West. They *have to be 'national allegories' and serve up signs of their being authentically Indian.*

Mukherjee's argument could be extended to other postcolonial writers, especially the diasporic ones (about whom, more in the following chapter), who seek to emphasize their representative nature: *this novel* is a synecdoche for a *national condition*. Graham Huggan refers to a process of postcolonial exoticizing (2001) where a Rushdie or a Tutuola or an Adichie is marketed as 'authentic' Third World writing, what Huggan calls the 'hypercommodified status of the "multicultural" or "Third World" writer' (p. 19). Marginality is the single greatest virtue these writers thrive upon in the global literary marketplace, suggests Huggan. Lisa Lau (2007) speaks of a 're-Orientalism' where the postcolonial writer is doing what the colonials used to: offer orientalized images of their own cultures. Lau writes:

> Orientalism is no longer only the relationship of the dominance and representation of the Oriental by the non-Oriental or Occidental,

but that this role appears to have been taken over (in part at least) by other Orientals, namely, the diasporic authors. (p. 2)

Lau echoes Mukherjee when she writes: 'quite a number of diasporic South Asian women writers are under pressure to demonstrate so-called recognizably "South Asian characteristics"' (p. 12). I would suggest that one of the selling points of Monica Ali's *Brick Lane* and Kiran Desai's *The Inheritance of Loss* (the first shortlisted for the Booker, the second a Booker winner) is their focus on communities that have not, thus far, received much attention in fiction. This is the Bangladeshi community in London (about which there are no novels, to the best of my knowledge) in Ali and the Gorkhas in Desai. Both function, I suggest, as 'ethnofictions', introductions to communities and their cultural practices. The greater the emphasis on cultural practices and ways of life in these works, the greater their appeal to Western audiences in what is an instance of the postcolonial exotic. Both writers underscore their cultural belonging through such ethnographic fictions. Diasporic authors seek 'felicitous spaces' and 'analogues of home' in community and neighbourhood in a metaphoric embeddedness in their 'original' cultures and spaces. But it is precisely in this imaginative return to roots and cultural spaces that a process of exoticizing works.

The postcolonial is thus interested in *spaces of belonging* – cultural, geographical and even metaphoric. It signifies a space where one's possessions, lives and loves find safety and comfort. It becomes a space to which one remains connected in spite (or because) of geographical displacement. This space of belonging is what comes under scrutiny by women, minorities and other marginal groups in the postcolonial condition, as we shall see in the following section.

Before concluding this section a reference to new forms of postcolonial space – that of diaspora – is in order (it will receive more sustained attention in the chapter on cosmopolitanism). For exiles, immigrants and the displaced, space and belonging are severely problematized. Inhabiting a new territory while remaining culturally rooted in a 'home' country results in a fractured condition where the citizenship-territory link is called into question. In Kureishi's *The Buddha of Suburbia* he maps the disparate and contrasting experiences of space between generations: '[With] fifteen . . . [years] lived in the South London suburbs . . . [my father] stumbled around the place like an Indian off the boat.' In contrast Karim 'knew all the streets and very bus route' (1990, p. 7).

Until such time as the home *territory* continues to call out to the migrant, she/he remains an exile. The migrant, writes Chandani Lokugé, 'ceases to be an exile when the homeland loses its haptic meaning' (2000, p. 26). As Lokugé points out in the case of Bharat in Gooneratne's *A Change of Skies*, it is only 'when Bharat is able to respond meaningfully to the Australian space that he can think of Australia as home' (p. 27). Lokugé correctly draws attention to territorial and cultural locations of 'belonging' in her reading. I have elsewhere argued (Nayar 2008a, pp. 195–7) that diasporic cultures are caught up in a peculiar condition. Exiles tend to hold on to their traditions in an almost desperate effort to retain/reclaim their 'original' culture. This is a process of acquiring a 'cultural citizenship', defined as the 'maintenance and development of cultural lineage through education, custom, language and religion and the positive acknowledgement of difference in and by the mainstream' (Toby Miller 2001, p. 2). Thus we see two senses of 'belonging' emerge here: *legal belonging* as a citizen, but also a *cultural belonging* as a member of an ethnic group/community. Caught up in a 'national' culture in whose *cultural* life the migrant community may have little or no role to play (this is especially the case with *first* generation immigrant communities), the community clings to its own customs and cultural codes. The migrant seeks a cultural citizenship within her/his own community while also seeking legal citizenship within the nation. This tension between (and negotiation of) cultural and legal citizenship is what constitutes a rewriting of the 'First World' space by immigrants.

SUBALTERN SPACES

THE CITY BELONGS TO YOU!
KEEP IT BEAUTIFUL!
FOOD FOR THE HUNGRY! HOMES FOR THE HOMELESS!
THE NATION IS ON THE MOVE! (Mistry 1995, p. 373, emphasis in original)

This is a slogan the poor and the displaced are treated to in Rohinton Mistry's *A Fine Balance*. Ironically, the beautification of the city is to be achieved when the poor are taken away from the city. They do not 'belong' to the beautiful space of the city – they are the postcolonial nation's subalterns.

In this section I explore the postcolonial subaltern's negotiation with space. How do Aboriginals, minorities, women and social outcasts treat (and are treated by) the space of the nation? How do such subalterns in presumably sovereign (i.e. postcolonial) nations negotiate spaces? What identities are bestowed, possible or imposed on these subalterns by the territory and cultural processes of the postcolonial state? Minority and subaltern writers in the postcolonial condition are therefore interested in

- the physical-spatial organization of cities and spaces into classed, racialized and majoritarian-minoritarian spaces through which rights of residence, movement and belonging are restricted and controlled;
- the cultural spaces where minority, marginal and non-dominant cultural spaces find possible expression (or not);
- the gendered nature of space – of the home, neighbourhood, community and city – and the differential nature of safety, duties and work for men and women in each of these spaces.

First, let us look how the Aboriginals and tribal cultures have dealt with the question of space in the postcolonial age.

Aboriginal writer Jackie Huggins (1995) documents the enforced displacement her people endured because of the white man's regulations and reorganization of the Australian land. The contrast Huggins makes is worth noting some detail:

My born country is the land of the Bidjara-Pitjara people, and is known now as Carnarvon Gorge . . . There were huge cliffs and rocks, riddled with caves where many of my people's paintings were. Most caves and rock faces showed my people's stencilled hands, weapons and tools, and there were engravings here, too . . . This place is old. My people and their art were here long before the whiteman came . . . As had happened for my mother and her mother before her, going back generation after generation, I was born in the sanctuary of one of those caves. My mother would tell us how my grandmother would wash my mother's newborn babies in the nearby creek, place them in a cooliman and carry them back to suckle on my exhausted mother's breast. (p. 168)

Then they are taken away in cattle trucks to 'reservations':

This new country was so different from our country – flat, no hills, and valleys, arid and cleared of trees . . . It was Barambah Reserve (renamed Cherbourg in 1932) . . . Here we were separated from each other into rough houses – buildings that seemed so strange to me then, with their walls so straight. Each family was fenced off from the other into their own two little rooms where you ate and slept. The houses were little cells all next to each other in little rows. A prison . . . The place in fact had its own gaol. A prison in a prison. There were white and Aboriginal areas. (p. 169)

Huggins makes it clear that the white man had no right to Aboriginal lands:

No one had the right to remove us from our traditional lands and to do what they did to us. We were once the proud custodians of our land and now our way of life became controlled by insensitive people who knew nothing about us but thought they knew everything. They even chose how and where we could live. We had to stay in one place now while the white-man could roam free. (p. 169)

Writing from India, Dalit activist Baby Kamble speaks of the so-called lower castes' attachment to the land:

We may be coarse and ignorant, yet you must admit that we have been the most devoted children of Maharashtra, this land of our birth, and it is we who are the true heirs of this great land. You played with our lives and enjoyed yourself at our expense. But remember, we may have lost everything, but never the truth. (2008, p. 37)

Activist Janu, who has been fighting for the land rights of the tribals in South India writes:

The life cycle of our people, their customs and very existence are bound to the earth. This is more so than in any other society. When projects are designed without any link to this bond, our people suffer. This may be wrong if looked at from the point of view of civil society. But it is self-evident when we go to the newly formed colonies. (2004, p. 47)

Ironically, tribal lands are taken over by the postcolonial state, colluding with big business and industrial houses. The tribal is displaced from his/her land under the pretext of national 'development', 'modernization' and 'progress'. Janu writes:

Our people had turned into mere wage labourers. Mother Forest had turned into the Departmental Forest . . . All the land belonged to the migrants. (p. 30)

In Leslie Marmon Silko's *Ceremony* (1986) the homeless Indian mother and her young son live in a makeshift shack, and the mother has to prostitute herself in order to support herself and her son. The boy's memories are of poverty, squalor and filth when he rummaged 'for garbage in the alleys behind the houses' (p. 108). The once-great culture is reduced to such a vermin-like life. The spaces of life for Native Americans, suggests Silko, are meager. Later Silko underscores this sense of loss and displacement:

He [Betonie] turned and pointed to the city dump east of the Ceremonial grounds and rodeo chutes. 'They keep us to the north side of the railroad tracks, next to the river and their dump. Where none of them want to live'. (p. 117)

Betonie escapes the squalor of his immediate surroundings by retreating into his mind-scapes (Dennis 2007, p. 66). In the Aboriginal Waipuldanya's autobiography he speaks of the horrors of spatial and cultural displacement:

My mother died in a lazaret, confined like a convict in a barren Alcatraz in Darwin Harbour, abjectly miserable with a motley of other social outcasts, white, yellow, brown, and black, who had committed the unpardonable offence of being infected with an alien disease. Leprosy! (p. 154)

Waipuldanya describes how she was 'cast out of the camp, to dwell all the rest of her days in a foreign land' (p. 154). Here Waipuldanya conflates spatial, biomedical and cultural isolation. The mother is incarcerated because of her foreign disease. She is physically isolated from her own family and culture. Some of course do want to abandon their 'home/land', as Waipuldanya himself admits: 'One year I was a primitive blackfellow living by the tribal law . . . next year I was an embryo citizen in another world' (p. 181).

In each of these cases what we see is the postcolonial marginalized agonizing over spaces of belonging. The Aboriginal and the tribal is mourning not just the loss of physical territory but their cultural space. The loss is of tradition, ways of living and cultural memory because, for the Aboriginal, these are all rooted in a sense of place. In other words, *the loss of the land is also the loss of tribal memory, history, cultural practices and way of life.* Such narratives document the yearning for home-spaces, of the exclusion and expulsion of people from the land. Cartography, political mapping and social structures constitute modes of legitimizing belonging or non-belonging.

For women in postcolonial states the problem is of a different kind. For long inured to and indoctrinated with the idea that their space is that of the home and the family, the woman in the postcolonial state finds the public sphere (i) closed off to her and (ii) inimical to her participation. With modernization and greater employment opportunities, postcolonial women have begun to step out of the circumscribed limits of the home and family, but only to find that these opportunities are also skewed against them.

Autobiographies and fiction from postcolonial women writers have since the 1990s questioned the nature and functioning of both the domestic as well as the public spaces – both in the sense of the physical territory of, say, the city and the processes that constitute the public sphere. Postcolonial women writers are therefore interested in

- the space of domesticity which is designated 'feminine' and its possible reconfigurations,
- the cultural and social space of the family and the feminine 'duties and responsibilities' that are willed upon the women,
- the nature of public spaces (including parks, recreational spaces, transport, shopping areas),
- the gendered social relations that 'take place' in urban spaces,
- their participation (or lack thereof) in the public sphere – politics, administrative decision-making, etc.

In Indian novelist Shashi Deshpande's *The Dark Holds No Terrors* (1990 [1980]) the space of the home is transformed into a horrifying space for the woman. The accomplished and socially respectable doctor-wife is abused within the space of the home by the husband. In Nayantara Sahgal's *A Situation in New Delhi* (1988 [1977) a student is raped within the official space of the University as Sahgal shows how public space remains threatening to its women. Arundhati Roy's *The God of Small Things* (1997) is about returns and exits of women from public and social spaces. Ammu gets married because she does not want to return to Ayemenem (p. 39). After her marriage fails, Ammu makes an 'unwelcome' return to Ayemenem (p. 42) because divorcee women are not respectable enough for the public space of the town/village. In R. K. Narayan's *The Dark Room* (1998 [1938]) the nature of cultural spaces, in terms of how women respond to them, is described using two sets of women, Ramani and Shanta Bai, and Savitri and Ramani. There is a category of Indian women who are seduced by 'Western' values, as contrasted with Indian women who stay within the 'proper' Indian one, suggests Narayan's novel. Savitri viewing a religious film is moved deeply:

> The picture carried Savitri with it, and when in the end Kuchela stood in his 'pooja' room and lit camphor and incense before the image of god, Savitri brought her palms together and prayed. (p. 30)

When Ramani goes with Shanta-bai the latter's response is in sharp contrast to Savitri's:

> What rubbish the whole thing is! . . . Till our film producers give up mythological nonsense there is no salvation for our films. Let us get out. I can't stand this any more. (p. 91)

Women like Shanta-bai who do not accept the dominant cultural codes – admiration and devotion to the traditions – are problematic residents of the cultural spaces of the nation, suggests Narayan.

In postcolonial nations the regulation of public space becomes a key feature. Ironically, the sovereignty of the nation-state is asserted in the shutting out of public spaces to its citizens. For example, youth in African public spaces are seen as threats with their bodies, ideas of pleasure and their sexualities. Debates about the loss of morality among youth, their aggression and their indifference in postcolonial countries like India suggest that the space of the nation is something that has to be preserved in certain ways, and strategies of inclusion and exclusion – who is authorized to use this space – are put in place. Writing about this reorganization of space in postcolonial Africa, Mamadou Diof (2003) says:

> Excluded from the arenas of power, work, education, and leisure, young Africans construct places of socialization and new sociabilities whose function is to show their difference, either on the margins of society or at its heart, simultaneously as victims and active agents, and circulating in a geography that escapes the limits of the national territory. (p. 5)

The youth are labelled 'delinquent', notes Diof when actually what they seek is recognition:

> The function of these spaces, which escape the logics of public and administrative control, communitarian prescriptions, and state surveillance, is to serve as supports for acts that express within the public sphere, in a violent, artistic, or spiritual way, a desire for recognition and a presence. (p. 5)

South American fiction and testimonies document how postcolonial nations have erased their own citizens from national spaces, torturing, incarcerating and executing any dissenter. In Isabel Allende's *Of Love and Shadows* under the dictatorship several of its citizens have 'disappeared'. Irene and Francisco having discovered mass graves are unable to decide how best to make it public. 'Justice', writes Allende of the unnamed postcolonial nation, 'was an almost forgotten term, no longer mentioned because, like the word "liberty", it had subversive overtones' (p. 220). In Alicia Partnoy's fictionalized account of her incarceration in Argentina, *The Little School* (1998), she lists people who have been 'disappeared' by the government. I have elsewhere argued (Nayar 2009) that such narratives as Partnoy's call into question the commitment of a postcolonial state to its own citizens, and suggested that these narratives disrupt the mainstream nationalist narrative by documenting those who do not belong, and that they must be read alongside similar accounts of suffering and human rights violations from other parts of the world.

In discussions of such spaces the woman's dress code has often been at the core of the debates. The Taliban in Afghanistan, the Islamic groups in Kashmir, the Hindu right-wing party in India have all sought to impose 'appropriate' dress codes upon its women. Under the guise of 'protecting' their culture from Western modernization and globalization – where the woman becomes the reservoir of native culture and tradition – these groups ordered women from their faiths to observe a dress code. Those who didn't fall in line were victims of physical attacks. This is another instance of the policing of cultural spaces and the attempts, in postcolonial societies, to define who 'belongs': the woman in the veil 'belongs' to the space of the nation/community/faith (in the case of Afghanistan or Kashmir).

Such debates around 'belonging' are always about identity politics, and very often have much to do with larger questions of modernization and globalization. Thus, Nivedita Menon notes how Egyptian feminists came out in defence of the veil. The veil became, in this argument, a mode of resisting Westernizaton and the commodification of the native Muslim woman for the white male gaze. In other words, the voluntary return to and adoption of the veil becomes a liberatory move where the Muslim woman rejected the excessively Western and consumer culture in favour of her own traditions (Menon 2007, p. 211). In this reading, postcolonial feminism explicitly situates the *woman's right to choose the veil* as a marker of her identity. Menon argues that in some postcolonial cultures like India the cultural hegemony of globalization – the dominance of particular kinds of looks for women – produces cultural nationalist responses, such as the ones by right-wing parties (p. 215). Menon argues, correctly in my opinion, that in the woman's adoption of the veil or such traditions what 'operates is not free will in the feminist/modernist sense, but . . . it cannot be characterized by a lack of free will either' (p. 219). True, the woman here *might choose to belong to a patriarchal, cultural nationalist framework that is not congenial to the woman's freedom, but it still remains a 'free will' of a kind.* Does the autonomy of the individual – to choose the *burqa* or the beauty parlour, to return to Menon's key terms – contradict, contest or endorse the patriarchal space of culture? Does the woman choose to belong to such a cultural space even when her values and beliefs are not the dominant ones of that space? It is a difficult political dilemma. On the one hand is the feminist espousal of the right to choose the beauty parlour – but this becomes the woman's subjectification to and commodification by (Western) consumer cultures of modernity. On the other is the cultural nationalist espousal of the *burqa* – but this becomes the woman's subjectification to a patriarchal space. But what if the woman *chooses* either of these positions?

ECOLOGY, ENVIRONMENTALISM AND POSTCOLONIALISM

'This was the story that gave the land its life,' writes Ghosh in his *The Hungry Tide* (p. 354). The Bon Bibi legend, suggests Ghosh is the story that gives the land its history, character and even philosophy (pp. 102–5). The story's narrative, Nirmal discovers in the novel, is a curious analogy to the tide country itself. The narrative had been created 'from elements of legend and scripture, from the near and the far, Bangla and Arabic.' It has Arabic invocations at what looks like a Hindu *puja* (pp. 246–7).

> The mudbanks of the tide country are shaped not only by rivers of silt, but also by rivers of language: Bengali, English, Arabic, Hindi, Arakanese and who knows what else . . . the tide country's faith is something like one of its great mohonas, a meeting not just of many rivers, but a circular roundabout people can use to pass in many directions. (p. 247)

Here Ghosh weaves narrative with ecology, story-telling with the landscape in an astute linkage of environmentalism and postcolonialism. The entire novel deals with displacement of people, of the loss of territory (physical as well as social spaces) and of story-telling. How the people stay with the land, how stories grow out of the land and inform the peoples' experience of locale and locality is the subject of Ghosh's amazing novel.

If colonialism appropriated non-European lands for its own economic purposes, the postcolonial condition in many nations of Africa, South America and Asia has been marked by a linkage between the nation-state and global, transnational corporations that utilize these same natural resources and lands. This utilization is primarily exploitative of the natural resources in the interests of global capital and secondarily of the labour of the non-European peoples.

A new turn within postcolonial studies is visible in the writings of Ken Saro-Wiwa in Africa and Arundhati Roy in India. Saro-Wiwa, at the time of his execution, was battling the arrival of US oil companies in Nigeria. More importantly, his resistance to the oil companies was explicitly situated within a discourse of environmentalism (Nixon 2007), where he saw Nigerian ecosystems being devastated by global capital in active collusion with the Nigeria (postcolonial) state. Arundhati Roy writing about the politics of dams, consumer culture and globalization has pointed to the devastating effects of these upon native (mainly Aboriginal) cultures. Like Saro-Wiwa, Roy also gestures at the postcolonial state's alignment with global capital for the exploitation of the *land*. Thus these writers call into question the very notion of postcolonial independence because postcoloniality seems to extend colonialism's anti-environment themes, only this time in *conjunction* with the exploiter.

This is not to romanticize the precolonial land, or to idealize nature in the postcolony. National definitions have been always aligned with territory and sense of *place*, but it runs the risk of lapsing into such a localized and therefore xenophobic cultural nationalism. Environmentalism is a localized condition, where bioregionalism dominates cosmopolitanism and displacement.

In eco-activist C. K. Janu, fighting for the rights of tribals in Kerala, India, we see a postcolonialism which is about the oppression by independent states. The First Peoples' link with the land is broken due to 'development projects' and advancing modernity. At one point in her narrative, *Mother Forest*, Janu writes:

The life cycle of our people, their customs and very existence are bound to the earth. This is more so than in any other society. When projects are designed without any link to this bond, our people suffer. This may be wrong if looked at from the point of view of civil society. But it is self-evident when we go to the newly formed colonies. (2004, p. 47)

Numerous works from Native Americans, African tribes, Aborigines and First Peoples from postcolonial nations as well as settler colonies like Australia and Canada demonstrate a disillusionment with postcolonial politics where their traditional lands and ways of life have been taken away from them. Restricted to reservations and ghettoes, and modernized, sometimes, against their will, these First Peoples battle not only a colonial legacy but also postcolonial indifference and a neocolonial structural exploitation. Rob Nixon (2007) has astutely pointed out that because high-profile postcolonial theory – exemplified by Spivak, Bhabha, Appiah and others – showcases hybridity and dislocation, ecological writing, with its 'bioregionalism' do not quite fit into the 'theory'. Nixon argues that bioregional writing demonstrates a locatedness and embeddedness that militates against displacement and also seems to suggest a certain xenophobia. However, Nixon argues, using the example of Saro-Wiwa, that one cannot think of a postcolonialism which does not address the question of the environment because lands, natural resources and people continue to be exploited by First World structures and mechanisms, just as it used to be in the colonial age. In this context it is important to look at the work of activists like Ken Saro-Wiwa and Arundhati Roy, along with the writings of Aboriginals and First Peoples as intertwining

- postcolonialism's emphazis on emancipation from exploitation and
- an ecological consciousness rooted in both space and cultural traditions of tribes, ethnic groups and communities.

While it is true that there is a serious deterioration of the environment in countries like India, the shortages of and struggles over natural resources are determined by the economic divide between peoples and groups. Hence environmental historians and scholars like Ramachandra Guha and Martinez-Alier (1998) have argued for an 'environmentalism of the poor'. Nature-based conflicts have evolved, Guha and Martinez-Alier argue, from the 'lopsided, iniquitous and environmentally destructive process of development in independent India (p. 17). Hence environmental movements in such contexts emerge from 'resource shortages' and rely on 'traditional networks of organization, the village and the tribe' (p. 17). The 'environmentalism of the poor' originates as a clash over productive resources, where these resources, with the active collusion of the state, are in the grip of the elite landlords. Guha and Martinez-Alier list the features of 'southern' (postcolonial) environmentalism thus:

- Refuse to exchange the world they know for an uncertain future (often presented as 'modernization' or 'development');

- Interlinked with questions of human rights, ethnicity and distributive justice;
- Defend the local and the locality against the nation;
- Closer to subsistence and survival;
- Critique consumerism and uncontrolled economic development (p. 18).

Arundhati Roy writing of the displaced peoples of the Narmada dam project notes how the inhabitants have been 'scattered to 175 separate rehabilitation sites'. 'Social links,' writes Roy, 'have been smashed, communities broken up' (2001, pp. 102–3). Ken Saro-Wiwa notes how oil-rich southern Nigeria had been neglected while arid, Northern Nigeria 'there were wide expressways constructed at great cost with the petrodollars which the delta belched forth' (1995, p. 19). Later he spells out the differential development in the postcolonial country:

The population of Lagos had exploded once oil money from the delta had been cornered by the nation's rulers and transferred to lagos from hapless communities like the Ogoni and the Ijaws who were too few to defend their inheritance. (p. 33)

Saro-Wiwa also reprints the petition presented by the Ogonis to the Nigerian government in which they point out that:

Oil has been mined on our land since 1958 . . . by Shell Petroleum Development Company (Nigeria) Limited . . .

In over 30 years of oil mining, the Ogoni nationality have provided the Nigerian nation with a total revenue estimated at over forty billion naira, thirty billion dollars . . .

That in return for the above contribution, the Ogoni people have received NOTHING. (pp. 67–8, emphasis in original)

The document also points out that several Ogoni languages are disappearing whereas 'other Nigerian languages are being forced' upon them (p. 68). Saro-Wiwa's narrative clearly implicates economic exploitation and neo-colonialism as causal factors in the continuing marginalization of the tribe. The narrative is an instance of the close alignment of postcolonialism and environmentalism.

Roy's and Saro-Wiwa's narratives illustrate the force of Nixon's arguments. Neither of these two postcolonials – one from India and one from Nigeria – sees cultural hybridity, displacement or multiple locations as empowering experiences. Indeed, their entire effort is to address the specificity of location, of locale and local cultures. The 'smashed' and 'broken up' communities signify the loss not only of land/territory but also of a traditional social space.

In the case of Third World (postcolonial) nations environmentalism is limited by the economic conditions of its peoples. In Amitavh Ghosh's *The Hungry Tide* Piya is furious when the villagers of the Sunderbans set about killing a tiger. She pleads for the tiger's life much to the villagers' surprise. Kanai points out to her that her environmentalism and animal-conservation ideas are Western: they ignore the realities of life in the Sunderbans. Kusum, one of the inhabitants of the tiger-infested spaces bitterly criticizes the animal conservation movement (pp. 261–2). Kanai says of the animal conservation movement: it made a 'push to protect the wildlife here, without regard for the human costs' (p. 301).

* * *

This chapter has demonstrated how postcolonialism's interest in space and place begins with a critique of colonial domination – through cartography, military conquest – of native spaces. The figure of the 'discoverer', *terra nullius* or the feminine landscape in colonial discourse often anticipated and invited colonial conquest, as postcolonial readings have shown. Postcolonialism's spatial dynamics, the chapter argued, is also reflected in the ways in which independent nations construct spaces of belonging. Questions of cultural belonging, it showed, involve identity politics, especially when territory and social spaces are both denied some groups. It has argued that several sections of the population – minorities, women, subalterns – do not find a place within the space of the postcolonial nation-state. The sense of belonging is the privilege, in many cases, of a few. It also demonstrated postcolonialism's close, but not unproblematic, relationship with environmentalism.

CHAPTER SIX

COSMOPOLITANISMS

Everywhere was now a part of everywhere else. Russia, America, London, Kashmir. Our lives, our stories, flowed into one another's, were no longer our own, individual, discrete. This unsettled people. There were collisions and explosions. The world was no longer calm.

(Rushdie 2005, p. 37)

When Agha Shahid Ali, the Indian poet settled in America, recalls his home, Kashmir, he finds he can only 'hold' it in the form of a 'neat four by six inches' postcard. The 'half-inch Himalayas' of the postcard, he writes, will be the 'closest' he will ever be to home (1996, p. 752). Pico Iyer (2000), who divides his time between India and the USA and travels extensively all over the world, on the other hand, describes himself as a 'global soul' (the title of one of his works). Ali and Iyer embody two key moments in postcolonialism's negotiation of displacement, diaspora consciousness and its nostalgic recall of 'home' and an emerging postcolonial cosmopolitan vision of the world. This chapter deals with both these key moments.

The sense of displacement and nostalgia in Ali is emblematic of a whole new postcolonial sensibility that makes its appearance from the 1970s in literature produced by Asians in the USA and European nations: the *literature of diaspora*. Iyer's is the *postcolonial cosmopolitanism* of the globalizing-globalized Asian who is at home in the USA, India or any part of the world, whose 'Indianness' is not the 'core' component of his writings.

Postcolonialism in the last decades of the twentieth century has had to accept as material conditions and states of consciousness

- global displacement as a central feature of its populations,
- nostalgia as a condition of sensibility,

- multiculturalism as a context in which its writers live and work,
- global mobilities, globalized cultures,
- hybrid sensibilities and feelings of multicultural citizenship of its writers.

Monica Ali, Salman Rushdie, V. S. Naipaul, Hanif Kureishi, Rohinton Mistry, Syam Selvadurai, Jhumpa Lahiri and Michael Ondaatje are writers of 'Third World' origin who have lived in Anglo-European, Canadian nations and cultures for the larger part of their lives. The writings of George Lamming, Derek Walcott, like Rushdie and the others mentioned above, grapple with the cultural memory of their 'homelands', even when the homeland remains an unreachable place, and the contexts in which they now live. The 'places' in which such immigrants live have themselves been transformed. A metropolis like London or New York, for example, has been transformed into a postcolonial location with the predominance of Third World populations. Conversely, metropolises like Bangkok, Colombo or New Delhi in Third World nations have seen Westernization and global products/fashions/trends disseminating and sharing space with local, traditional and ethnic cultures. In other words, metropolises across the world have lost their traditional dominant populations and cultures and seen the mixing of cultures and traditions in a 'hybridization' of place.

This chapter explores this new dominant within postcolonial literature and thought: the rise of a diasporic sensibility, the new hybridization of cultures, multiculturalism and cosmopolitanism. It moves from a discussion of the literature and sensibility of postcolonial diaspora to the rise of a postcolonial cosmopolitanism in the transnational novel.[1]

DIASPORA, DISPLACEMENT AND SPACE

Diaspora literature commonly includes the following themes:

i. the relation between centre (or 'home') and the 'periphery' into which they and their families dispersed;
ii. a diaspora consciousness or sensibility marked by

    a. nostalgia, both individual and communal, for home,
    b. a sense of alienation in a new society/culture/land,

c. a desire to retain features from the 'homeland' – this includes a determined effort to retain rituals, language, forms of behaviour,

d. an anxiety over acculturation and adaptation.

iii. a conscious attempt to assert ethnic identity in terms of the homeland, while simultaneously seeking acceptance/assimilation in the new cultures.

Diaspora Consciousness

In Bharati Mukherjee's *The Tiger's Daughter* (1971) she writes:

> *For years Tara had dreamt of returning to India. She had believed that all hesitations, all shadowy fears of the time abroad would be erased quite magically if she could just return to Calcutta.*
>
> *(p. 30, emphasis added)*

Mukherjee captures an important aspect of diaspora consciousness: the nostalgia for a lost world. In fact diaspora novelist-poet-critic, Meena Alexander, refers to the very act of literary creation as 'writing in search of a homeland' (1993, p. 4). Diaspora consciousness is very often identifiable by a sense of loss (for 'home') and a sense of estrangement (from the new home). It is thus double-sited, in other words, caught between two spaces and cultures. Writing is an attempt to recreate this mythic lost space, and eventually escape from it, if M. G. Vassanji, another diaspora writer believes:

> This reclamation of the past is the first serious act of writing. having reclaimed it, having given himself a history, he liberates himself to write about the present. (1985, p. 63)

Diasporic cultures, as Robin Cohen defines them, are communities living together in one country who

> acknowledge that 'the old country' – a notion often buried deep in language, religion, custom or folklore – always has some claim on their loyalty and emotions . . . a member's adherence to a diasporic community is demonstrated by an acceptance of an inescapable link with their past migration history and a sense of co-ethnicity with others of a similar background. (Cohen 2001, p. ix)

Theorists of diaspora such as James Clifford and Robin Cohen speak of identifications, alignments and affiliations in the immigrant consciousness. William Safran argues that diaspora implies a 'polycentrism', the 'notion of at least two centers of ethnonational culture: the homeland and the diaspora' (2008, p. 76). These identifications are identities in *process*, where the immigrant has to negotiate between an inherited identity and acquire a new one in the adopted space, country and culture. This 'processual' nature of diaspora consciousness is, as Safran argues, space-related, '*between* the hostand and homeland, or *between* several hostlands' (p. 77, emphasis added). A diaspora consciousness, James Clifford argues, is constructed both positively and negatively. It is negatively constructed through discrimination and exclusion. It is positively constructed through 'identification with world-historical cultural/political forces' (Clifford 1999, pp. 256–7). Clifford exploring the structure of a diaspora consciousness writes:

> identifications not identities, acts of relationship rather than pregiven forms: this tradition is a network of partially constructed histories, a persistently displaced and reinvented time/space of crossings. (p. 268)

'Diasporic' suggests an individual's linkage to the former home and the present one, to a culture left behind and to a culture now adopted. Thus 'diaspora' suggests *two* (spatial) sites, (geographical) locations and (cultural) affiliation. The 'former' is located within nostalgic recall, and the 'present' as an experiential reality, of the pain of transculturation and acculturation. (Bella Adams 2008, argues for a 'split' identity of the immigrant, pp. 128–31.) In Rohinton Mistry's scatology-driven short story, 'Squatter', Sarosh is unable to get used to the Western toilet, even after ten years in Toronto. He detects, writes Mistry, 'something malodorous in the air: the presence of xenophobia and hostility' (1996, p. 916). 'Diaspora', argues Steven Vertovec (1999), is at once a social form (which involves social relations, political orientation to the homeland and economic strategies that link diasporic groups with their 'home' countries), a type of consciousness and a mode of cultural production. There is a *collective* consciousness of being 'Indian in America' or 'Black British' in diaspora communities. Roger Bromley suggests that every diaspora narrative is 'both an individual story and, explicitly, a cultural narrative' (Bromley 2000, p. 21). A diaspora consciousness emerges in the acknowledgement of difference, and the resistance to homogenized identities. Thus 'Asian British' constitutes a diaspora identity because it refuses to be simply British, and reinforces the difference that 'Asian' stands for. 'British' is a cultural norm and normative identity that would subsume the 'Asian' component – and diaspora consciousness resists such a process (Kalra et al. 2005, pp. 30–4).

A sense of 'home' and the 'original' (home) culture in its *place* haunts all diasporic fiction. 'Home', notes Avtar Brah, 'is a mythic place of desire in the diasporic imagination' (1996, p. 192). The key words in Brah's perspicacious comment are 'mythic' and 'imagination' – a structure of fantasy, a desire and longing for a place that exists only in the mind. Rushdie, anticipating Brah's theorization of diaspora, speaks of 'imaginary homelands, Indias of mind' (Rushdie 1991, p. 10).

Tara in Mukherjee's *The Tiger's Daughter* had longed for the sights, smells and shapes of Camac Street, Calcutta so that she could feel connected to her roots (1971, p. 10). These representations of the immigrant suggest a strong nostalgic sensibility, where the sense of home refuses to go away even after years of 'exile'. Such immigrants of course see displacement almost exclusively as exile, and carry idealized versions and visions of their home with them. Mukherjee makes it clear that the diaspora sensibility functions with a fantasy-vision of home when she paints the Calcutta of Tara's dream a nasty place:

> There is, of course, no escape from Calcutta. Even an angel
> concedes that when pressed. Family after family moves from
> the provinces to its brutish center, and the center quivers a little,
> absorbs the bodies, digests them, and waits. (p. 4)

In fact the entire space of Calcutta, Tara realizes after her experience of the city, is falling apart with corruption, violence and Maoist rebellions. There is no ideal home to return to, suggests Mukherjee in a damning indictment of the diaspora penchant for nostalgic recalls.

In similar fashion we see nostalgia as a structure of consciousness in Meena Alexander's *Manhattan Music* (1997). Sandhya is described this way:

> She [Sandhya] kept returning to her childhood home, a house with a red-tiled roof and a sandy courtyard where the mulberry bloomed. (p. 41)

Another character, Sakhi, describes the painful process of diasporic life and cultural adaptation:

> Travelling places was hard, staying was harder. You had to open your suitcase, lay out the little bits and pieces into ready-made niches. Smooth out the sari, exchange it for a skirt, have your hair trimmed a little differently . . . Then you tucked the suitcase under the bed and forgot about it, started accumulating the bric-a-brac that made you part of the streets around. (p. 207)

In both these citations we see an emphasis on space, displacement from childhood spaces and the imagination. The spatial imagination, as we have already noted in the earlier chapter, is a key constituent of the postcolonial literary work. In the case of postcolonial diaspora writings the spatial imagination is once more the predominant one, and to this I now turn.

Diaspora and the Spatial Imagination

Metaphors of travelling, displacement and spaces in dozens of diaspora and immigrants suggest a concern with space and place. Mobility, Sau-ling Cynthia Wong has argued, is one of the key 'motifs' in the case of Asian American literature (1993).[2] A very large number of diasporic writing has *spatial location* or *travel* implied in its very title: *A Change of Skies* (Yasmine Gooneratne), *Asylum, USA* (Boman Desai), *An Area of Darkness*, *The Middle Passage*, *The Enigma of Arrival*, *Miguel Street* and *A House for Mr Biswas* (VS Naipaul), *Such a Long Journey* and *Tales From Ferosha Bagh* (Rohinton Mistry), *The Famished Road* (Ben Okri), *Unaccustomed Earth* (Jhumpa Lahiri), *Days and Nights in Calcutta* (Bharati

Mukherjee and Clark Blaise) *The Nowhere Man* (Kamala Markandaya), *Bombay Duck* and *Poona Company* (Farrukh Dhondy), *Brick Lane* (Monica Ali), *Nampally Road* and *The House of a Thousand Doors* (Meena Alexander), *In An Antique Land, The Shadow Lines* and *The Calcutta Chromosome* (Amitav Ghosh). It is spatial displacement that the sense of 'home', 'feeling at home' and 'rootlessness' emerges in diaspora and migrant writing. In this section I explore diaspora consciousness in the literature through the space-travel-displacement theme.

Diaspora writings of space are often thematized as the search for a 'home' away from homelands, to discover and delineate a space of affections and mutual dependency in a new land. This requires a dialectic between intimate and community spaces. Community spaces are *parergonal* spaces (parergonal, literally, the frames of a work) which frame and constitute intimate spaces. This parergonal space decides the specific location/residence/relationships of people. Parergonal space is thus communal/community space and corresponds to what Avtar Brah (1996) has termed 'diaspora space'. It is the space where race, gender, class intersect and influence the location of the individual.

In Boman Desai's novel, *Asylum, USA* (2000) Noshir Daruvalla attempts to stay on in the USA *and* find a suitable home and partner to share his intimate space. The attempts are characterized by a tension between the very real *practices of power* over space and *symbolic power* over these same spaces. That is, Noshir's attempts are keyed to altering the real power structures that govern his intimate space, even though many of these attempts are only symbolic.

The home, as the geographer David Ley informs us, is the 'most articulate expression of the self' which can 'reinforce either a positive self-image' or, in the 'case of dreary public housing in an unwanted location' induce an identity of a 'peripheral and low status member of society' (1981, p. 220). Noshir's 'peripheral' identity is constructed when he finds that the intimate space of the home excludes him. Barbara and Noshir enter into a contract: for a certain amount of money they will get married to facilitate Noshir's stay in the USA and eventual citizenship. When Barbara emphasizes that the marriage is 'not for real' Noshir responds: 'but we *will* need to live together' (pp. 8–9, emphasis in original). The emphasis on both, the shared space of a 'home' and the affordability of a space, conflate in these thoughts. Noshir suggests a transformation, or at least a compromise, between a *symbolic* control over *space* (where they live together though their marriage is 'not for real') and the actual *space* of the house. Noshir moves in with Barbara and *her* girlfriend Carmen. Noshir's very first experience of the supposedly intimate space of the house is not of inclusion but of exclusion. Carmen ignores Noshir and addresses him in derogatory and rude language (p. 33) before shutting him out in a *spatial act of exclusion*: 'She didn't look at me as she strode past and slammed the bathroom door behind her' (p. 34). Barbara consoles Noshir: 'She thinks you're trespassing on her turf . . .' (p. 34). Not at ease in his own 'home', Noshir begins a ritual of walking the dog: 'our walks alone were pockets of privacy from the household' (p. 54). When Noshir invites a vagabond home Barbara informs Noshir: 'If you want bring him into your own apartment, feel free, but not here. Get that straight. Otherwise you're out of here.' Carmen adds: 'if you want bring strangers here, all right, but your home, not here' (p. 62). Noshir's thoughts run like this: 'It was my apartment too; I paid my share of the rent; but I was more their dependent than they were mine and I hated her threat' (p. 62). By denying him the right to invite people to their home, Barbara and Carmen are, in effect, denying him any rights of sovereignty over space.

For the immigrant there is a dialectic between intimate and the parergonal spaces in which she/he formulates identity. It is necessary to, therefore, understand the actual parergonal spaces that 'frame' the intimate ones of house/home. To begin with there is the largest of parergonal spaces: America itself. Desai refers to America itself as 'Disneyland' and Americans as possessing a 'Disneyland syndrome' (pp. 17, 185). Disneyland is a 'pseudo-place', one whose myths and legends become generative tropes for people in poorer nations like India. A pseudo-place, as Paulo Prato and Gianluca Trivero define it, is one that everyone recognizes immediately, which does not require any interpretation. Disneyland and Switzerland are examples of such pseudo-places (Prato and Trivero 1985, p. 28). Disneyland is that mythical paradise that all Indians hope to reach some day. Noshir says: 'Don't get me wrong. I'm not saying India is Hell. It's a more spiritual country than America' (p. 17). Noshir has set up the characteristics of the parergonal space that is America (materialist, stimulating, wealthy) and, in contrast, India (spiritual, poor). Disneyland/America is the framing, parergonal space: one that is already constructed in the Indian imagination:

> He [Noshir's father] wanted a soninAmerica because that put him ahead in the rat race, being the first, like putting a man on the moon. All his friends were planning to have soninAmerica. Then is someone asked Do you have any kids? You could say I have a son in America, as if you had a superson. He wanted a sonin-America. Who can blame him? I wanted to come to America. Who can blame me? Everyone wants to come. Everyone came. Germans, Irish, Swedes, Italians, Mexicans, Asians . . . if you were in America you were Somebody – a myth, maybe, yes, of course, but THE myth about America. (pp. 20–1, emphasis in original)

America is readily recognizable: the myths are so powerful that generations of Indians (and others) are brought up on them. When he is in trouble with the Immigration authorities, Noshir is saved by old friends of his family. Noshir describes the situation of his rescue thus: '(S)aved by suburbanites I was. Disneyland people, barbecues and malls' (pp. 25).

I suggest that Noshir being 'saved' by 'Disneyland people' is a construction of the parergonal space because it reflects a sense of community. The effect of this act is to enable Noshir to stay on and find an intimate space. Thus Noshir's search for 'home' can begin only when the community/parergonal space sanctions and enables him to do so. In other words, this space allows Noshir the chance to be assimilated into Disneyland. So the first and largest parergonal space is Disneyland-America. But this same parergonal space becomes inimical when he is attacked by neighbouring kids (pp. 12–14). This is one of his first experiences of being an 'outsider' in the USA. Ironically, the community within which Noshir hopes to find his 'place' is full of home-less or displaced/transplanted people seeking to make a home in a new place: Helen is unwanted by both her cousin and her friend with whom she was staying (p. 107), Roma is thrown out of her boyfriend Leo's apartment (p. 109), Blythe takes in 'strays' (p. 126), Brij is running away from her foster-parents (p. 129), Sheila Waggoner has left her home (p. 137).

This community of the displaced becomes an integrative par-ergonal space where everyone is estranged and no one is nostalgic.

In the dialectic between intimate and parergonal spaces, Noshir's diaspora *identification* (and identity) with American culture is forged.

HYBRIDITY, MIMICRY AND POSTCOLONIAL MULTICULTURALISM

You stole from me my first-born, sent him to your own country so you could turn him into something in your own image.
(Soyinka 1984, p. 205)

Soyinka's character, Elesin, is accusing the Englishman, Pilkings, of transforming his son into something other than African, of erasing the boy's 'Africanness' and cultural identity so that he (the son) was more white than African. Elesin's anger is directed at the colonial's assumption that native cultures could simply be replaced with their own white one. 'He [the white man] has put a knife on the things that held us together and we have fallen apart', writes Achebe in *Things Fall Apart* (1969, p. 162). If Soyinka is pointing to a troubled condition that the son endures – of not being fully white (since he remains, for all practical purposes, black-skinned) and of not being truly African (since he has acquired European habits and modes of thinking) – Achebe is speaking of a loss of tradition. Hybridity is what Soyinka's character is referring to.

Hybridity is problematically linked to an imperial legacy that seems at odds with globalization and its emphazis on multiculturalism. In Kiran Desai's *The Inheritance of Loss* Lola describes Naipaul's *A Bend in the River* thus:

I think he's strange. Stuck in the past . . . He has not progressed. Colonial neurosis, he's never freed himself from it. Quite different thing now. (p. 46)

Despite globalization, Desai suggests, the legacy of imperialism endures. Globalization of Indianness or ethnic food does not reverse imperial legacies. It is within this complex negotiation of a 'neurotic' colonial legacy, a globalized culture and multiculturalism that the postcolonial evolves today.

Edward Said identifies the rise of a hybrid consciousness and acculturation as a response to both colonial and nationalist projects of the early twentieth century. Said writes:

> We begin to sense that old authority cannot simply be replaced by new authority, but that new alignments across borders, types, nations and essences are rapidly coming into view, and it is these alignments that now provoke and challenge the fundamentally static notion of identity that has been the core of cultural thought during the era of imperialism. (Said 1994b, p. xxviii)

These 'new alignments' pose serious and troubling questions to notions of 'pure' identity and cultural 'roots'. Hybridity in post-colonial diaspora narratives finds expression in the form of two main themes:

- Hybridity and Mimicry,
- Hybridity, Acculturation and Multiculturalism.

Hybridity and Mimicry

In Yasmine Gooneratne's *A Change of Skies*, Vera, on hearing of her brother, Bharat's decision to move to the Southern Cross University in Sydney, asks with a touch of irony: 'will you be regarded as honorary whites?' (1991, p. 33). Her question turns out to be prophetic, for Bharat, in order to erase the 'foreign' element in him, reinvents himself. He changes his name to 'Barry Mundy' and takes to wearing contact lenses. The irony is heightened by the pride his wife, Navaranjini, has taken in his native name's significance:

> My husband's name, Bharat, means "India" in just about every Indian language there is . . . Giving up Bharat seemed to us a betrayal of everything he had stood for. (p. 119)

This process of 'whitening' and de-racination is at once a hybrid-ization of the postcolonial as well as the pathetic mimicry of the white race/culture.

Hybridity, postcolonialism discovers, is inherent to all cultures. Thus hybridity figures as a prominent theme in many postcolonials.

In most cases, the native is *already* a hybrid because of the colonial past and its inheritance – a theme to be found in numerous postcolonial novels. Here the postcolonial novel deals with the painful legacy of the colonial past which has altered the native's psyche and culture.

Some of the most devastating critiques of this aspect of postcolonial hybridity are to be found in the fiction of Caribbean novelist of Indian origins, V. S. Naipaul. Naipaul argues that native society and minds have lost their souls to the European. In *The Middle Passage* he writes:

> In the immigrant colonial society with no standards of its own . . .
> minds are rigidly closed; and Trinidadians of all races and classes
> are remaking themselves in the image of the Hollywood B-man.
> (Naipaul 1969, p. 65)

The 'mimic men' are the postcolonials who have been hybridized and are unable to come to terms with their dualisms: they cannot abandon their native cultures but want to acquire the English/ colonial one in which they are not at ease either. In Naipaul's *A House for Mr Biswas* (1961) Ganesh seeks to improve his social standing by acquiring literacy in English and aspiring to become as English as possible. Ganesh's house mixes Indian and Western cultures, is at once cosmopolitan and native, and he is caught between the vernacular and the English language. He remains trapped in his strong belief in Hinduism and its rituals and yet wants to be known as a cosmopolitan. Ganesh's entire life, Naipaul suggests, is one of role-playing, but never fitting a role well enough. It is this sheer incompatibility of imperial demands and national-native aspirations that marks the postcolonial hybrid.

The making of the postcolonial hybrid is also marked by the legacy of colonial corruption, argues Naipaul. In *The Mimic Men* he notes with both anger and grief in Ralph Singh's words:

> We pretended to be real, to be learning, to be preparing ourselves
> for life, we mimic men of the New World, one unknown corner of
> it, with all its reminders of corruption that came so quickly to the
> new. (1967, p. 147)

The key term here is 'pretended'. Naipaul is savage in his attack on the superfluous, ignorant aping of Western cultures without any real understanding of the complexity of these. In *The Middle Passage* he adds:

> a combination of historical accidents and national temperament has turned the Trinidad Indian into a complete colonial, even more Philistine than the white. (1969, p. 89)

Yasmine Gooneratne, the Sri Lankan novelist and critic, writes of her own family's mimic nature in *Relative Merits*:

> Cultivating English modes of living and thinking, the members of my father's clan had imbibed a very proper English prejudice against Jews, 'frogs', 'chinks', 'niggers', 'japs', 'huns', 'fuzzy-wuzzies', 'wops' and 'wogs' of every description. (1986, p. 84)

And Attia Hosain writes in her *Sunlight on a Broken Column* of a grandfather who,

> alone, beardless . . . dressed in a suit, with shining pointed boots and spats . . . with a group of strained pompous Englishmen standing behind Englishwomen. (p. 32)

Mrs Wadia is another such mimic postcolonial:

> Her perfumes, and shoes and lace and linen and silver came from the most expensive shops in Paris and London. She . . . was prouder of Western culture than those who were born into it, and more critical of Eastern culture than those outside it. (p. 129)

In Rushdie's *Midnight's Children* the Methwold Estate is full of mimic men and women, where Indians affect British accents and live in houses called 'Buckingham', 'Sans Souci', 'Escorial' and 'Versailles'.

Hybridity, Acculturation and Multiculturalism

If Gooneratne and Naipaul find the colonial legacy problematic because of the postcolonial's unconditional and unquestioning acceptance of it, Salman Rushdie shifts the terms of the debate. Is cultural appropriation and hybridization exclusively a curse, or has every culture always been hybridized?

Rushdie is arguably one of the most famous proponents of hybrid cultures. His description of Bombay city in *The Moor's Last Sigh* (quoted in Chapter 5) captures the sense of cultural hybridization. This is a city where 'all Indians met and merged', writes Rushdie (p. 350). It is the loss of this multicultural, tolerant, multi-lingual, multi-religious Bombay to Hindu fundamentalism that Rushdie mourns in every novel after *The Moor's Last Sigh*.

We have already noted how diaspora consciousness refuses to adhere to a single, normative identity. Being 'black British' is to resist incorporation into a British identity alone, and keeping alive one's Caribbean or African cultural legacies. In effect, such a consciousness resists homogenization into a unitary national identity. Arjun Appadurai summarizes this feature of the diaspora consciousness:

> Diasporic diversity actually puts loyalty to a non-territorial trans-national first . . . The question is how can a post-national politics be built around this cultural fact? (1996, p. 173)

Such a politics is suggested by Paul Gilroy (2002 [1987], 1993) who argues that we need to see 'British' identity as constituted by Black culture within it. That is, we cannot see racial or ethnic difference as absolute categories. We need to see how every racial identity is built through a relationship with another. Thus British identity cannot exclude the creative expressions of Asians and Blacks within Britain. Bhangra or rap music, films and food, for instance, from diverse cultures have been commodified for the British to consume. Their being British increasingly includes such a multicultural experience. Likewise, Third World postcolonials experience American and European products within their own cultures now.

Bharat in Yasmine Gooneratne's *A Change of Skies* is a postcolonial who is multicultural in his education, thinking and knowledge. Thus he is already familiar with England:

> Long before I saw Britain for the second time (as a postgraduate student), I knew London . . . I knew . . . what muffins tasted like . . . For generations my relatives had been either going to, or returning from England. And so firmly has their gaze been focused on the metropolitan centre of a pink imperium that they had never so much as glanced in any other direction. (1991, p. 19)

Bharat shows an *awareness* of two distinct cultures – his own as well as England, in roughly equal measure. He is the product of a multicultural condition.

A multicultural society is one where several cultures co-exist, and where there is the notion of the distinctiveness of each culture (Watson 2002, p. 1). It is increasingly taken to include the cultural rights of minorities (including sexual minorities) and women.

Assimilation and acculturation are key moments in postcolonial diaspora narratives that deal with multiculturalism. When Jasmine, the heroine of Bharati Mukherjee's eponymous novel (1989) arrives in the USA as an illegal immigrant, Jyoti, she does *not* carry with her a sense of nostalgia for a lost home (she has had to flee India after her husband is assassinated). Mukherjee here maps an entirely new kind of diaspora sensibility – one that actively and eagerly seeks new cultural experiences and roles. Mukherjee's key metaphor is a gynaecological one: rebirthing. Jasmine hopes to 'rebirth [herself] in the image of [her] dreams' (p. 25). Jyoti, upon her marriage had become 'Jasmine' in what is surely a mimic identity. When she arrives in the USA she transforms into 'Jazzy' and then, subsequently, 'Jase' and 'Jane'. The change of name indicates the change of her ethnic identity into something else, with little nostalgia for her old, native names. But most significant in Jasmine's acculturation is her strategic refusal to work with the parergonal spaces of the Indian community. Boman Desai's Noshir, as we have seen earlier, also deals with the community space in order to create an intimate space for himself. Here Jasmine chooses an entirely all-American parergonal space in which to construct her new identity. Jasmine's Americanization includes taking language classes to improve her skills, working as a caregiver to a child of two whites. The Vadhera family is satirized by Mukherjee for trying to retain a sense of Indianness.

This kind of postcolonial diaspora is also generational – a theme seen in much of Hanif Kureishi's works – where the second and third generation of immigrants find themselves easily multicultural.

GLOBAL SOULS, THE COSMOPOLITAN NOVEL AND THE POSTCOLONIAL PARASITE

Increasingly, of late, and particularly when I drink, I find my thoughts drawn into the past rather than impelled into the future. I recall my

*drinking sherry in California and dreaming of my earlier student days
in England, where I ate* dalmoth *and dreamed of Delhi. What is the
purpose, I wonder, of all this restlessness? I sometimes seem to myself
to wander around the world merely accumulating material for future
nostalgias.*

(Vikram Seth 1987, p. 35)

Seth, one of India's most well-known novelists, is here explicitly
defining a cosmopolitan condition, of restlessness, constant displacement, distancing from one's cultural origins and nostalgia.
Cosmopolitanism, as articulated in the European intellectual tradition since the Greeks, 'endorses reflective distance from one's cultural
affiliations, a broad understanding of other cultures, and customs,
and a belief in universal humanity' (Amanda Anderson 1998, p. 267). It
is usually aligned with 'transnationalism', though a major distinction
needs to be made between the two. Transnationalism explicitly refers to
a new geographical condition/location (e.g. across nation-state borders,
for example) while cosmopolitanism is an intellectual-cultural condition. Cosmopolitanism in the works of writers like Salman Rushdie,
Pico Iyer, V. S. Naipaul and others celebrate their rootlessness and
their ability to occupy multiple cultural locations. If, as William
Safran has argued, diaspora is 'space-related . . . between hostland
and homeland, or between several hostlands' (2008, p. 77), then it is
also true that 'it is not always clear to what extent the positions of
homeland and hostland have been confounded' (p. 77). In the case of
a Salman Rushdie or a Ben Okri, they seem to be at home in several
hostlands. This cultural polycentricity of being 'at home in the world'
is a transnational or cosmopolitan sensibility.[3]

Cosmopolitanism is an intellectual project whereby the writer
seeks to assimilate 'foreign' cultures and not stay embedded in her/
how 'original' cultures. Thus Seth's familiarity with Western classical
music (which he deploys in *An Equal Music*) or Rushdie's use of
Persian, Hindi and European poetic traditions in his novels or, more
recently Italian Renaissance cultures in *The Enchantress of Florence*
(not to mention his now-established debt to magical realism, the
Latin American Gabriel Marquez, the German Gunter Grass, the Irish
James Joyce and others) suggests a cosmopolitan imagination, the
ability to absorb multiple cultural traditions. What we see here is
the rise of a new form of the 'Third Worlder' – whom Anna Kurian

terms the 'global Indian' – one who travels in multiple cultures and worlds with *equanimity*, engages with new cultural practices and is already transculturated (Kurian 2008, pp. 257–8, emphasis added). Robert Young, like Kurian, also sees a 'new stability, self-assurance and quietism' in the multiple and hybrid identities of the present day postcolonial (Young 1995, p. 4).

Cosmopolitanism must be contextualized within globalization, fluid nation-state boundaries, global flows of capital, commodities and people, especially since the 1990s. Cosmopolitanism manifests in the 1990s postcolonial novel in the following themes:

- multiple geographical locations (transnational),
- acculturation,
- travel and displacement,
- absence of nostalgia for 'lost' homelands,
- co-existence of multiple cultures/identities.

Yet this cosmopolitanism is not unitary or of the same kind across all postcolonials. One can discern two kinds of postcolonial cosmo-politanism in the transnational novel of the 1990s.

Two Versions of Cosmopolitanism

In Rushdie's novel, *Fury*, Malik Solanka declares: 'No longer a historian but a man without histories let me be. I'll rip my lying mother tongue out of my throat and speak your broken English instead' (Rushdie 2001, p. 51). Here we see a version of cosmopol-itanism where roots, origins and cultural affiliations are abandoned in favour of a new cosmopolitan tendency. When Malik Solanka in the novel surrenders his 'native' culture to the power of New York's neo-imperial cultures (which he describes as possessing a 'hybrid, omnivorous power', p. 44), he becomes a particular kind of cosmopol-itan, an 'imperial cosmopolitan' (Srivastava 2008, p. 175). 'Imperial cosmopolitanism' is an extension of the colonial-era thinking into postcolonial conditions. Whereas the colonial era was marked by the subjection of the native cultures to the white/European one, in 'imperial cosmopolitanism' the postcolonial cheerily surrenders her/his native identity to the metropolitan cultures of the First World. Rushdie's celebration of multiple locations often seems to promote a *voluntary* subjection of his 'roots' to a new form of imperialism: the American/European one. He writes in *Shame*:

> What is the best thing about migrant peoples . . .? I think it is their hopefulness . . . And what's the worst thing? It's the emptiness of one's baggage. We've come unstuck from more than land. We've floated upwards from history, from memory, from Time. (p. 91)

Like Rushdie, Bharati Mukherjee, another Indian immigrant writer now settled in the USA maps her own writing trajectory as moving from 'the aloofness of expatriation' to 'the exuberance of immigration' (1985, p. xv). This celebratory displacement has become a characteristic of several Asian diasporic writers since the 1990s. This postcolonial cosmopolitanism

- does not wallow in nostalgia for the lost home,
- does not feel alienated in a new land/culture,
- does not see displacement as exile,
- celebrates multiculturalism (but also critiques it),
- champions assimilation into the new, adopted culture,
- rejects exclusion and cultural ghettoization.

In short, what Srivastava identifies as an 'imperial cosmopolitanism' is a vibrant, assimilatory cosmopolitanism where migrancy and displacement are seen as causes for celebration. Rushdie, Naipaul, Baharti Mukherjee and Neil Bisoondath represent this variety of postcolonial cosmopolitanism.

But this is only one kind of postcolonial cosmopolitanism. A second kind of postcolonial cosmopolitanism is discernable in diasporic postcolonial writers like Hanif Kureishi, Vikram Seth and Amitav Ghosh. Neelam Srivastava has correctly argued that in Seth, 'a responsible and located cosmopolitanism is actually linked to a strong national sense', where his cosmopolitanism is a 'precondition for the articulation of a nationally oriented secularism that attempts to engage with India's most "present needs", i.e., the problems of governing a multicultural and multi-religious polity' (Srivastava 2008, pp. 168–9). Emily Johansen has recently argued a case for 'territorialized cosmopolitanism' (2008), 'a cosmopolitanism located in specific, though often multiple, places' (p. 2). Johanssen defines 'territorialized cosmopolitanism' as a marker of those 'people who . . . see themselves as having ethical and moral responsibilities to the world *and* a specific local place – or even places' (p. 3). Novelist Nayantara Sahgal anticipates such a cosmopolitanism when she argues that even the burden of an ancient inheritance such as Hinduism makes her feel 'fragmented' because she assimilates several cultures. Sahgal writes:

> The question of direction is itself no longer relevant when the migration of cultures is leaving cultures open-ended, and when migration can take place without ever leaving one's soil. Where does one culture begin and end when they are housed in the same person? (1992, p. 36)

Sahgal is gesturing at a migrant imagination (what she terms 'schizophrenic') and a cosmopolitanism that is not exclusive to the migrant alone: one can be a localized cosmopolitan as well.

This would be the kind of cosmopolitanism that characterizes Amitav Ghosh (Johanssen's example is of Ghosh's *The Hungry Tide*), especially in his *The Shadow Lines*. A 'territorialized cosmopolitanism' in the postcolonial is marked by

- A cosmopolitan vision and a universal, inclusivist worldview,
- A detached appraisal – rather than a celebratory one – of the 'native' country,
- A concern for secularism, democracy and anguish at corruption and decadence in the 'home' country,
- A balance between native and global cultures,
- A careful evaluation of global(ized) agendas, projects and their limitations.

A dominant theme of *The Shadow Lines* is secular Indian democracy in the time of communal tensions and nation-building. Towards the end of *The Hungry Tide* the cosmopolitan Piya and Kanai are forced to admit that their 'global souls' cannot do them much good in the harsh realities of the Sundarbans. As I have argued elsewhere (Nayar, 'The Postcolonial Uncanny', forthcoming), all their cosmopolitan knowledge cannot help ensure a feeling of security in their 'original' culture. A sense of home is possible only when they take recourse to an 'indigenous canny', or local knowledge in the form of Fokir. At the conclusion of the novel Piya states:

All the routes Fokir showed me are stored here . . . Fokir took the boat into every little creek and gully where he'd ever seen a dolphin. That one map represents decades of work and volumes of knowledge. It's going to be the foundation of my own project. That's why I think it should be named after him. (Ghosh 2004, p. 398)

Piya then is able to refer to the place as 'home' (p. 399). This is 'territorialized' (Johannsen) and 'located or responsible' (Srivastava 2008) cosmopolitanism where a sense of ethical obligations 'grounds' the globe-trotting intellectual.

A critique of Third World, or postcolonial, cosmopolitanism has been made by Timothy Brennan (1997). Reading Rushdie, Brennan argues that Rushdie and other cosmopolitans treat politics as mere play. Brennan is alert to the linkage between cosmopolitanism and globalization. Graham Huggan (2001) likewise, sees the *marketability* of the 'hybrid' writer and cosmopolitan immigrant writer in the global literary circles, a major factor in the excessive valorization of 'cosmopolitanism'. Dominic Head is more sympathetic. Head admits that economic and political contexts explain the large-scale celebrity success of the migrant, cosmopolitan writer working out of New York or England. But Head also argues that 'the success of the hyper [around multicultural writing] has surely more to do with the perceived importance of multiculturalism as a topic, for both publishers and readers' (2008, pp. 97–8). Asian American literary production has increased because white America sees Asian Americans as 'culturally different others', and even exotic – and these authors have catered to the white reader by emphasizing their own cultural otherness, ethnic identity as being essentially different. Thus, while the immigrants of European descent 'seemed to have virtually no boundaries to the subject matter of their literary representations, descendants of non-whites such as Asians have actually focused on issues surrounding their ethnicity and related matters' (Chae 2007, p. 14). There is, in other words, a suspicion that ethnicity sells, and the Asian Americans have foregrounded cultural difference for commercial and publishing success.

These multicultural and cosmopolitan writers who celebrate multiple locations, shifting allegiances and rootlessness often ignore the very racialized nature of identities and locations. For the Third World migrant labourer in New York city, there is no cosmopolitanism: she/he is a clearly *racially marked* figure who is *restricted* to and *defined* by her/his racial identity and not as a 'global soul' absorbing multiple cultures. In Kiran Desai's *The Inheritance of Loss*, she underscores this racially marked identity of the poor Third Worlder when she speaks of the illegal immigrants working the kitchens in New York city. Cosmopolitanism, then, is a matter of class.

The Postcolonial Parasite

The cosmopolitan-transnational novel resists the binary of home-abroad, past culture/present culture that is a characteristic of diaspora writing, especially Asian-American novels like those by Bharati Mukherjee or Indo-Canadian ones like Rohinton Mistry. The transnational or cosmopolitan novel from postcolonial authors is a 'global' novel whose characters occupy *multiple* national and cultural spaces. Elleke Boehmer describes the immigrant writer thus: 'ex-colonial by birth, "Third World" in cultural interest, cosmopolitan in almost every other way', these writers work 'within the precincts of the Western metropolis while at the same time retaining thematic and/or political connections with a national background' (2006 [1995, p. 233). I would qualify that last phrase in the case of figures like Rushdie or Vikram Seth or Jhumpa Lahiri: the connections are less national than transnational.

The transnational postcolonial is what I have termed a 'parasite'. Michel Serres writes of the parasite:

It was only noise, but it was also a message, a bit of information producing panic: an interruption, a corruption, a rupture of information . . . A parasite who has the last word, who produces disorder and who generates a different order. (1982, p. 3)

The parasite 'does not play at being another; it plays at being the same' (p. 202). The host has to mimic the guest, the parasite, itself to survive. Thus the subject and object roles are reversed for both the host and the parasite. Finally, the death of the host means the death of the parasite. Parasites, according to Serres, can be biological, anthropological or informational. I suggest a fourth mode of the parasite: the cultural.

A parasite that disrupts and interrupts information and induces a different order asserts agency, consciously or unconsciously. The Third World is the parasite that *disrupts* and *fractures* the flow of the First World, interrupts it and reorients it. Economically, in the age of neo-colonialisms and the new empires, the Third World is dependent, as a parasite on foreign aid (from food to arms). Aid flows *from* First World *to* Third World. Tourism is primarily about the First World *in* the Third World. Yet the parasite initiates something else: change.

The cultural parasite is not necessarily the mere presence of an Indian or a Bangladeshi in London or New York. I see the cultural parasite as an *event* where Third World cultural artifacts – Bollywood films, African masks, ethnic commodities from South American cultures as well as Native American artifacts – interrupt the unitary cultural narrative of London or New York. The cultural parasite is therefore a process of *mutually transformative exchange*. It is 'noise', in Serres' terms, that alters the meaning of the 'original' message and interrupts it, and thereby creates a different order.

The parasite is produced in the interstices of cultural negotiations. It has multiple identities, and cannot be reduced to any one of them. A good example would be the characters in Hanif Kureishi's writings. In works like *The Buddha of Suburbia* (1990) for instance, Kureishi locates identity at the intersection of multiple categories and locations: ethnic (Asian-Pakistani), gender (male), community (Asian-British), sexuality (bisexual), class (middle-class) and geography (metropolitan London). While on the one hand this might appear to be a very unstable formation, it also resists the solidifying and unchanging structure of essentialism.

In order to situate the context for the cultural parasite I would like to look at London's cultural and physical geography after the 1950s, basing my arguments on Jane Jacobs' work (1996). Spitalfields, London, has been home to large numbers of people from the sub-continent. When Prince Charles toured the community, with its large population of migrants, he said it reminded him of a 'Third World country' (*Guardian* 2 July 1987, cited in Jacobs 1996, p. 70). What is interesting is that it is no longer possible to see the migrants as a community or 'space' that occur(s) elsewhere. They may have been outsiders, but they were still part of a system that included them: the empire. That is, the migrant from Bangladesh or India was now part of the core. The Third World was not out there, at the periphery of Britain, it was a part of the core itself. Englishness was now a multicultural Englishness, as Bengalis (the largest component of the population in Spitalfields, Jacobs p. 70) made it their new home. Brick Lane, the arterial road of Spitalfields, has a predominantly Bengali population, whose life Monica Ali explored in detail in *Brick Lane* (2003). As Ali demonstrated, even though the Lane was a community in and of itself, it took in the rest of London, while London itself was 'contaminated' by the effects of activities in Brick Lane. Historically, of course, Ali's Brick Lane has been at the centre of racial, ethnic and national tensions, and her novel, with its tightly-knit community marks a new cosmopolitan geography, with the ethnic minority at the heart of 'white' London.[4] A crucial development in this reconfiguration of geography is the support Spitalfields secured from London's Left. The Left supported the Bengali community and thereby, as Jane Jacobs has argued, transformed a 'foreign' group into the 'natural' inhabitants of Spitalfields. This is what I am calling the 'noise' generated by the parasite, where the disruption in Britain's national narrative of Englishness – basically, the right wing discourse of 'pure' Englishness, characteristic of Enoch Powell – results in a new social order and discourse: multicultural Britain. The naturalization that Jane Jacobs speaks of is the transformation of Britain itself: the host modifies itself in response to the actions of the parasitic guest, even as the guest modifies its behaviour to suit the host. Here is Monica Ali's description of Brick Lane:

And the streets were stacked with rubbish, entire kingdoms of rubbish piled high as fortresses with only the border skirmishes of plastic bottles and grease-stained card-board to separate them . . .

The communal bins ring the courtyard like squat metal warriors, competing in foulness, contemplating the stand-off. One has keeled over and spilled its guts. A rat flicks in and out of them . . . The bins have been evicted. Bhangra. That's what they play . . . Bhangra and Shakin' Stevens . . . (pp. 43–4, 70)

This could very well be the description of any Indian city. What Ali's description does is to demonstrate how an Asian geography has been carved out of the London landscape.

This is postcolonial agency, the ability to appropriate and *modify* any culture and contexts. It is the function of the parasite, and is fundamentally 'transruptive'. 'Transruption' is a series of 'contestatory cultural and theoretical interventions which, in their impact as cultural differences, unsettle social norms and threaten to dismantle hegemonic concepts and practices' (Hesse 2000, p. 17). They cannot, as Hesse underscores, be silenced or repressed. In Monica Ali's novel a racist slur is scribbled on a wall in Brick Lane.

Someone had written in careful flowing silver spray over the wall, Pakis. And someone else, in less beautiful but confident black letters, had added, 'Rule'. (Ali 2003, p. 194)

The language game here is worked out as a disruption through addition. One word and the racist slur is transformed into a subaltern voice. The English language itself is subverted through this process, a transruption that dismantles the rhetoric of race.

The postcolonial parasite in the form of the 'noise', and asserts its postcolonial agency through a rectangulation of affiliations (I adapt the model of rectangulation from Vinay Dharwadker 2001). The transnational parasite is affiliated to – emotionally, culturally, economically – family, nation, city and ethnic community. Biju in Kiran Desai's Booker novel *The Inheritance of Loss* (2006) demonstrates this quadrangulation of affiliations, all in the first few chapters of the tale. Desai's novel, incidentally, does not demonstrate a postcolonial agency, since it is intended as a tragic tale of destroyed ambitions. Biju's story opens with a brief, terse description of New York:

Biju at the Baby Bistro.
Above, the restaurant was French, but below in the kitchen it was Mexican and Indian. And, when a Paki was hired, it was Mexican, Indian, Pakistani.
Biju at Le Colonial for the authentic colonial experience.
On top, rich colonial, and down below, poor native. Colombian, Tunisian, Ecuadorian, Gambian.
On to the Stars and Stripes Diner. All American flag on top, all Guatemalan flag below.
Plus one Indian flag when Biju arrived. (p. 21)

The new cosmopolitanism of New York is built on affiliations that are multiple, though they appear to be serving the same purpose (the American food industry). An image gestures one of the most crucial of affiliations: 'Biju felt he was entering a warm amniotic bath' (p. 23). The affiliation to mother/land is clear.

The second affiliation is given almost immediately alongside that of the mother. In America and in such 'basement kitchens', writes Desai, 'every nationality confirmed its stereotype' (p. 23). Later, Biju is deeply moved by the Hindi film songs he hears: 'Biju felt so proud of his country's movies he almost fainted' (p. 53). The nation theme and affiliation is emphasized for us here.

The third affiliation is within the adopted city, the culture of the dispossessed. Biju, states Desai,

> joined a shifting population of men camping out near the fuse box, behind the boiler, in the cubby holes, and storage rooms at the bottom of what had been a single-family home, the entrance still adorned with a scrap of colored mosaic in the shape of a star. (p. 51)

The dispossessed are all the same: suffering tribulations in the world's wealthiest country. Their affiliation with the city is of the parasite, working to keep the kitchens running, even when the adopted culture does not help them or even acknowledge them.

The fourth, and perhaps most tragic affiliation is with the ethnic community: Indians across the world. Biju learnt about how the world treated Indians. The Indians were hated in Tanzania, Uganda, Nigeria, Fiji, Madagascar, Hong Kong, Germany, Italy, Japan, Guam, Singapore, Burma, South Africa and China (p. 77). Their ethnicity marks them out as targets. And yet this ethnic identity is also transformed into a theme of postcolonial agency.

In Salman Rushdie's *Fury* (2001), Rhinehart underscores the indispensable necessity of the Indian diaspora for the USA (or the First World). He tells Solanka:

> In the eighteen-nineties her ancestors went as indentured labourers to work in what's-its-name. Lilliput-Blefuscu. Now they run the sugarcane production and the economy would fall apart without them, but you know how it is wherever Indians go. People don't like them. Dey works too hard and dey keeps to deyself and dey acts so dang uppity. Ask anyone. Ask Idi Amin. (p. 61)

Here the immigrant is accused of not assimilating while/despite being successful. Their ethnicity and economic success present a dangerous combination to the 'true' natives of the 'First World'. Once again the postcolonial parasite has disturbed the conditions of the host. On the one hand the parasite is dependent yet indispensable, and on the other, its presence restructures the society. The society needs and does not need the parasite.

The question of the transnational parasite and 'its' postcolonial agency is perhaps best underscored by Shankar, a member of the Indian Doctors' Association in England, in Kavery Nambisan's *The Hills of Angheri*:

We can do more for our country by staying on here and being successful . . . It's not just the money we send home. If each of us can pull out three or four people from India and help them start life here, it would be a service . . . (p. 251)

This is, I believe, an important mode of thinking about postcolonial agency. Nambisan makes a subtle shift from the individualism of the earlier section (cited above) to a community. Postcolonial agency is about not forgetting the community or ethnicity, but making sure that others succeed *along with* oneself. The First World will be transformed from the inside, even as the original 'home' itself gets transformed when the migrant succeeds elsewhere ('the money we send home'). It is therefore crucial to note, in this theme of the postcolonial transformation of the First World, Shankar's concluding statement in the above dialogue: 'these white bastards. We'll rule them one day, on their soil' (p. 251). This appropriation of a colonial rhetoric by the new immigrants is an instantiation of postcolonial agency, and marks much of the transnational novel where the nostalgia and yearning is replaced by poise and aggression. Thus Monica Ali's 'hero' Karim has a strange linguistic feature: 'When he spoke in Bengali he stammered. In English, he found his voice and it gave him no trouble' (p. 173). The postcolonial immigrant achieves agential powers through an appropriation of the First World's cultural icons, language and rhetoric.

Vikram Seth's *An Equal Music* (1999), set in London with no Indian characters, is an extraordinary example of transnational writing by virtue of being written by an Indian with no 'Indianness' in the novel's plot. As should be evident I am here shifting the terms of the debate between textual themes and authorial identity. Michael Holme, the *English* narrator and main protagonist, is a violinist based in London. He tutors Virginie, a young *French* girl. Michael constantly looks back at the time when he was a student in Vienna: Michael thinks of his time as a student in *Vienna*: 'What I lost there I have never come near to retrieving' (p. 5). In Vienna he was a student of the *Swedish* musician Carl Kall. There he falls in love with Julia, the daughter of an *Oxford* don and an *Austrian* mother. There is only one reference to multicultural London:

> I drive . . . past the Habib Bank and the Allied Bank of Pakistan, the clothing warehouses, a Jewish museum, a mosque, a church, a McDonalds, sauna, solicitors, pub, video shop, Boots, bakers, sandwich bar, kebab house . . . (p. 62)

The mix of cultural registers and identities in this novel written by an Indian makes it transnational. The transcendence of art becomes Seth's own transnational act of agency. Shobha De, Indian novelist and columnist, praised this aspect of Seth's work when she praised the universality and the emphasis on the transcending power of music (De 1999, p. 6). Another well-known novelist, Kushwant Singh praised the novel and cautioned its potential readers:

> Indian readers not familiar with the works of Bach, Beethoven, Mozart, Hayden and Schubert and know nothing about fugues, scherzos, adagios, arpeggios and movements in this or that letter of the alphabet . . . don't let such trivialities daunt you. (1999, Reference.com/Encyclopedia/Wikipedia. http://www.reference.com/browse/wiki/Vikram_Seth)

It is Seth's deliberate turning away from the politics of the postcolonial immigrant (nostalgia, anxiety) in this work that situates him as a transnational. Seth does not need to write about the diasporic experience, the inevitable 'search for identity'.

* * *

Theorists of cultural postnationalism like Jeremy Waldron have argued that since most individuals today anyway possess dual or even multiple cultural heritages, to even think of a unitary national or ethno-cultural identity is absurd (Waldron 1995, pp. 96–7, 103–5). Wilson Harris, the British-based Guyanan writer, spoke of the vast 'regenerative, cross-cultural possibility' of heterogeneity of cultures (1990, p. 176), and the writings of Seth, Mukherjee, Iyer, Ali, seem to fulfil this possibility. The postcolonial, it seems, is the new cosmopolitan.

CHAPTER SEVEN

NEW CONCERNS FOR THE POSTCOLONIAL

'As the world map is being redrawn after 1989, postcolonial studies has done little to keep pace with the changing forms of imperialism as an actual set of strategies and developments', complains critic Timothy Brennan (2007, p. 107). There is considerable merit in Brennan's complaint: postcolonial studies continues to work mainly with the colonial period, the legacies of empire and imperial discourse. But all is not lost: one discerns a shift within postcolonialism towards an analysis of the way empire and imperialism have *returned* to haunt Asia, Africa and other decolonized nations.

Postcolonialism has had to grapple, as noted throughout this book, with colonial legacies in intellectual thought and culture even as it sought to craft a new agenda for inquiry into the present state of postcolonial nations. Postcolonialism has also had to deal with the problems of multicultural societies and the rise of fundamentalism and secessionism in Asian, African and South American cultures. It has also had to deal with 'end of racism' debates and new configurations of the human itself in technology. Since the 1990s Human Rights debates have often disturbed postcolonial societies and their notions of sovereignty in their concern for the rights of minorities and women (the recognition and enforcement of human rights across state borders has become a major issue today).

Newer concerns for the postcolonial have emerged in the age of economic globalization, neocolonialism and cultural imperialism (often coded as 'Westernization' or even 'Americanization') in post-colonial societies. Dissolving nation-state boundaries, transnational linkages (of voluntary organizations, capitalism) and transnational terror have tested postcolonialism's emphasis on territoriality. The rise of cosmopolitanism as both an ethic and a political philosophy (Derrida 2001, Habermas 2001) challenges the theme of nativism, even as 'vernacular cosmopolitanism' (Pollock et al. 2000) proposes a postcolonizing of the very idea of the cosmopolitan. In this short chapter I outline what I take to be the key elements in a re-orientation of postcolonial thought. It explores the increased transnational linkages of the postcolonial nation in this age of globalization. It then moves on to a discussion of cybercultures and the new Information and Communications Technologies (ICTs) and their impact on postcolonial cultures.

GLOBALIZATION AND THE POSTCOLONIAL NATION

The men of the village had all the busy restlessness of airline passengers in a transit lounge. Many of them had worked and travelled in the sheikhdoms of the Persian Gulf . . . of them had passports so thick they opened out like concertinas.

(Ghosh 2002 [1986], p. 5)

Globalization, especially of the twentieth century, is the expansion of trade, the development of transnational and global communication networks, the diminished role of the nation-state, the rise of transnational cultural, economic, political networks and the increased circulation of Western consumer products and cultural artifacts. Globalization has a significant cultural component. 'Cultural globalization' is the circulation of Western media: television, pop/rock music and Hollywood icons, sartorial fashions and Pepsi-Coca Cola in a *global consumer culture*. But globalization is not simply a one-way traffic of Western culture across the world. A commodification of ethnic products is essential to a global consumer culture. The mobility of the (non-European) native that Amitav Ghosh captures in his description above, is also a consequence of globalization. Local products such as Indian cuisine and ethnic wear have now reached global markets: the 'curry' was famously identified as UK's 'national dish', African music and Italian pizza are now as much global as Coca Cola. Migration of software and communications workers into all parts of the world has altered demographic, and therefore cultural, constitution of various countries in Europe. A 'glocalization' of the world is also visible. Roland Robertson speaks of 'glocalization' as being at the heart of globalization. Glocalization is 'the creation and incorporation of locality, processes which themselves largely shape, in turn, the compression of the world as a whole' (Robertson 1995, p. 40).

All globalization theory – explanatory models of the phenomenon – suggests that globalization is not simply about trade and finance but has cultural and social aspects as well. Globalization is a move towards an integration of social and cultural spaces of products and commodities. Critics of capitalism and globalization see the emergence of a new 'Empire' (see the section on Hardt and Negri in Chapter 1).

Postcolonialism has, since the 1990s, negotiated

- the globalization of the Third World economy;
- a cultural globalization involving both, American and European products supplanting local/native ones and the global circulation of ethnic products (such as the Indian 'curry' or Hindi cinema);
- a facile and commercialized multiculturalism;
- increasing fundamentalisms internally, accompanied by revanchist, reactionary cultural nationalisms;
- greater hybridity of Third World citizens;
- the erosion of the powers of the nation-state in the age of multinational capital and newer forms of imperialism by bodies like the IMF.

Postcolonialism, Globalization and Continuing Imperialism

Postcolonial studies has been concerned, as this book has demonstrated, with imperialism and its racialized effects. Its interest in globalization stems from this concern. Globalization in its economic and cultural form in the twentieth century is only *an accelerated and newer version of imperialism*. Imperialism was a form of globalization – the unification of the territories around the world under one imperial power, the use of these territories as sources of raw material and as markets and the constant mobility – mostly one-way – of European towards the Asian or African. But what links postcolonialism with globalization today is the ethical and intellectual concern with domination, power and subjugation.

Postcolonialism's interest in globalization results in certain questions that stem from a similar set of concerns when dealing with the colonial legacy. That is, the questions postcolonialism once asked of nineteenth century colonialisms provide the framework in which the interrogation of *current* versions of Empire is possible. These questions include (and I keep it deliberately broad):

- What forms of agency does the local, non-white native have in the context of globalization?
- What power relations regulate the centre (Euro-American) and periphery (Asian, African, South American) relation?
- How does a native culture contest, co-opt or get erased in the globalization of culture?
- What are the techniques – economic, political, social, juridical – through which a globalization of culture occurs today?
- What are the parallels between say, the rhetoric/discourse of British imperialism in the nineteenth century and the neocolonialism of the American Empire today?

As these questions indicate, postcolonialism is interested in the social and cultural aspects of the new Empire, globalized capital. It sees economic control and exploitation as continuing older forms of European control over Asia and Africa but also as appropriating/ echoing the discourses and techniques of social and cultural control from the European 'tradition'.

Imperialism and colonialism were modes of social control and intellectual inquiry by the Europeans over the Asians. 'Subjugation' was not merely military conquest but the civilizational and cultural domination of the white race over the Asian or African, argues postcolonial studies. That is, postcolonialism has treated imperialism and colonialism as an exercise in cultural domination, in the imposition of Eurocentric ideas (whether of the superiority of the white race or ideas about development) over native ones, and the slow erasure of native (non-European) cultures under the onslaught of European 'development', 'improvement' and museumization. Postcolonialism has revealed colonialism and imperialism as producing hybridized cultures through the cultural apparatus of education, religion, literature and the law (see Chapter 2).

In a sense globalization becomes a natural subject of study for postcolonialism because, like colonialism earlier, globalization is marked by a European (or rather Euro-American) domination of global culture. Local cultures and nation-states become irrelevant to the global flow of Hollywood, Barbie, IMF aid and McDonalds. Asian and African spaces are treated as markets for these products. Native characteristics are marginalized, local traditions erased as Western aid, medicine, development, economic systems ('free trade' as an economic system is never really 'free' for the Asian or African nation).

If postcolonialism showed how European thought erased local traditions by classifying it as 'barbaric', its present subject of inquiry is the transformation of native cultures into hybrid forms where the European component dominates. As we shall see in the following section, cybercultures and technologies of globalization work towards such an erasure of non-European identities through the imposition of Western names, accents and modes of functioning. Geographer Denis Cosgrove has argued persuasively in his *Apollo's Eye* that the Enlightenment ideology of 'encirclement' and universal cartographics was a totalizing European vision of the globe (2001, pp. 195–9). The latitudinal arc of the late eighteenth and early nineteenth centuries, writes Cosgrove, sought to 'appropriat[e] global space by bringing East and West together within a single imaginative realm' (p. 207). Studies of cartography's politics (Edney 1997) have shown how the European map-making projects often 'flattened' the earth, consigned Asian and African cultures to the periphery (even as colonialism drew these in, in a dependent, exploitative relationship with the European nation). Postcolonialism has been interested in margins, localities, smaller traditions that have resisted, co-opted or contested this kind of European totalizing visions and practices. Thus, logically, it is interested in globalization which extends colonialism's practice of 'unifying' the world under a European umbrella by ignoring difference, local cultures and native traditions.

Hardt and Negri argue that postcolonialism's emphasis on the politics of difference has become irrelevant because the new Empire subtly champions difference in order to incorporate it into new forms of 'modern sovereignty'. Bhabha's emphasis on colonial discourse's failure to implement its binaries is, they argue, based on a flawed assumption that 'power . . . operate[s] exclusively through a dialectical and binary structure' (2009a [1994], p. 145), but in the modern Empire, the form of the dominating power does not operate through binaries. It harnesses difference, locality and heterogeneity for its purposes. Hardt and Negri describe this new form of imperial control thus:

> The globalization or deterritorialization operated by the imperial machine is not in fact opposed to localization or reterritorialization,

but rather sets in play mobile and modulating circuits of differentiation and identification. (p. 43)

Thus postcolonialism needs to engage with totalizing, homogenizing discourses within globalization while being alert to the deliberate celebration of difference and locality for, as Hardt and Negri warn, the emphasis on differentiation is itself a 'regime' (p. 43) that serves the purposes of the new Empire. If traditional colonialism highlighted difference in order to show how the Other is inferior, the Empire now celebrates difference in order to co-opt it, navigate through it and harness it. 'Continuing imperialism', as I have called it, is postcolonialism's concern, but with an awareness that older forms of colonial domination, discourse, Othering have been transmuted into what look benign, philanthropic and praisesongs of difference.

The Postcolonial, the Postnational and the Refugee

Globalization renders the nation-state's borders porous. Indeed there is a suspicion that the nation-state is being transcended in the globalization of finance, capital, trade, migration and technology. Critics therefore speak of the 'postnational' condition (Appadurai 1996, Habermas 2001). The survival of the sovereign state is at stake. Territorially concentrated national identities are increasingly troubled. Postnationalists argue in favour of 'transnational identities and citizenship practices that transcend boundaries of national political communities' (Harty and Murphy 2005, p. 134).

This rise of the postnational and the concomitant reduction in the nation-state's significant sovereignty resonates with a particular problem that postcolonialism has been interested in since Frantz Fanon: of nationalism and national consciousness. The ambivalence towards nationalism and national consciousness that we see in Fanon is aligned with the celebration of the postnational and the cosmopolitan in Bhabha (1995b) and Appadurai, as Ali Behdad points out (Behdad 2007, pp. 72–3). Behdad also notes that such 'boosters' of globalization often ignore the 'uneven nature of global flow' (p. 76) where migrant cultures do not significantly alter European or American politics and where the distribution of wealth and privilege is not really global at all – that it remains raced, as it used to be in colonial times. Behdad warns that postcolonialism must address the 'unequal geography of globalization and its historical links with European colonialism and the process of decolonization' (p. 77). What Behdad directs us to is the racialized aspects of contemporary globalization – something that postcolonialism must address. Economic benefits from global trade linkages rarely deliver the same benefits to Asian and African nations as they do to the European and American one. Does this indicate that the 'postnational' simply means that the dissolution of national borders primarily benefits Euro-American firms, corporations and governments? What happens to the national economy in the postnational context?

A major contribution, to my mind, to the postcolonial reading of globalization/postnational versus local/national comes from Aihwa Ong (2003). Ong turns to the figure of the refugee in late twentieth century. In the twentieth century the volume of migration and the consequent demands have been severe, testing humanitarian organizations, legal systems, health authorities and nation-states as never before. Extreme consequences of migration and the resultant multiculturalization of societies/nations include genocides and ethnic cleansing (Bosnia is a recent case). Countries now seek to screen refugees and enact requirements for allowing them in (the Baltic states introducing language as a criterion for citizenship, for instance).

Ong detects three 'technologies of subject-making' (p. 70). First, the USA has always worked on a logic of racial bipolarity and 'orientalism'. Whiteness becomes established as an identity through the contrast with African slaves, and fear and longing have influenced American interactions with and attitudes towards Chinese and Asian immigrants. Slaves and immigrants were 'cleansed' of ethnic tendencies through technologies of paternalism, care, welfare capitalism's 'reform' and disciplining. Second, the attempts to assimilate ethnic groups into standardized American moulds were manifest as the 'moral politics of poor relief' (p. 74). Reforms aimed at the poor immigrant and the urban poor (usually migrants from the country to the industrial city) and the rise of the welfare mode were crucial in aligning poverty, race and morality in the discourse of 'deserving/undeserving' and citizenship. Third, the refugee's resettlement and return to citizenship has been a major project for most First World nation-states. The state and the refugee are often, Ong argues, situated as polarized positions. But, she notes, different kinds of refugees have also been differently perceived and received by peoples. National policies about refugees have often changed the 'moral status of the refugee' (p. 79).

Ong's key argument is that the refugee and the citizen are not irreconcilable opposites. Rather, she writes, 'the refugee and the citizen are the political effects of institutional processes that are deeply imbued with sociocultural values' (p. 79). As I have suggested elsewhere (Nayar 2010a, pp. 238–40), Ong's reading of the refugee throws up several race-related concerns that intersect with Critical Race Studies:

- the category of the refugee and citizen are constructions within discourses;
- these discourses are informed and are controlled by social contexts of receiving societies, cultures and states;
- these social contexts encode particular values and ideas about family, duty, responsibility and individual;
- the refugee becomes the subject of these discourses and, to be accepted as citizen might require to fulfil what the receiving society/culture perceives as the markers of a 'true' citizen.

That is, once the refugee has been instituted as refugee (in opposition to the citizen) then mechanisms and technologies that change her/his status will come into play. Here racialized discourses about the refugees' health, welfare, economic means come into force. As Ong notes:

the legacy of racializing expectations with regard to market potential, intelligence, mental health, and moral worthiness came to influence at the practical, everyday level the experiences and understanding of both the newcomers and the long-term residents who assisted them. (2003, pp. 82–3)

Ong's work demonstrates how racial discourses merge with discourses of health, economy, nationalism, morality and welfare in order to position the refugee in particular ways. These discourses determine the ease or difficulty of the refugee becoming a citizen. The task of postcolonialism within contexts of global migration, increasing refugee populations and globalized capitalism is to inquire into how the refugee is constructed within discourses of charity, responsibility and eligibility. Just as the native was once subject to scrutiny as a 'good citizen' of the empire, the refugee becomes an ethical figure who needs to qualify as a citizen in the postnational, globalized context. Postcolonialism must, therefore, examine the conditions under which the Third World refugee is 'evaluated' as a possible citizen. Does the refugee have to subscribe to Euro-American notions of the family and the individual? Can the refugee who retains her/his native cultures – for which she/he has been targeted, attacked – yet be a responsible citizen in any part of the globe? Or are the obligations of the Euro-American globalized worlds such that 'difference' is respected and protected? In an age where most individuals already have mixed cultural identities and heritages, can we think of a distinctive ethno-cultural or national identity, even in the case of the nostalgic refugee?

POSTCOLONIALISM IN THE AGE OF TRANSNATIONAL TERROR

Since 9/11 the world's chief concern has been terrorism. New paradigms of transnational terror have obsessed the First World mainly because they locate its origins in a civilizational battle (Huntington's notorious thesis, 1996, but also of 'jihad versus McWorld', Barber 1995) between Islamic and Christian civilizations. Postcolonial theory's valorization of ambivalence and hybridity, in particular, took a devastating body blow in the aftermath of 9/11 when the USA and other nations reaffirmed national and cultural boundaries: 'either you are with us or you are with the terrorists'. There was no ambivalence here at all. It returned to colonial binaries:

White (Euro-American)	Non-white (Asian, also Middle East)
Christian	Islamic
Civilized	Barbaric
Seeks reform & advancement	Promotes revivalism
Forward-looking	Backward-looking
Pro-women	Anti-women
Respect for individual	Communitarian, anti-individual
Defender of Rights	Violator of Rights

This restored to the rhetoric colonial dichotomies. Multiculturalism – a pet theme in postcolonialism – came under the scanner for having encouraged and idolized difference (of Asians and other cultures from white, Christian ones) and rejected assimilation, for retaining 'their' cultures in a white America. Post-9/11 writings, especially from within evangelical America, paint Islam as inherently violent and a false religion. Richard Cimino (2005) argues that where previously America's multiculturalism was a matter of pride, in the post-9/11 scenario, the pluralism in American society challenged evangelical identity, and lead to the erection of new boundary markers between Christianity and other religions.

Postcolonial studies of colonial textbooks/education/literacy missions (Viswanathan 1990, Priya Joshi 2002) have shown how education, pedagogy and the English language itself served imperial purposes by carefully positioning the natives as primitive requiring European intervention, native civilization as barbaric, etc. In the wake of 9/11 American school textbooks apparently did the same. A study shows how 9/11 was explained merely as a 'terrorist attack led by Bin Laden' with little reference to American foreign policies. These also placed 9/11 in a patriotic framework, and roused greater nationalist sentiments concomitant with a deep suspicion of Arabs and Muslims (Romanowski 2009). Steven Salaita (2005) has demonstrated how Arab Americans had to present an 'imperative patriotism' after 9/11 – and this once more returns us to the relevance and necessity of multiethnicity and homogenization. Kalra, Kaur and Hutnyk put it succinctly: 'in the wake of the "war on terror", Arab-Americans and South Asian-Americans were required to undo the hyphen and drape themselves in the US flag as a sign of their unadulterated patriotism' (2005, p. 130).

Transnational terrorism and the resultant 'war on terror' have created a crisis of sorts in postcolonialism because all their key themes of ambivalence, diaspora and hybridity have been called into question. On the one hand borders have become porous to terror and migration, and the other countries police their borders far more than before. Reproductions of ethnic identities have strengthened as never before. USA and the West returns to a colonial-style discourse, speaking of 'us' and 'them', and constructing itself in an antagonistic relationship with the Islamic and Asian Other. Stereotypes of the barbaric Muslim have come to haunt the visual cultures of the post-9/11 West. Foreigners, immigrants, asylum-seekers turbaned or veiled figures became emblematic of the 'threat within'. Ali Behdad writes of 'the figure of the immigrant/foreigner once again provided the differential other through whose threatening presence in the nation a state of emergency was declared' (2005, p. 4). Turbaned men were targeted (even Indian Sikhs). The discourses after 9/11 brought back the image of the monster – this time as a Muslim terrorist.

Edward Rothstein (2001) and other commentators used 9/11 as an excuse to attack postcolonialism's cultural relativism, its rejection of 'Western' ideals of humanism and protest. Rothstein wrote:

the rejections of universal values and ideals leave little room for unqualified condemnations of a terrorist attack, particularly one against the West. Such an attack, however inexcusable, can be seen as a horrifying airing of a legitimate cultural grievance. (http://www.nytimes.com/2001/09/22/arts/connections-attacks-us-challenge-perspectives-postmodern-true-believers.html? pagewanted=2, 4 November 2009)

Rothstein went on to declare that eventually the 'Western relativism of pomo and the obsessive focus of poco will be widely seen as ethically perverse' (http://www.nytimes.com/2001/09/22/arts/connections-attacks-us-challenge-perspectives-postmodern-true-believers.html? pagewanted=2, 4 November 2009). Stanley Kurtz testifying before the Subcommittee on Select Education, Committee on Education and the Workforce and the US House of Representatives, explicitly referenced Edward Said as the prime mover in whipping up academic antagonism to American foreign policy. Kurtz in fact argued that there must be a monitoring of the grants given to programs that teach courses critical of US foreign policy (Ray 2005, pp. 577–9). Sangeeta Ray points out that the Kurtz kind of backlash against 'poco' has an interest consequence. Whereas colonialism located the foreigner and the stranger out there in the colony, this post-9/11 rhetoric warns of the 'circulation of the "stranger in our midst"' (580). In each case what we see is the crisis of postcolonialism.

Postcolonialism's emphasis on contamination, impurity, dualism, ambivalence and the rejection of notions of cultural purity and stereotypes are turned around by post-9/11 commentators to imply a rejection of America and Israel, while actively championing terrorism. Postcolonialism sees the self and Other as mutually constitutive (Edward Said in *Orientalism* showed how the West was able to construct its identity only because of the constitutive presence of the Asian-Arab Other). It rejects the notion of absolute difference – and this is what sets Kurtz and company against postcolonialism. After 9/11 they wish to see the world in absolute binaries: us and them, Muslim villain and Christian hero. Ambivalence is frowned upon, and stereotypes reinstated. The backlash against Said and postcolonialism in general is the attempt to return to older forms of thinking about 'culture' itself.

In terms of literature the success of novels and memoirs dealing with Arab or Muslim cultures, or with 'threatening' spaces such as Afghanistan or Iran suggests a revival of interest in this Other. One thinks of Khaled Hossaini, Marjane Satrapi, Kamila Shamsie, Azar Nafisi and their phenomenal success in the Western and global marketplace. Nafisi's memoir, *Reading Lolita in Tehran* (2003) shows the oppressive conditions under which women live in Iran. Marjane Satrapi's graphic memoir, *Persepolis*, documented the Iranian revolution and the several oppressive methods used in the revivalist Islamic republic. Khaled Hossaini's portrayal of a Talibanized Afghanistan likewise, fed the images of a brutal culture already circulating in the West. Is this the new postcolonial in the age of terror?

In the chapter on nations and nationalism (Chapter 3) I had reason to refer to Lisa Lau and the idea of 're-orientalism' (2009). Graham Huggan wrote of the 'postcolonial exotic' (2001), arguing that the postcolonial remains an exotic commodity, yearned for, promoted and consumed in the West. Writers like Nafisi and Mohammed do give us the sense that their success is at least partly attributable to 9/11 where the 'barbaric' native becomes the subject of legal, juridical, military and literary inquiry. Dominic Head reading Martin Amis' *Yellow Dog* sees in the novel's portrait of violence a 'symbolic portrait' of 'Western civilization destroying itself in precisely the manner that its great global antagonist would expect' (2008, p. 103). Don De Lillo's *Falling Man* (2007) seeks to explore a scarred American psyche after 9/11, and John Updike's *Terrorist* (2006) attempts to get inside the mind of the terrorist.

Pal Ahluwalia calls for the adoption of a postcolonial 'ethical stance for the other'. Instead of the imperial one of reductive binaries which treated the Other as inferior or monstrous, a postcolonial ethics sees the self as constituted by the Other. This means, rather than seeing the Self as coherent, unified and distinct from the Other, a postcolonial ethics situates the 'I' within a system of social relations (2007, pp. 267–9). Susan Koshy shifts the terms of the debate slightly when she asks why 9/11 serves as an epochal moment at all. Koshy frames the 'problem' as a series of questions:

What alternative histories could we write if we substituted 9/11 with other events, such as the 1984 Bhopal disaster or the 1956 Suez Crisis? Or, alternatively, if 9/11 was not just a national tragedy but an event that was telematically witnessed by and involved other countries, what meanings did it have in other parts of the world? Can a historicism that focuses on national contexts address the far-reaching meanings of the events? What narratives of US ascendancy or decline and what new geopolitical align-ments can we discern if we view the events in an international frame? (2008, p. 301)

Koshy's believes that the 'answers to these questions would not only take us away from the framework of Orientalism and Islamophobia, which identify Western anxieties and axiomatics', and because 'there are other Asias than the ones authored by the West' (p. 301).

The onus will be, I suggest, on these 'other Asias' to take post-colonialism forward. These 'other Asias' disrupt the discourse of stereotyping (reinstated after 9/11) by being

- Multicultural
- Tolerant
- Adaptive

It pays attention to the rights of minorities (of all kinds) and refuses to be restricted to stereotypes. It builds alliances across regions and cultures. One trajectory of such a postcolonialism is visible in the work of Ashis Nandy. In 'Towards a Third World Utopia' (2004 [1987) and 'A New Cosmopolitanism: Toward a Dialogue of Asian Civilizations' (1998) Nandy has offered a new vision of cosmopol-itanism and globalization where the 'Third World' plays a major role. Nandy writes:

The only way the Third World can transcend the sloganeering of its well-wishers is, first, by becoming a collective representation of the victims of man-made suffering everywhere in the world and in all past times, second, by internalizing or owning up the outside forces of oppression and, then, coping with them as inner vectors and third by recognizing the oppressed or marginalized selves of the First and Second Worlds as civilizational allies in the battle against institutionalized suffering. (p. 441)

Nandy argues that Third World nations can align themselves with the 'repressed' and oppressed within First World nations. This means, cosmopolitanism can be built on a common ethics of recognition: where we *acknowledge the suffering of the Other* and work to fight institutional forms of suffering everywhere. I have argued that this argument in Nandy is a Utopic vision based on *affect*, a recognition of and response to the suffering of Others. This locates Nandy within what I have termed 'affective cosmopolitanism' (Nayar 2008c). Leela Gandhi has in similar fashion spoken of 'affective communities' (2006). Judith Butler (2004) refers to a rising consciousness of the 'precarity' of our lives when we see suffering. 'Despite our differences', writes Butler, 'in location and history, my guess is that it is possible to appeal to a "we," for all of us have some notion of what it is to have lost somebody. Loss has made a tenuous "we" of us all' (p. 20). Feelings of loss, bereavement and the anxiety of vulnerability (sentiments) are accompanied by a political reasoning where we recognize the condition of precarity and the need for *interdependence*. As Butler puts it, 'if my fate is not originally or finally separable from yours, then the "we" is traversed by a relationality that we cannot easily argue against' (pp. 22–3). Postcolonial ethics is this sense of precarity that drives our sense of interdependence. The Other is not out there somewhere – I am connected to the Other through a mutuality of potential destruction, precarity and harm. It is this new awareness that makes me see the Other in a new way.

CYBERCULTURE FORMATIONS AND THE POSTCOLONIAL

Information and Communications Technologies (ICTs) have been a central cog in the machine of globalization. The online environment generated by New Media enables the creation of alternate and fluid identities, instant communications and new forms of leisure (computer gaming, online movies). Sites of production and financial control have become widely dispersed through outsourcing, flexi-production, production-on-demand and the increasing dominance of 'knowledge work'. Families, communities and groups separated by geographical distances now find sociality on the www. The nature of social interaction itself has changed with social networking, the mobile telephone and e-mail. Virtual worlds like *Second Life* offer an alternate domain for socialization, profit-making and leisure. Parts of everyday life are now lived in cyberspace.

The Cultural Studies approach to New Media and cybercultures – a short hand term to describe a variety of technologies, experiences and 'spaces', from mobile phones to online gaming to the rise of cybercommunities – treats it as a set of social relations with its own politics of gender, race and class. If, as Pierre Lévy suggests, cyberculture is a 'set of technologies . . . practices, attitudes, modes of thought and values' (2001, p. xvi) then it becomes imperative that we should look at material infrastructure, political ideologies, emotional responses, subversive appropriations and exploitative potential of cyberculture. We need to locate technological 'devices' and processes within ideologies, economic policies and politics.

Critical Cyberculture Studies combines race studies with postcolonialism. The work of Lisa Nakamura (2002), Beth Kolko et al. (2000) among others have addressed the issue of race in cyberspace. Fatima Jackson (1999, 2001) has examined the role of race in massive scientific projects such as the Human Genome Project (the databasing of the human genome). D. J. Leonard's work (2005) has revealed the inherent racism of computer games.

Since ICTs are central to the process of globalization and globalization becomes a newer form of colonial exploitation (called 'neo-colonialism'), race studies needs to scrutinize the new technologies for the differential power relations between the races in cyberspace, its technologies and economy. Race, the marker of difference between the First World and the Third World, is a crucial factor in the way these technologies are created (in sweatshops in Third World), used, represented and controlled (how many Africans or Asians own software companies?). ICTs that generate cyberspaces are built and embedded in the 'real' world, through material artifacts (such as machines and buildings) and through the labour of actual people (construction workers, software engineers), many of whom are non-white (by 1996 nearly half of the 55,000 temporary visas issued by the US government to high-tech workers went to Indians).

Thus, while cyberspace may be built by *non-white* workers the profits and administrative control are rarely in their hands. Global media and the www are western owned and administered. Further, many of these conglomerates and companies are located in countries that have had a long history of racism. When these companies project the idea of a multicultural workplace they are actually generating what Lisa Nakamura correctly terms 'cosmetic multiculturalism', a false sense of racial equality, which masks the centrality of cheap immigrant labour from other races in their profit-making industry (Nakamura 2002, p. 21). Materialist critiques of the new informational economy (Terranova 2000, Downey 2002) have shown how the so-called 'virtual' masks real labour, for whom identity remains embodied, grounded and embedded in concrete conditions.

The Internet, or rather cyberspace, is a space where identities are fluid and fragmented, where the colour of their skin is of no consequence. This has been the focus of several Internet scholars who see cyberspace as liberating (Rheingold 1994 [1992], Turkle 1995). However, the minorities, blacks and mixed-race peoples are already, in the real world, marginalized and fragmented in the real world: they already lack economic and political power. Lisa Nakamura writes:

> The celebration of the "fluid self" that simultaneously lauds post-modernity as a potentially liberatory sort of worldview tends to overlook the more disturbing aspects of the fluid, marginalized selves that already exist offline in the form of actual marginalized peoples, which is not nearly so romantic a formulation. (2002, p. xvi)

For minorities and other races the internet is not a liberating space. In fact for such ethnicities there is an urgent need to foreground their racial and ethnic identity and not dissolve or alter it. When political power, welfare, employment are all based on their racial identity, they cannot afford to become 'deracinated' in cyberspace. That luxury remains the privilege of the ethnic groups who already possess power and for whom their race has ceased to matter, in one sense.

However, minorities and other racial 'types' have increasingly taken to the internet, discovering within the new technologies enormous potential for ethnic group work, community resources and means of political empowerment. Subcultural group's diasporic communities have emerged. Rhythm of Life (*www.rolo.org*) is a non-profit organization that raises money to provide both computer skills and job training to the black working poor and working class in the San

Francisco Bay Area. The Afro-Futurist collective (*www.afrofuturism. net*) is an online community for African-American and African Diasporic artists and intellectuals. In India Cybermohalla is a popular digital culture initiative by New Delhi, India's Centre for the Study of Developing Societies' Sarai project and an Ankur, an NGO, *www.sarai.net*). Cybermohalla mixes street language with English, the topos of the 'sarai' and the 'mohalla' (literally 'locality') with that of a-geographic cyberspace, street conversation and the intimate diary with that of a documentary, a glocalization of the digital (Nayar 2007a).

Cybercultures celebrate the end of the body. Just when the blacks or the Hispanics seek and establish a presence on the www cybercultures promote a fragmented and non-identitarian politics. This continues the Western/white strategy of marginalizing non-white identities. If during colonialism they rejected the 'native' as barbaric, they now reject the native as *non-raced*. Since the battle for equality and democracy has been on the basis of race, and since exploitation is governed mainly by the colour of the skin, to do away with racial identity is to refuse any chance of agency to the black or the Hispanic.

Contemporary empirical studies have shown how online identities rework established racial stereotypes (see Nakamura 2002 in particular). This reinforces racial difference, but a difference that is stereotyped in ways that demean the non-white races. Thus D. J. Leonard's work on computer games (2005) has shown how the black men are invariably excessively violent and black women hypersexual in numerous games.

Globalization today expands the network of slaving voyages, transoceanic trade links, travel and conquest that linked various locations on the earth for centuries before the present one. Capitalism is increasingly *technocapitalism* because the distributed nature of production, marketing and consumption demands technological linkages, synchronous and 24×7 communications. Indeed, as Manuel Castells has argued (1989), capitalism itself has been restructured through 'informationalism'. One of the tasks of the postcolonial is to critique the new forms of racial discourse and racialized cultural practices that are enabled by and within 'informationalism'. 'Post-colonizing cyberculture', as I term it (Nayar 2010b) refers to a process of interpretation and appropriation of cyberspace and cybercultural practices that is alert not only to the racially determined exploitative conditions of globalized ICT labour, but also to the emancipatory potential of cybercultures.

If cyberspace is rooted in, recursively linked to and informed by the real, as I have proposed elsewhere (Nayar 2010b), then it means

- our real life identities inform our attitudes, responses and experiences of cyberspace.
- We bring back our experience as an 'avatar' (online identity) into our real one. The real (racial, ethnic, gender) identity enters online spaces through various means
- The language used in online communication, as researchers have demonstrated, reveal racial identities (Warschauer 2000);
- Racial identities are commodified and circulate in cyberspace and popular representations of cyberspace (in films, for instance) just as they have been in other media;
- Dedicated African, Chicano and minority websites seek to locate race and particular cultures in cyberspace, in many cases seeking an online community formation (diasporic groups, for instance, as studied by Franklin 2004).

Call centre work and outsourcing presents a good example of the problematic (racialized) politics of the informational economy. Outsourcing subordinates vast numbers of Indians, Chinese and, increasingly Hispanics in South American countries, to First World economic and industrial needs. The cost differential of labour here might be promising to the Western industry, and even offer higher pay to non-white workers, but it also produces serious work and organizational issues. Take, for instance, the matter of identity. Accent training, the use of Western pseudonyms by the postcolonial call centre worker ('Sham' becomes 'Sam') and acculturation (the Indian is given a crash course in American culture and forms of speech) are troubling in the sense it seems to reinstate the colonial paradigm of 'converting' the native into the almost-white. As Phil Taylor and Peter Bain point out (2005), these are neo-imperialist and indeed racist practices. Cyberculture's space-time compression and flows are the consequence, indeed construction, of such racialized labour practices (Shome 2006). Nearly a decade ago Timothy Luke had pointed to the uneven power relations in cyberspace:

> The cyberspatial resources of global computer nets permit virtual enterprises to employ thousands of poor women in Jamaica,

Mauritius or the Philippines in low-paid, tedious data entry or word-processing jobs for firms in London, Paris, or San Diego. Cyberspace permits dromo-economic entrepreneurs to virtualize segments of a core workplace at these peripheral locations. (1999, p. 37. Also Downey 2002)

Luke gestures here at the centre-periphery divide of cybercultures – a divide that returns to the nineteenth century's colonial structure.

Globalization thrives on resource (labour, intellect, natural materials and markets) exploitation of Third World by First World, a feature of colonialism from the very beginning. Migrant workers from India and Asia built Silicon Valley that eventually headquartered the research *and* commercial aspects of computer revolution. The new ICTs grew out of the labour generated by 'Third World', non-white workers – in the Silicon Valley with its vast numbers of Asian software workers. Business Process Outsourcing (BPO) works that enable global networking depend almost entirely on Asian labour (India, from where I write, is a centre for the BPO industry). Postcolonial studies in the cybercultural era examines how discourses of racial, ethnic and national identity are embedded, contested and rejected by discourses of a globalized world and 'free' markets.

Postcolonial approaches to cyberculture also interrogate the digitization and databasing of information and populations in projects such as the Human Genome Project (HGP). The HGP will store data of the ethnic and racial populations of the world. For the postcolonial and the ethnic minority this poses some crucial questions:

- Who will own this data?
- Will the indigenous populations whose samples have been taken to database the DNA of the community/tribe have access to it?
- Will they be allowed to determine the dissemination of information?

Originally African Americans were *not* included in the genomic survey of the human race. After persistent demands, DNA samplings from African Americans were also included. This exclusion is a throwback to the colonial age when Africans did not figure in tracts on humanity, except as primitives and animal-like species. In effect this would have meant a normative human genetic code drawn from a narrow section of the population, as 'representative' of all humans. If future medicine and medical research will rely on such data (genomic medicine is one such rapidly growing domain), then a related question emerges: if a racial or ethnic group is not genetically profiled in the database will genomic medicines be developed for such groups at all? (see Jackson 1999, 2001, Nayar 2006). A postcolonial approach to such projects maps the underlying ideologies and exploitative mechanisms at work within contemporary techno-science, and links such projects with older colonial ones such as cartography, population studies and ethnography.

But cybercultural technologies can also be empowering. The post-colonial era has seen the rise of a global civil society. Ethnic identities are now asserted on multiple, global locations without (necessarily) a territory (such as the nation-state). The Other who has been written out of history is being brought back by ethnic-specific projects thanks to new technologies. The solidarity forged between ethnic identities in Asia and America (by Asians of American origin) reshapes the very contours of 'Asia' and 'America', and the relation between the two. Such solidarities are increasingly facilitated by the global telecommunications technologies. A whole new geography of the diaspora is emerging, as contemporary studies (Franklin 2004) have shown. Non-governmental organizations, trans-governmental organizations and activists link across the globe through these technologies. In a postcolonial world, such a network can be the source of a democratic, interventionary and resistant civil society. Local communities, building solidarities with other like-minded communities, often become postcolonial in that they resist imperialism from within the metropolis.

* * *

This chapter has argued that postcolonialism needs to move beyond its obsession with colonial history and address new concerns – technology, globalization and transnational terrorism that have called multiculturalism into crisis. Its commitment to a new form of the human – which Frantz Fanon had argued for in all his works – is an *ethical* one. Postcolonialism's ethics, often put into crisis in the wake of 9/11, must be one of addressivity to the Other, the different and the silent. It has stakes in political economy, global geopolitics, militarism, cultural practices, consumer culture – in short everything where power plays out in racialized relations. Postcolonialism accepts the continuing impact of imperialism, albeit in new forms. Postcolonialism, therefore, as Couze Venn brilliantly summarizes it, 'develops an oppositional analytical standpoint that targets the conditions, the narratives, the relations of power that, in their combined effects, support the iniquitous forms of sociality and the varieties of pauperizations that characterize the current world order' (2006, p. 3). Elleke Boehmer's suggestion towards the end of her *Colonial and Postcolonial Literature* remains a salutary agenda: that postcolonial literature 'offers ways of articulating, of putting into play this justice- and respect-driven struggle', as a 'gateway to *feeling* otherness' (p. 258, emphasis added). It is this responsibility to the injured, the marginal – subsumed under one head, the 'Other' – of history, technology, politics that marks the continued relevance of the postcolonial.

NOTES

CHAPTER 1

1 'Discourse' is the context in which knowledge is produced and all conversation and communication occurs. It defines the limits of what can be said, and what is prohibited. It is the context of representation, speech and language. The law, religion, medicine, literature are all 'discourses' in which the body, the human, beauty, truth are defined and made acceptable (legitimate). Likewise, all aspects of life have a discursive context: race, identity, class, economy, politics rely on certain modes of articulation, representation and reproduction

2 Cabral's argument here anticipates Partha Chatterjee's famous thesis that the 'inner' sphere of domesticity and home remained distinct and untouched by the colonizer's beliefs and systems of thought in the colonial condition (Chatterjee 1993). See Chapter 4 in this book for an account.

3 Edward Said was not really the first to speak of the prejudices in Western writings about Asia or Islam. KM Panikkar (*Asia and Western Domination*, 1953), PJ Marshall (*British Discovery of Hinduism in the Eighteenth Century*, 1970), Talal Asad (*Anthropology and the Colonial Encounter*, 1973), Hichem Djait (*Europe and Islam*, 1985) and Syed Hussein Alatas (*The Myth of the Lazy Native*, 1977) had all pointed to the politics of Western representations of the Orient in anthropology, religious studies, historiography and literature.

CHAPTER 2

1 'Ideology' is a mode of *not* recognizing the true nature of our material lives and social roles when we consume a cultural artefact such as literature or film. It is a system of ideas, values, beliefs that we live by. This system of values is usually put in place by the dominant classes, and the subject classes are fed them so that they begin to live and believe in the values.

2 Mukherjee's kind of postcolonialism has found its early arguments in the work of critics like Bruce McCully (*English Education and the Origins of Indian Nationalism*, 1942, and David Kopf's *British Orientalism and the Bengal Renaissance*, 1969) which argued that Indian nationalism found its

inspirational ideas and even its political thought in the texts of English/ European liberal thought. Gauri Viswanathan argues, however, that both these early texts in fact end up valorizing English education by showing how the Indians would never have modernized themselves but for English education (Viswanathan, 1990, pp. 14–16).

CHAPTER 4

1 While Mangaliso treats the woman revolutionary as a proto-feminist, this cannot be the only reading. Neloufer de Mel's recent work on Sinhala drama and films shows how the body of the female suicide bomber in the LTTE's revolutionary struggle sexualizes her and as a result, generates a moral public discourse about her (2007, pp. 192–245).
2 For a collection of essays on gender and nationalism, see Lois West (ed.) *Feminist Nationalism* (1997).

CHAPTER 5

1 Critics have argued that Rushdie treats nationalism as an illusion and a myth (Ahmad 1987).
2 For a comparative perspective of African and Australian literary uses of land and spatial tropes see Simon Darian-Smith et al. (1996).

CHAPTER 6

1 'Transnational' differs from 'international' in the sense it refers to relations that run across states but refers to people and groups and not necessarily to official bodies. Eliezer Ben-Rafael and Yitzak Sternberg speak of transnational disaporas' 'anchorage in allegiance that imply a reference to a common narrative and plight' (2008, p. 2). This 'common narrative' could be of African slavery, Judaism's exile or the dispersion of Catholic missionaries (p. 2).
2 The labels 'ethnic' and 'Asian American' have been sometimes in conflict with the 'postcolonial', as Bella Adams has argued (2008, pp. 15–16). This is driven, at least partly by the intraracial debates where some Asian American texts have been accused of racism against other Asian races.
3 Where early generations of Asian American and diaspora authors struggled with their identities in a new place, the 1990s saw a much more confident and strident identity politics. The Asian Americans had done well, politically and economically, and hence could not simply be aligned with Blacks or Chicanos as 'disadvantaged' races. It also meant that intraracial differences with Asian American communities could be talked about and *other* affiliations based on class, gender, ethnicity and sexuality forged (Lowe 1991).
4 In 1978 a young Bengali clothing worker, Altab Ali was murdered here leading to anti- racist protests.

BIBLIOGRAPHY

Achebe, C. (1967), *Arrow of God*. New York: John Day.
—(1969), *Things Fall Apart*. 1958. New York: Fawcett.
—(1988), *Anthills of the Savannah*. London: Heinemann.
—(1999), 'Colonialist Criticism', in B. Ashcroft, G. Griffiths and H. Tiffin (eds), *The Postcolonial Studies Reader*. 1975. London and New York: Routledge, pp. 57–61.
—(2001), 'An Image of Africa: Racism in Conrad's *Heart of Darkness*', in G. Castle (ed.) *Postcolonial Discourses: An Anthology*. 1977. Oxford: Blackwell, pp. 210–20.
Acholonu, C. O. (1995), *Motherism: The Afrocentric Alternative*. Nigeria: Afa.
Adams, B. (2008), *Asian American Literature*. Edinburgh: Edinburgh University Press.
Adichie, C. N. (2009), 'Cell One', in *The Thing Around Your Neck*. London: Fourth Estate, pp. 3–21.
Ahluwalia, P. (2007), 'Afterlives of Post-colonialism: Reflections on Theory Post-9/11', *Postcolonial Studies*, 10, 3, 257–70.
Ahmad, A. (1987), 'Jameson's Rhetoric of Otherness and the "National Allegory"', *Social Text* 17, 3–25.
—(1997), 'The Politics of Literary Postcoloniality', in P. Mongia (ed.) *Contemporary Postcolonial Theory: A Reader*. Delhi: Oxford University Press, pp. 276–93.
Aidoo, A. A. (1988), *Our Sister Killjoy Or, Reflections from a Black-Eyed Squint*. 1977. Haklow, Essex: Longman.
—(2001), *Anowa*, in H. Gilbert (ed.) *Postcolonial Plays*. 1970. London and New York: Routledge, pp. 101–27.
Alatas, S. H. (1977), *The Myth of the Lazy Native*. London: F. Cass.
Alexander, M. (1993), *Fault Lines: A Memoir*. New York: The Feminist Press.
—(1997), *Manhattan Music*. San Francisco: Mercury House.
Ali, A. S. (1996), 'Postcard from Kashmir', in J. Thieme (ed.) *The Arnold Anthology of Post-colonial Literatures in English*. 1993. London: Arnold, p. 752.
Ali, C. R. (1970), 'The Idea of Pakistan', in E. Kedourie (ed.) *Nationalism in Asia and Africa*. New York: Meridian, pp. 245–9.
Ali, M. (2003), *Brick Lane*. 2001. London: Doubleday.

Allen, P. G. (1983), *The Woman Who Owned the Shadows*. San Francisco: Aunt Lute.

Allende, I. (1994), *Of Love and Shadows*. Tr., M. S. Peden. 1987. New York: Corgi.

Alp, T. (1970), 'The Restoration of Turkish History', in E. Kedourie (ed.) *Nationalism in Asia and Africa*. New York: Meridian, pp. 207–24.

Amadiume, I. (1997), *Re-Inventing Africa: Matriarchy, Religion and Culture*. London: Zed.

Anderson, A. (1998), 'Cosmopolitanism, Universalism, and the Divided Legacies of Modernity', in P. Cheah and B. Robbins (eds), *Cosmopolitics: Thinking and Feeling Beyond the Nation*. Minneapolis: University of Minnesota Press, pp. 265–89.

Anderson, B. (1991), *Imagined Communities: Reflections on the Origins and Spread of Nationalism*. London and New York: Verso. Rev. ed.

Anderson, G. and Subedar, M. (1921), *The Development of an Indian Policy (1818–1858)*. London: G. Bell and Bombay: AH Wheeler.

Anon, (1858), 'Christianity in India', *Dublin University Magazine* 312, 3, 641–50.

Anzaldúa, G. (1994), *Borderlands/La Frontera: The New Mestiza*. 1987. San Francisco: Spinsters/Aunt Lute.

Appadurai, A. (1996), *Modernity at Large: Cultural Dimensions of Globalization*. Minneapolis: University of Minnesota Press.

Armah, A. K. (1988), *The Beautyful Ones are Not Yet Born*. Portsmouth: Heinemann.

Armstrong, J. (1985), *Slash*. Penticton: Theytus Books.

—(1996), 'This is a Story', in J. Thieme (ed.) *The Arnold Anthology of Post-colonial Literatures in English*. 1993. London: Arnold, pp. 428–33.

Arnold, D. (1993), *Colonizing the Body: State Medicine and Epidemic Disease in Nineteenth-century India*. Berkeley and London: University of California Press.

Arteaga, A. (1997), *Chicano Poetics: Heterotexts and Hybridities*. Cambridge: Cambridge University Press.

Asad, T. (ed.), (1973), *Anthropology and the Colonial Encounter*. London: Ithaca.

Ash-Shamlan, S. (1998), 'Zainab', in A. Bagader, A. M. Heinrichsdorff and D. S. Akers (eds), *Voices of Change: Short Stories by Saudi Arabian Women Writers*. London: Lynne Reiner, pp. 39–41.

Bagader, A., Heinrichsdorff, A. M. and Akers, D. S. (1998), (eds), *Voices of Change: Short Stories by Saudi Arabian Women Writers*. London: Lynne Reiner.

Bagchi, J. (1991), 'Shakespeare in Loin Cloths: English Literature and the Early Nationalist Consciousness in Bengal', in S. Joshi (ed.) *Rethinking English: Essays in Literature, Language, History*. New Delhi: Trianka, pp. 146–59.

Ballhatchet, K. (1980), *Race, Sex and Class under the Raj: Imperial Attitudes and Policies and their Critics 1703–1905*. London: Weidenfeld and Nicolson.

Banerjea, S. (1970), 'The Study of Indian History', in E. Kedourie (ed.) *Nationalism in Asia and Africa.* New York: Meridian, pp. 225–44.

Barber, B. (1995), *Jihad vs McWorld.* New York: Times.

Barringer, T. J. (ed.), (1998), *Colonialism and the Object: Empire, Material Culture and the Museum.* London and New York: Routledge.

Bayly, C. A. (1999), *Empire and Information: Intelligence Gathering and Social Communication in India, 1780–1870.* Cambridge: Cambridge University Press.

Behdad, A. (2005), 'Nation and Immigration', *Portal Journal of Multidisciplinary International Studies* 2, 2, 1–16.

Behdad, A. (2007), 'On Globalization, Again!' in A. Loomba, S. Kaul, M. Bunzl, A. Burton and J. Esty (eds), *Postcolonial Studies and Beyond.* Durham and London: Duke University Press, pp. 62–79.

Ben-Rafael, E. and Sternberg, Y. (2008), 'Introduction: Debating Transnationalism', in E. Ben-Rafael and Y. Sternberg, with J. B. Liwerant and Y. Gorny (eds), *Transnationalism: Diasporas and the Advent of a New (Dis)Order.* Leiden: Brill, pp. 1–25.

Beveridge, W. (1947), *India Called Them.* London: n.p.

Bewell, A. (1999), *Romanticism and Colonial Disease.* Baltimore: Johns Hopkins University Press.

Bhabha, H. K. (1995a). 'Introduction: Narrating the Nation', in H. K. Bhabha (ed.) *Nation and Narration.* 1990. London and New York: Routledge, pp. 1–7.

—(1995b), 'DissemiNation: Time, Narrative, and the Margins of the Modern Nation', in H. K. Bhabha (ed.) *Nation and Narration.* 1990. London and New York: Routledge, pp. 291–322.

—(2009a), 'Of Mimicry and Man: The Ambivalence of Colonial Discourse', in *The Location of Culture.* 1994. London and New York: Routledge, pp. 121–31.

—(2009b), 'Signs Taken for Wonders: Questions of Ambivalence and Authority under a Tree Outside Delhi, May 1817', in *The Location of Culture.* 1994. London and New York: Routledge, pp. 145–74.

—(2009c), 'Sly Civility', in *The Location of Culture.* 1994. London and New York: Routledge, pp. 132–44.

Billig, M. (1995), *Banal Nationalism.* London: Sage.

Blyden, E. W. (1970), 'The Negro in Ancient History', in E. Kedourie (ed.) *Nationalism in Asia and Africa.* New York: Meridian, pp. 250–74.

Boehmer, E. (2005), 'Versions of Yearning and Dissent: The Troping of Desire in Yvonne Vera and Tsitsi Dangarembga', in F. Veit-Wild and D. Naguschewski (eds), *Body, Sexuality, and Gender: Versions and Subversion in African Literature I.* Amsterdam and New York: Rodopi, pp. 113–28.

—(2006), *Colonial and Postcolonial Literatures: Migrant Metaphors.* 1995. Oxford: Oxford University Press.

Bolt, C. (1971), *Victorian Attitudes to Race.* London: Routledge and Kegan Paul.

Brah, A. (1996), *Cartographies of Diaspora: Contesting Identities.* London and New York: Routledge.

Brantlinger, P. (1988), *Rule of Darkness: British Literature and Imperialism, 1830–1914*. Ithaca and London: Cornell University Press.

Brathwaite, E. K. (1981), *The Arrivants: A New World Trilogy*. 1973. London: Oxford University Press.

—(1999), 'Nation Language', in B. Ashcroft, G. Griffiths and H. Tiffin (eds), *The Post-colonial Studies Reader*. 1984. London and New York: Routledge, pp. 309–13.

Brennan, T. (1995), 'The National Longing for Form', in H. K. Bhabha (ed.) *Nation and Narration*. 1990. London and New York: Routledge, pp. 44–70.

—(1997), *At Home in the World: Cosmopolitanism Now*. Cambridge, MA: Harvard University Press.

—(2007), 'The Economic Image-Function of the Periphery', in A. Loomba, S. Kaul, M. Bunzl, A. Burton and J. Esty (eds), *Postcolonial Studies and Beyond*. Durham and London: Duke University Press, pp. 101–22.

Brockway, L. H. (1979), *Science and Colonial Expansion: The Role of the British Royal Botanic Gardens*. London: Academic.

Bromley, R. (2000), *Narratives for a New Belonging: Diasporic Cultural Fictions*. Edinburgh: Edinburgh University Press.

Bruton, W. (1638), *News from the East-Indies, or, a Voyage to Bengalla*, London: J. Oakes.

Butler, J. (2002), 'Is Kinship always Heterosexual?' *Differences* 13, 1, 14–44.

—(2004), *Precarious Life: The Powers of Mourning and Violence*. London: Verso.

Carby, H. V. (1987), *Reconstructing Womanhood: The Emergence of the Afro-American Woman Novelist*. Oxford: Oxford University Press.

—(2000), 'White Women Listen! Black Feminism and the Boundaries of Sisterhood', in L. Back and J. Solomos (eds), *Theories of Race and Racism: A Reader*. London and New York: Routledge, pp. 389–403.

Castells, M. (1989), *The Informational City: Information Technology, Economic Restructuring and the Urban-Regional Process*. Oxford: Blackwell.

—(1996), *The Rise of the Network Society*. Oxford: Blackwell.

—(2000), *End of Millenium*. Malden, MA: Blackwell, 2nd edn.

Cecil, E. (1902), 'The Needs of Africa, II. Female Emigration', *The Nineteenth Century* April, 683.

Césaire, A. (1972), *Discourse on Colonialism*. Tr. Joan Pinkham. New York: Monthly Review Press, 1972.

Chae, Y. (2007), *Politicizing Asian American Literature: Towards a Critical Multiculturalism*. London: Routledge.

Chakrabarty, D. (1997), 'Postcoloniality and the Artifice of History: Who Speaks for "Indian" Pasts?', in Padmini Mongia (ed.) *Contemporary Postcolonial Theory: A Reader*. Delhi: Oxford University Press, pp. 223–48.

—(2000), *Provincializing Europe: Postcolonial Thought and Historical Difference*. Delhi: Oxford University Press.

Chandra, V. (2000), 'The Cult of Authenticity', *Boston Review*, February–March 2000. http://bostonreview.net/BR25.1/chandra.html. Accessed 2 September 2009.

Chatterjee, P. (1999a). *Nationalist Thought and the Colonial World: A Derivative Discourse*. 1986, in *The Partha Chatterjee Omnibus*. New Delhi: Oxford University Press.

—(1999b), *The Nation and Its Fragments: Colonial and Postcolonial Histories*. 1993. In *The Partha Chatterjee Omnibus*. New Delhi: Oxford University Press.

—(2001), 'The Nationalist Resolution of the Women's Question', in G. Castle (ed.) *Postcolonial Discourses: An Anthology*. 1990. Oxford: Blackwell, pp. 152–66.

Cheah, P. (2003), *Spectral Nationality: Passages of Freedom from Kant to Postcolonial Literatures of Liberation*. New York: Columbia University Press.

Chinchilla, N. S. (1997), 'Nationalism, Feminism, and Revolution in Central America', in L. A. West (ed.) *Feminist Nationalism*. London and New York: Routledge, pp. 201–19.

Cimino, R. (2005), '"No God in Common": American Evangelical Discourse on Islam after 9/11', *Review of Religious Research* 47, 2, 162–74.

Clarkson, W. (1850), *Missionary Encouragements in India: Or, The Christian Village in Gujarat*. London: John Snow, 9th edn.

Clatworthy, J. F. (1969) 'The Formation of British Colonial Education Policy, 1921–1961'. US Department of Health, Education and Welfare, Office of Education, Bureau of Research. http://www.eric.ed.gov/ERICDocs/data/ericdocs2sql/content_storage_01/0000019b/80/37/5d/de.pdf. Accessed 7 August 2009.

Clifford, J. (1999), *Routes: Travel and Translation in the Late Twentieth Century*. Cambridge, MA: Harvard University Press.

Cohen, R. (2001), *Global Diasporas: An Introduction*. London: Routledge.

Cohn, B. S. (1997), *Colonialism and Its Forms of Knowledge: The British in India*. 1996. New Delhi: Oxford University Press.

Collins, P. H. (1990), *Black Feminist Thought: Knowledge, Consciousness and the Politics of Empowerment*. Cambridge, MA: Unwin Hyman.

Cook, J. (1969), *The Journals of Captain James Cook on his Voyages of Discovery, II: The Voyage of the Resolution and Adventure, 1772–1775*, J. C. Beaglehole, (ed.) Hakluyt Society Extra Series XXXV. Cambridge: Cambridge University Press for the Hakluyt Society.

Cooper, F. (2007), 'Postcolonial Studies and the Study of History', in Ania Loomba, Suvir Kaul, Matti Bunzl, Antoinette Burton and Jed Esty (eds), *Postcolonial Studies and Beyond*. Durham and London: Duke University Press, pp. 401–22.

Cosgrove, D. E. (2001), *Apollo's Eye: A Cartographic Genealogy of the Earth in the Western Imagination*. Baltimore: Johns Hopkins University Press.

Crane, R. J. (2001), 'Out of the Center: Thoughts on the Post-colonial Literatures of Australia and New Zealand', in G. Castle (ed.) *Postcolonial Discourses: An Anthology*. 1990. Oxford: Blackwell, pp. 390–8.

Daly, M. W. (2007), *Darfur's Sorrow: A History of Destruction and Genocide*. Cambridge: Cambridge University Press.

Dangarembga, T. (1988), *Nervous Conditions*. London: The Women's Press.

Darian-Smith, K., Gunner, L. and S. Nuttall. (1996), *Text, Theory, Space: Land, Literature and History in South Africa and Australia*. London: Routledge.

Daruwalla, K. (1982), 'Mistress', *The Keeper of the Dead*. Delhi: Oxford University Press, pp. 22–3.

—(2002), 'The Map-maker', in *Collected Poems*. New Delhi: Penguin, pp. 334–6.

—(2006), *Collected Poems*. 2002. New Delhi: Penguin.

Das, K. (1996), 'An Introduction', in J. Thieme (ed.) *The Arnold Anthology of Post-colonial Literatures in English*. 1993. London: Arnold, p. 717.

—(1996), *My Story*. 1976. New Delhi: Sterling

Dattani, M. (2000), *On a Muggy Night in Bombay*, in *Collected Plays I*. 1998. New Delhi: Penguin.

Davidson, F. E. and Blackman, M. B. (1992), *During my Time*. Washington: University of Washington Press.

Davis, A. (1971), 'The Black Woman's Role in the Community of Slaves', *Black Scholar* 3, 4, 2–15.

Dawson, G. (1994), *Soldier Heroes: British Empire, Adventure and the Imaging of Masculinity*. London and New York: Routledge.

Dayan, J. (1995), 'Haiti, History and the Gods', in G. Prakash (ed.) *After Colonialism: Imperial Histories and Postcolonial Displacements*. Princeton, MJ: Princeton University Press, pp. 66–97.

De, S. (1999), 'There's Something about Vikram'. *The Sunday Observer*, 11 April, 6.

De Alba, A. G. (1999), *Sor Juana's Second Dream*. Albuquerque: University of New Mexico Press.

De Lillo, D. (2007), *Falling Man*. New York: Scribner.

De Mel, N. (2007), *Militarizing Sri Lanka: Popular Culture, Memory and Narrative in the Armed Conflict*. London: Sage.

De Mel, N. and Samarakkody, M. (eds), (2002), *Writing and Inheritance: Women's Writing in Sri Lanka, 1860–1948* Vol 1. Colombo: Women's Education and Research Centre.

Defoe, D. (2007), *Robinson Crusoe*. 1719. Oxford: Oxford University Press.

Dennis, H. M. (2007), *Native American Literature: Towards a Spatialized Reading*. London and New York: Routledge.

Derrida, J. (2001), *On Cosmopolitanism and Forgiveness*. Tr. Mark Dooley and Michael Hughes. London: Routledge.

Desai, A. (1982), *Fire on the Mountain*. 1977. New York: Penguin.

Desai, B. (2000), *Asylum, USA*. New Delhi: HarperCollins.

Desai, K. (2006), *The Inheritance of Loss*. New Delhi: Viking.

Deshpande, S. (1990), *The Dark Holds No Terrors*. 1980. New Delhi: Penguin.

Dharker, I. (1988), *Purdah*. Delhi: Oxford University Press.

Dharwadker, V. (2001), 'Cosmopolitanism in its Time and Place', in V. Dharwadker (ed.) *Cosmopolitan Geographies: New Locations in Literature and Culture*. London and New York: Routledge, pp. 1–13.

Diesel, A. (2002), 'Tales of Women's Suffering: Draupadi and other Amman Goddesses as Role Models for Women', *Journal of Contemporary Religion* 17, 1, 5–20.

Diof, M. (2003), 'Engaging Postcolonial Cultures: African Youth and Public Space', *African Studies Review*, 46, 2, 1–12.

Diop, C. A. (1970), 'The Contribution of Ethiopia-Nubia and of Egypt to Civilization', in E. Kedourie (ed.) *Nationalism in Asia and Africa.* New York: Meridian, 1970. 275–82.

Dirks, N. B. (2003), *Castes of Mind: Colonialism and the Making of Modern India.* New Delhi: Permanent Black.

—(2006), *The Scandal of Empire: India and the Creation of Imperial Britain.* New Delhi: Permanent Black.

Dirlik, A. (1997), 'The Postcolonial Aura: Third World Criticism in the Age of Global Capitalism', in Padmini Mongia (ed.) *Contemporary Postcolonial Theory: A Reader.* 1994. Delhi: Oxford University Press, pp. 294–320.

—(2002), 'Literature/Identity: Transnationalism, Narrative and Representation', *Review of Education, Pedagogy and Cultural Studies* 24, 209–34.

Dirom, A. (1793), *Narrative of the Campaign in India, which Terminated the War with Tippoo Sultan, in 1792.* London: W. Bulmer.

Djait, H. (1985), *Europe and Islam.* Tr. Peter Heinegg. Berkeley and London: University of California Press.

Djebar, A. (1992), *Women of Algiers in their Apartment.* Tr. Marjolijn de Jager. Charlottesville and London: University Press of Virginia.

Docker, J. (1999), 'The Neocolonial Assumption in University Teaching of English', in B. Ashcroft, G. Griffiths and H. Tiffin (eds), *The Post-colonial Studies Reader.* 1972. London and New York: Routledge, pp. 443–6.

Documents of the Chicano Struggle. New York: Pathfinder Press, 1971.

Downey, G. (2002), 'Virtual Webs, Physical Technologies, and Hidden Workers: The Spaces of Labor in Information Internetworks', *Technology and Culture* 42, 2, 209–35.

Duff, A. (1839), *India, and India Missions.* Edinburgh: J. Johnstone.

Durrani, T. (1991), *My Feudal Lord.* Lahore: n.p.

Eagleton, T. (1985), *Criticism and Ideology: A Study in Marxist Literary Theory.* 1975. London: Verso.

Edmond, R. (2006), *Leprosy and Empire: A Medical and Cultural History.* Cambridge: Cambridge University Press.

Edney, M. H. (1997), *Mapping an Empire: The Geographical Construction of British India, 1765–1843.* Chicago and London: Chicago University Press.

El Saadawi, N. (1980), *The Hidden Face of Eve: Women in the Arab World.* Tr. and ed. Sherif Hetata. London: Zed.

—(1983), *Woman at Point Zero.* Tr. Sherif Hetata. London: Zed.

—(1994), *The Innocence of the Devil.* Tr. Sherif Hetata. Berkeley: University of California Press.

Elwood, A. K. (1830), *Narrative of a Journey Overland from England, by the Continent of Europe, Egypt, and the Red Sea, to India; Including a Residence there, and Voyage Home, in the Years 1825, 26, 27, and 28.* London: Colburn and Bentley, 2 vols.

Ezekiel, N. (1989), *Collected Poems 1952–1988.* 1976. Delhi: Oxford University Press.

Fanon, F. (1963), *The Wretched of the Earth*. Tr. Constance Farrington. New York: Grove Press.

—(1967a), *Black Skin, White Masks*. Tr. Charles Lam Markmann. New York: Grove Press, 1967.

—(1967b), *Toward the African Revolution: Political Essays*. Tr. Haakon Chevalier. New York: Grove Press.

—(1967c), *Studies in a Dying Colonialism*. Tr. Haakon Chevalier. New York: Monthly Review Press.

Farah, N. (1999), *Maps*. New York: Arcade.

Forna, A. (2000), 'Mothers of Africa and the Diaspora: Shared Maternal Values among Black Women', in K. Owusu (ed.) *Black British Culture and Society: A Text Reader*. London and New York: Routledge, pp. 358–72.

Forster, G. (1798), *A Journey from Bengal to England through the Northern part of India, Kashmire, Afghanistan, and Persia, and into Russia, by the Caspian Sea*. London: R. Faulder, 2 vols.

Forster, J. R. (1778), *Observations Made during a Voyage Round the World*. London: G. Robinson.

Franklin, M. (ed.), (2000), *Representing India: Indian Culture and Imperial Control in Eighteenth-Century British Orientalist Discourse*. London and New York: Routledge, 9 vols.

Franklin, M. I. (2004), *Postcolonial Politics, the Internet and Everyday Life: Pacific Traversals Online*. London: Routledge.

Füredi, F. (1994), *Colonial Wars and the Politics of Third World Nationalism*. London: Tauris.

Gandhi, L. (1999), *Postcolonial Theory: A Critical Introduction*. Delhi: Oxford University Press.

—(2006), *Affective Communities: Anticolonial Thought and the Politics of Friendship*. Delhi: Permanent Black.

Gandhi, M. K. (1909), *Hind Swaraj*. 'The Condition of India', Online edition, http://www.mkgandhi.org/swarajya/coverpage.htm. Accessed 7 August 2009.

Ganguly, D. (1997), 'G. N. Devy: The Nativist as Postcolonial Critic', in M. Paranjape (ed.) *Nativism: Essays in Criticism*. New Delhi: Sahitya Akademi, pp. 129–52.

Garcia, A. M. (1997), 'The Development of Chicana Feminist Discourse', in L. A. West (ed.) *Feminist Nationalism*. London and New York: Routledge, pp. 247–68.

Gates, H. L. Jr. (1992), *Loose Canons: Notes on Culture Wars*. New York: Oxford University Press.

General Report on the Census of India, 1891. (1893), London: Her Majesty's Stationery Office.

Ghose, I. (1998), *Women Travellers in Colonial India: The Power of the Female Gaze*. Delhi: Oxford University Press.

Ghosh, A. (1988), *The Shadow Lines*. New Delhi: Ravi Dayal.

—(2002), 'The Imam and the Indian'. 1986, in *The Imam and the Indian: Prose Pieces*. Hyderabad: Orient Longman.

—(2004), *The Hungry Tide*. Delhi: Ravi Dayal.

Gibson, N. C. (2003), *Fanon: The Postcolonial Imagination*. Cambridge: Polity.

Gilroy, P. (1993), *The Black Atlantic: Modernity and Double Consciousness*. 1987. London: Verso.

—(2002), *There Ain't No Black in the Union Jack: The Cultural Politics of Race and Nation*. 1987. London and New York: Routledge.

Godimer, N. (1996), 'Six Feet of the Country', in J. Thieme (ed.) *The Arnold Anthology of Post-colonial Literatures in English*. 1993. London: Arnold, pp. 96–103.

Godono, E. (undated), 'Postcolonial Motherism: A Brand New Woman in the African Novel'. African Postcolonial Literature in English in the Postcolonial Web. http://www.thecore.nus.edu.sg/post/africa/godona1.html. Accessed 8 August 2009.

Goh, R. B. H. (2005), *Christianity in Southeast Asia*. Singapore: Institute of Southeast Asian Studies.

Gooneratne, Y. (1986), *Relative Merits: A Personal Memoir of the Bandaranaike Family of Sri Lanka*. London: C. Hurst.

—(1991), *A Change of Skies*. Sydney: Pan-Picador.

Gopinath, G. (1996), 'Funny Boys and Girls: Notes on a Queer South Asian Planet', in R. Leong (ed.) *Asian American Sexualities: Dimensions of the Gay and Lesbian Experience*. New York and London: Routledge, pp. 119–27.

—(2002), 'Local Sites/Global Contexts: The Transnational Trajectories of Deepa Mehta's *Fire*', in A. Cruz-Malavé and M. F. Manalansan IV (eds), *Queer Globalizations: Citizenship and the Afterlife of Colonialism*. New York and London: New York University Press, pp. 149–61.

Graham, J. (2009), *Land and Nationalism in Fictions from Southern Africa*. London and New York: Routledge.

Graham, M. (2000), *Journal of a Residence in India*. 1812. New Delhi: Asian Educational Services.

Grant, C. (1999), Part of Chapter IV of Charles Grant's *Observations on the State of Society among the Asiatic Subjects of Great Britain*, in L. Zastoupil and M. Moir (eds), *The Great Indian Education Debate: Documents Relating to the Orientalist-Anglicist Controversy, 1781–1843*. Richmond: Surrey: Curzon, pp. 81–9.

Green, M. (1980). *Dreams of Adventure, Deeds of Empire*. London: Routledge.

Greenblatt, S. (1991), *Marvelous Possessions: The Wonder of the New World*. Chicago: University of Chicago Press.

Gregg, H. (1897), 'The Indian Mutiny in Fiction', *Blackwood's Magazine* 161, 218–31.

Groover, K. (1999), *The Wilderness Within: American Women Writers and Spiritual Quest*. Fayetteville: University of Arkansas Press, 1999.

Guerrero, M. A. J. (2003), ' "Patriarchal Colonialism" and Indigenism: Implications for Native Feminist Spirituality and Native Womanism', *Hypatia* 18, 2, 58–69.

Guha, R[amachandra]. and Martinez-Alier, J. (1998), *Varieties of Environmentalism: Essays North and South*. Delhi: Oxford University Press.

Guha, R. (1982a), 'Preface', in R. Guha (ed.) *Subaltern Studies I: Writings on South Asian History and Society.* New Delhi: Oxford University Press, pp. 7–8.

—(1982b), 'Some Aspects of the Historiography of Colonial India' in R. Guha (ed.) *Subaltern Studies I: Writings on South Asian History and Society.* New Delhi: Oxford University Press, pp. 1–8.

—(1987), 'Chandra's Death', in R. Guha (ed.) *Subaltern Studies I: Writings on South Asian History and Society.* New Delhi: Oxford University Press, pp. 135–65.

Gupta, D. (2000), *Culture, Space and the Nation-state: From Sentiment to Structure.* New Delhi: Sage.

Habermas, J. (2001), *The Postnational Constellation: Political Essays.* Tr. and Ed. Max Pinsky. Cambridge: Polity.

Haggard, H. R. (2005), *King Solomon's Mines.* 1885. http://DigiReads.com. Accessed 7 August 2009.

—(undated), *She.* 1886–1887. http://www.gutenberg.org/etext/3155. Accessed 7 August 2009.

Halhed, N. Tr. and Ed., (1776), *A Code of Gentoo Laws.* London: n.p.

Hall, C. (2002), *Civilising Subjects: Colony and Metropole in the English Imagination, 1830–1867.* Chicago and London: University of Chicago Press.

Hardt, M. and Negri, A. (2000), *Empire.* Cambridge, MA: Harvard University Press.

Harris, W. (1988), *The Palace of the Peacock.* 1960. London: Faber and Faber.

—(1990), 'The Fabric of the Imagination', *Third World Quarterly* 12, 1, 175–86.

—(1999), 'The Limbo Gateway', in B. Ashcroft, G. Griffiths and H. Tiffin (eds), *The Post-colonial Studies Reader.* 1981. London and New York: Routledge, pp. 378–82.

Harrison, M. (1999), *Climate and Constitutions: Health, Race, Environment, and British Imperialism in India, 1600–1850.* Delhi: Oxford University Press.

Harty, S. and Murphy, M. (2005), *In Defence of Multinational Citizenship.* Vancouver: University of British Columbia Press.

Head, D. (2008), *The State of the Novel: Britain and Beyond.* Malden, MA and Oxford: Wiley-Blackwell.

Helie-Lucas, M.-A. (1993), 'Women's Struggles and Strategies in the Rise of Fundamentalism in the Muslim World: From Entryism to Internationalism', in H. Afshar (ed.) *Women in the Middle East: Perceptions, Realities and Struggles for Liberation.* New York: St. Martin's Press, pp. 206–41.

Hesse, B. (2000), 'Introduction: Un/settled Multiculturalisms', in B. Hesse (ed.) *Un/settled Multiculturalisms: Diasporas, Entanglements, Transruptions.* London and New York: Zed, pp. 1–30.

hooks, b. (1981), *Ain't I a Woman: Black Women and Feminism.* Boston, MA: South End Press.

Hooper-Greenhill, E. (1992), *Museums and the Shaping of Knowledge.* London and New York: Routledge.

Hope, A. D. 'Australia', in J. Thieme (ed.) (1996), *The Arnold Anthology of Post-colonial Literatures in English*. 1993. London: Arnold, pp. 193–4.

Horn, D. B. and Ransome, M. (eds), (1957), *English Historical Documents, 1714–1783*. London: Eyre and Spottiswoode.

Hosain, A. (1988), *Sunlight on a Broken Column*. 1961. New York: Penguin-Virago.

House of Commons. (1782), *Fourth Report from the Committee of Secrecy, Appointed to Enquire into the State of the East India Company*, Sheila Lambert, (ed.) *House of Commons Sessional Papers of the Eighteenth Century. Vol. 143. George III. Secret Committee Reports 4 and 5. 1782*, Delaware: Scholarly Resources, 1975.

Huggan, G. (1989), 'Decolonising the Map: Post-colonialism, Post-Structuralism and the Cartographic Connection', *Ariel* 20, 4, 115–31.

—(2001), *The Postcolonial Exotic: Marketing the Margins*. London and New York: Routledge.

Huggins, J. (1998), *Sister Girl: The Writings of Aboriginal Activist and Historian Jackie Huggins*. St. Lucia, Queensland: University of Queensland Press.

Huggins, J., Huggins, R. and Jacobs, J. M. (1995), 'Kooramindanjie: Place and the Postcolonial', *History Workshop Journal* 39, 164–81.

Hyam. R. (1990), *Empire and Sexuality: The British Experience*. Manchester and New York: Manchester University Press.

Ignatieff, M. (2001), *Human Rights as Politics and Idolatory*. Princeton, NJ: Princeton University Press.

Innes, C. L. (1992), 'Motherhood as a Metaphor for Creativity in Three African Women's Novels: Flora Nwapa, Rebeka Njau and Bessie Head', in S. Nasta (ed.) *Motherlands: Black Women's Writing from Africa, the Caribbean and South Asia*. New Brunswick, New Jersey: Rutgers University Press, pp. 200–18.

—(1996), ' "Forging the Conscience of Their Race": Nationalist Writers', in B. King (ed.) *New National and Postcolonial Literatures: An Introduction*. Oxford: Clarendon, pp. 120–39.

Iyer, P. (2000), *The Global Soul: Jet Lag, Shopping Malls and the Search for Home*. London: Bloomsbury.

Jackson, F. L. (1999), 'African-American Responses to the Human Genome Project', *Public Understanding of Science* 8, 3, 181–91.

—(2001), 'The Human Genome Project and the African American Community: Race, Diversity, and American Science', in R. A. Zilinskas and P. J. Balint (eds), *The Human Genome Project and Minority Communities: Ethical, Social, and Political Dilemmas*. Westport, CT: Praeger, pp. 35–52.

Jacobs, J. M. (1996), *Edge of Empire: Postcolonialism and the City*. London and New York: Routledge.

JanMohammed, A. R. and Lloyd, D. (1987), 'Introduction: Minority Discourse: What is to Be Done?' *Cultural Critique* 7, 5–17.

—(ed.), (1990), *The Nature and Context of Minority Discourse*. New York: Oxford University Press.

Janu, C. K. (2004), *Mother Forest: The Unfinished Story of CK Janu*. Written by Bhaskaran. Tr. N. Ravi Shanker. New Delhi: Kali for Women.

Jayawardene, K. (1986), *Feminism and Nationalism in the Third World*. London: Zed.

Jayawardene, K. (1995), *The White Woman's Other Burden: Western Women and South Asia during British Colonial Rule*. New York: Routledge.

Johansen, E. (2008), 'Imagining the Global and the Rural: Rural Cosmopolitanism in Sharon Butala's *The Garden of Eden* and Amitav Ghosh's *The Hungry Tide*'. *Postcolonial Text*, 4, 3. http://journals.sfu.ca/ pocol/index.php/pct/article/view/821/631. Accessed 7 August 2009.

Jones, W. (1807), *The Works of Sir William Jones. With a Life of the Author, by Lord Teignmouth [John Shore]*. London: John Stockdale, 13 vols.

Joshi, P. (2002), *In Another Country: Colonialism, Culture and the English Novel in India*. New Delhi: Oxford University Press.

Joshi, S. (1991), 'Rethinking English: An Introduction', in Svati Joshi (ed.) *Rethinking English: Essays in Literature, Language, History*. New Delhi: Trianka, pp. 1–31.

Journal of the House of Commons 48 (1793). New edn 1803.

Kalra, V. S, Kaur, R. and Hutnyk, J. (2005), *Diaspora and Hybridity*. London: Sage.

Kamble, B. (2008), *The Prisons We Broke*. Tr. Maya Pandit. Hyderabad: Orient Longman.

Kapur, M. (1998), *Difficult Daughters*. New Delhi: Penguin.

Katrak, K. (1992), 'Indian Nationalism, Gandhian "Satyagraha", and the Engendering of National Narratives', in A. Parker, M. Russo, D. Sommer, P. Yaeger (eds), *Nationalisms and Sexualities*. New York and London: Routledge.

—(2006), *Politics of the Female Body: Postcolonial Women Writers of the Third World*. New Jersey: Rutgers University Press.

Kedourie, E. (ed.), (1970), *Nationalism in Asia and Africa*. New York: Meridian.

Keneally, T. (1973), *The Chant of Jimmie Blacksmith*. Victoria: Penguin.

Kerr, I. J. (1995), *Building the Railways of the Raj, 1850–1900*. Delhi: Oxford University Press.

Khayyat, N. (1998), 'Had I Been Male', in A. Bagader, A. M. Heinrichsdorff and D. S. Akers (eds), *Voices of Change: Short Stories by Saudi Arabian Women Writers*. London: Lynne Reiner, pp. 19–22.

Kiberd, D. (2001), 'Inventing Ireland', in G. Castle (ed.) *Postcolonial Discourses: An Anthology*. 1996. Oxford: Blackwell, pp. 459–83.

Kindersley, J. (1777), *Letters from the Island of Teneriffe, Brazil, the Cape of Good Hope, and the East Indies*. London: J. Nource.

King, K. (2001), 'Global Gay Formations and Local Homosexualities', in G. Castle (ed.) *Postcolonial Discourses: An Anthology*. 1990. Oxford: Blackwell, pp. 508–19.

King, T. (1996), 'The One about Coyote Going West', in J. Thieme (ed.) *The Arnold Anthology of Post-Colonial Literatures in English*. 1993. London: Arnold, pp. 420–8.

Kolko, B., Nakamura, L. and Rodman, G. B. (eds), (2000), *Race in Cyberspace*. London and New York: Routledge.

Kopf, D. (1969), *British Orientalism and the Bengal Renaissance: The Dynamics of Indian Modernization, 1773–1835*. Berkeley: University of California Press.

Koshy, S. (2008), 'Postcolonial Studies after 9/11: A Response to Ali Behdad', *American Literary History* 20, 1–2.

Kumar, A. (2001), 'A Bang and a Whimper: A Conversation with Hanif Kureishi'. *Transition* 10, 4, 114–31.

Kumar, A[nil]. (1998), *Medicine and the Raj: British Medical Policy in India, 1835–1911*. New Delhi: Sage.

Kumar, D. (1997), *Science and the Raj 1857–1905*. 1995. Delhi: Oxford University Press.

Kumar, S. (1997), 'Nation Versus Nativism', in M. Paranjape (ed.) *Nativism: Essays in Criticism*. New Delhi: Sahitya Akademi, pp. 113–29.

Kureishi, H. (1986), *My Beautiful Laundrette*. London: Faber.

—(1990), *The Buddha of Suburbia*. New York: Viking.

—(2001), 'In Charge of His Own Definitions'. Conversation with Sandip Roy. *Trikone* 16, 3, 6.

Kurian, A. (2008), 'Going Places: Popular Tourism Writing in India', in M. Gokulsing and W. Dissanayake (eds), *Popular Culture in Globalized India*. London and New York: Routledge, pp. 252–63.

Lal, V. (2003), 'North American Hindus, the Sense of History, and the Politics of Internet Diasporism', in R. C. Lee and S.-L. C. Wong (eds), *Asian America.Net: Ethnicity, Nationalism, and Cyberspace*. Routledge, New York and London: Routledge, pp. 98–138.

Lakshmi, C. S. (1999), 'Bodies called Women: Some Thoughts on Gender, Ethnicity and Nation', in T. Selvy (ed.), *Women, Narration and Nation: Collective Images and Multiple Identities*. New Delhi: Vikas, pp. 53–88.

Lamming, G. (1979), *In the Castle of My Skin*. 1953. London: Longman.

Lau, L. (2009), 'Re-Orientalism: The Perpetration and Development of Orientalism by Orientals', *Modern Asian Studies* 43, 571–90.

Lazarus, N. (1990), *Resistance in Postcolonial African Fiction*. New Haven: Yale University Press.

—(1994), 'National Consciousness and the Specificity of (Post)colonial Intellectualism', in F. Barker, P. Hulme and M. Iversen (eds), *Colonial Discourse/Postcolonial Theory*. Manchester: Manchester University Press, pp. 197–220.

Lazreg, M. (1994), *The Eloquence of Silence: Algerian Women in Question*. New York: Routledge.

Leask, N.(1993), *British Romantic Writers and the East: Anxieties of Empire*. Cambridge: Cambridge University Press.

—(2002), *Curiosity and the Aesthetics of Travel Writing, 1770–1840: 'From An Antique Land'*. New York: Oxford University Press.

Leonard, D. J. (2005), 'To the White Extreme: Conquering Athletic Space, White Manhood, and Racing Virtual Reality', in N. Garrelts (ed.) *Digital Gameplaying*. Jefferson: McFarland, pp. 110–19.

Levine, P. (1987), *Victorian Feminism, 1850–1900*. London: Hutchinson.

Lévy, P. (2001), *Cyberculture*. Tr. Roberto Bononno. Minneapolis and London: University of Minnesota Press.

Ley, D. 'Behavioural Geography and the Philosophies of Meaning', in K. R. Cox and R. G. Golledge (eds), *Behavioural Problems in Geography Revisited*. London: Methuen, 1989, pp. 209–30.

Lloyd, D. (1994), 'Ethnic Cultures, Minority Discourse and the State', in F. Barker, P. Hulme and M. Iversen (eds), *Colonial Discourse/Postcolonial Theory*. Manchester: Manchester University Press, pp. 221–38.

Lockwood, D. (1978), *I, the Aboriginal*. 1962. Adelaide: Rigby.

Lokugé, C. (2000), ' "We Must Laugh at One Another, or Die" ': Yasmine Gooneratne's *A Change of Skies* and South Asian Migrant Identities', in R. J. Crane and R. Mohanram (eds), *Shifting Continents/Colliding Cultures: Diaspora Writing of the Indian Subcontinent*. Amsterdam: Rodopi, pp. 17–34.

Loomba, A. (1998), *Colonialism/Postcolonialism*. London: Routledge.

Lorimer, D. (1972), *Colour, Class and the Victorians: English Attitudes to the Negro in the Mid-Nineteenth Century*. Leicester: Leicester University Press.

Lowe, L. (1991), 'Heterogeneity, Hybridity, Multiplicity: Marking Asian American Differences', *Diaspora* 1, 1, 24–44.

Luke, T. (1999), 'Simulated Sovereignty, Telematic Territory: The Political Economy of Cyberspace', in M. Featherstone and S. Lash (eds.) *Spaces of Culture: City, Nation, World*. London: Sage, pp. 27–48.

MacKenzie, J. M. (1988), *The Empire of Nature: Hunting, Conservation and British Imperialism*. Manchester: Manchester University Press.

—(ed.), (1989), *Imperialism and Popular Culture*. Manchester: Manchester University Press.

Manalansan IV, M. F. (1993), '(Re)Locating the Gay Filipino: Resistance, Postcolonialism, and Identity', *Journal of Homosexuality* 26, 2–3, 53–72.

Mangaliso, Z. (1997), 'Gender and Nation-Building in South Africa', in L. A. West (ed.) *Feminist Nationalism*. London and New York: Routledge, pp. 130–44.

Mani, L. (1998), *Contentious Traditions: The Debate on Sati in Colonial India*. Delhi: Oxford University Press.

Mannoni, O. (1956), *Prospero and Caliban: The Psychology of Colonization*. Tr. Pamela Powesland. London: Methuen.

Marshall, P. J. (ed.), (1970), *British Discovery of Hinduism in the Eighteenth Century*. Cambridge: Cambridge University Press.

McClintock, A. (1995), *Imperial Leather: Race, Gender, and Sexuality in the Colonial Contest*. London and New York: Routledge.

McCully, B. T. (1940), *English Education and the Origins of Indian Nationalism*. New York: Columbia University Press.

Memorandum of the Census of India 1871–1872. (1875), London: George Edward Eyre and William Spottiswoode.

Menon, N. (2007), 'Between the Burqa and the Beauty Parlor? Globalization, Cultural Nationalism, and Feminist Politics', in A. Loomba, S. Kaul, M. Bunzl, A. Burton and J. Esty (eds), *Postcolonial Studies and Beyond*. New Delhi: Permanent Black, pp. 206–25.

Metcalf, T. R. (1989), *An Imperial Vision: Indian Architecture and Britain's Raj*. Berkeley: University of California Press.

Mignolo, W. D. (2003), *The Darker Side of the Renaissance: Literacy, Territoriality, and Colonization*. 1995. Michigan: University of Michigan Press.

Mill, J. (1978), *History of British India*. 1817. New Delhi: Associated Publishing, 2 vols.

Miller, T. (2001), 'Introducing . . . Cultural Citizenship'. *Social Text* 19, 4, 1–5.

Minhas, S. (2007), *Tunnel Vision*. Delhi: IndiaInk.

Mishra, V. (1989), 'The Texts of Mother India', *Kunapipi* 11, 1, 119–37.

Mistry, R. (1991), *Such a Long Journey*. New York: Knopf.

—(1996), *A Fine Balance*. London: Faber and Faber.

—(1996) 'Squatter', in J. Thieme (ed.) *The Arnold Anthology of Post-colonial Literatures in English*. 1987. London: Arnold, pp. 907–25.

Mitchell, J. M. (1889), 'Prefatory Note', in B. Padmanji, *Once Hindu, Now Christian: The Early Life of Baba Padmanji, An Autobiography*, (ed.), J. Murray Mitchell. New York: Fleming B. Revell, pp. 5–10.

Mitchell, T. L. (1839), *Three Expeditions into the Interior of Eastern Australia*. London: T. and W. Boone, 2nd edn, 2 vols.

Mitter, P. (1977), *Much Maligned Monsters: History of European Reactions to Indian Art*. Oxford: Clarendon.

Moghadam, V. M. (1997), 'Nationalist Agendas and Women's Rights: Conflicts in Afghanistan in the Twentieth Century', in L. A. West (ed.) *Feminist Nationalism*. London and New York: Routledge, pp. 75–100.

Mohanty, C., Talpade, A. R. and Lourdes, T. (eds), (1991), *Third World Women and the Politics of Feminism*. Bloomington: Indiana University Press.

Mohanty, C. T. (2003), 'Under Western Eyes: Feminist Scholarship and Colonial Discourses', in C. T Mohanty, *Feminism Without Borders: Decolonizing Theory, Practicing Solidarity*. 1984. New Delhi: Zubaan, pp. 17–42.

Mojab, S. (2001), 'Theorizing the Politics of "Islamic Feminism"'. *Feminist Review*, 69, 124–46.

Monhas, S. (2007), *Tunnel Vision*. New Delhi: IndiaInk.

Moorcroft, W. and Trebeck, G. (1841), *Travels in the Himalayan Provinces of Hindustan and the Panjab; in Ladakh and Kashmir; in Peshawar, Kabul, Kunduz and Bokhara, from 1819 to 1825*, H. H. Wilson (ed.) London: John Murray, 2 vols.

Moraga, C. (1997), *Waiting in the Wings: Portrait of a Queer Motherhood*. Ithaca: Firebrand.

—(2001), *The Hungry Woman* [including *The Hungry Woman: A Mexican Medea* and *Heart of the Earth: A Popul Vuh Story*]. Albuquerque: West End Press.

Morgan, S. (1987), *My Place*. Freemantle, W. A.: Freemantle Arts Centre Press.

Mukherjee, A. (2009), *This Gift of English: English Education and the Formation of Alternative Hegemonies in India*. Hyderabad: Orient BlackSwan.

Mukherjee, B. (1971), *The Tiger's Daughter*. New York: Fawcett.

—(1985), 'Introduction', in *Darkness*. New York: Penguin, pp. 13–16.

—(1989), *Jasmine*. New York: Fawcett Crest.

Mukherjee, M. (2000), 'The Anxiety of Indianness', in *The Perishable Empire: Essays on Indian Writing in English*. New Delhi: Oxford University Press, pp. 166–85.

Mukherjee, S. N. (1987), *Sir William Jones: A Study in Eighteenth-century British Attitudes to India*. Hyderabad: Orient Longman.

Mukhopadhyay, A. (2006), *Behind the Mask: The Cultural Definition of the Legal Subject in Colonial Bengal, 1715–1911*. Delhi: Oxford University Press.

Murray, L. A. (1992), 'Cumulus', in *The Daylight Moon: Poems*. Australia: Angus and Robertson, p. 4.

—(1992), 'Physiognomy on the Savage Manning River', in *The Daylight Moon: Poems*. Australia: Angus and Robertson, pp. 9–12.

Nafisi, A. (2003), *Reading Lolita in Tehran*. New York: Random House.

Nagel, J. (2005), 'Masculinity and Nationalism – Gender and Sexuality in the Making of Nations', in P. Spencer and H. Wollman (eds), *Nations and Nationalism: A Reader*. 1998. Edinburgh: Edinburgh University Press, pp. 110–30.

Naipaul, V. S. (1961), *A House for Mr Biswas*. New York: McGraw-Hill.

—(1967), *The Mimic Men*. London: Andre Deutsch.

—(1969), *The Middle Passage*. 1962. Harmondsworth: Penguin.

—(1987), *The Enigma of Arrival*. Harmondsworth: Penguin.

Nakamura, L. (2002), *Cybertypes: Race, Ethnicity, and Identity on the Internet*. London and New York: Routledge.

Nambisan, K. (2005), *The Hills of Angheri*. New Delhi: Penguin.

Namjoshi, S. (1989), *The Mothers of Maya Diip*. London: The Women's Press.

—(1996), *Building Babel*. Melbourne: Spinifex.

Nandy, A. (1983), *The Intimate Enemy: Loss and Recovery of Self under Colonialism*. Delhi: Oxford University Press.

—(1998), 'A New Cosmopolitanism: Toward a Dialogue of Asian Civilizations', in K-H Chen (ed.) *Trajectories: Inter-Asia Cultural Studies*. London and New York: Routledge, pp. 142–9.

—(2004), 'Towards a Third World Utopia', in *Bonfire of Creeds: The Essential Ashis Nandy*. 1987. Delhi: Oxford University Press, pp. 440–69.

Narayan, R. K. (1998), *The Dark Room*. 1938. Mysore: Indian Thought.

Nasta, S. (1992), 'Introduction', in S. Nasta (ed.) *Motherlands: Black Women's Writing from Africa, the Caribbean and South Asia*. New Brunswick: Rutgers University Press, pp. 13–30.

Nayar, P. K. (2002), 'The Imperial Sublime: English Travel Writing and India, 1750–1820', *Journal for Early Modern Cultural Studies* 2, 2, 57–99.

—(2006), 'The Rhetoric of Biocolonialism: Genomic Projects, Culture and the New Racisms', *Journal of Contemporary Thought* 24, 131–48.

—(2007a), 'The Digital Glocalized'. *Writing Technologies*. 1 (1) http://www.ntu.ac.uk/writing_technologies/Currentjournal/Nayar/index.html. Accessed 7 August 2009.

—(2007b), *The Great Uprising: India, 1857*. New Delhi: Penguin.

—(2007c), 'The Place of the Other: Arundhati Roy's *The God of Small Things*', *The Sri Lanka Journal of the Humanities* 33, 1–2, 15–28.

—(2008a), *Postcolonial Literature: An Introduction*. New Delhi: Pearson.

—(2008b), *English Writing and India, 1600–1920: Colonizing Aesthetics*. London and New York: Routledge.

—(2008c), 'Affective Cosmopolitanisms: Ashis Nandy's Utopia'. *E-Social Sciences Working Papers*. http://www.esocialsciences.com/articles/display-Articles.asp?Article_ID=1732. Accessed 7 August 2009.

—(2009), 'Human Rights and Testimonial Fiction: Alicia Partnoy and the Case of Argentina's Disappeared', *ICFAI University Journal of Commonwealth Literature* 1, 1, 61–78.

—(2010a), *Contemporary Literary and Cultural Theory: From Structuralism to Ecocriticism*. New Delhi: Pearson-Longman.

—(2010b), *An Introduction to New Media and Cybercultures*. Malden, MA and Oxford: Wiley-Blackwell.

—(forthcoming), 'The Postcolonial Parasite: The Transnational Indian Novel in English' in G. Pultar (ed.) *De/Construction of Ethnicity and Nationhood in the Age of Globalization*.

—(forthcoming), 'The Postcolonial Uncanny: The Politics of Dispossession in Amitav Ghosh's *The Hungry Tide*', *College Literature*.

Ngugi Wa Thiong' O. (1967), *A Grain of Wheat*. London: Heinemann.

—(1986), *Decolonising the Mind: The Politics of Language in African Literature*. London: J. Currey, Heinemann.

—(1999), 'On the Abolition of the English Department', in B. Ashcroft, G. Griffiths and H. Tiffin (eds), *The Post-colonial Studies Reader*. 1972. London and New York: Routledge, pp. 438–42.

Nichols, G. (1996), 'One Continent/To Another', in J. Thieme (ed.) *The Arnold Anthology of Post-colonial Literatures in English*. 1993. London: Arnold, pp. 582–3.

Nira, Y. –D. and Floya, A. (eds), (1989), *Woman-Nation-State*. New York: St. Martin' Press.

Nixon, R. (2007), 'Environmentalism and Postcolonialism', in A. Loomba, S. Kaul, M. Bunzl, A. Burton and J. Esty (eds), *Postcolonial Studies and Beyond*. New Delhi: Permanent Black, pp. 233–51.

Nnaemeka, O. (1998), 'This Women's Studies Business: Beyond Politics and History (Thoughts on the First WAAD Conference)', in N. Obioma (ed.), *Sisterhood, Feminism and Power: From Africa to the Diaspora*. Trenton, NJ and Asmara, Eritrea: Africa World Press, pp. 351–86.

Ondaatje, M. (1982), *Running in the Family*. New York: WW. Norton.

One Long Resident in India. (1877), 'Christianity in India', *Fraser's Magazine* 16, 73, 312.

Ong, A. (2003), *Buddha in Hiding: Refugees, Citizenship, and the New America*. Berkeley and London: University of California Press.

Orme, R. (1974), *Historical Fragments of the Mogul Empire, of the Morattoes and of the English. Concerns in Indostan from the year MDCLIX*, J. P. Guha (ed.) 1782. New Delhi: Associated.

Oyewùmí, O. (2000), 'Family Bonds/Conceptual Binds: African Notes on Feminist Epistemologies', *Signs* 25, 4, 1093–8.

Padmanji, B. (1889), *Once Hindu, Now Christian: The Early Life of Baba Padmanji, An Autobiography*. J. Murray Mitchell (ed.) New York: Fleming B. Revell.

Pandey, G. (1992), *The Construction of Communalism in Colonial North India*. New Delhi: Oxford University Press.

—(1999), 'Can a Muslim be an Indian?' *Comparative Studies in Society and History* 41, 4, 608–29.

Pannikar, K. M. (1974), *Asia and Western Dominance*. 1953. London: George Allen & Unwin.

Paranjape, M. (1995), 'Tradition, Modernity and Post-Modernity/Region, Nation and Inter-nation: Challenges in Theory', *LittCrit* 5, 4, 5–22.

—(1997a), 'Preface', in M. Paranjape (ed.), *Nativism: Essays in Criticism*. New Delhi: Sahitya Akademi, pp. 9–16.

—(1997b), 'Beyond Nativism: Towards a Contemporary Indian Tradition in Criticism', in M. Paranjape (ed.) *Nativism: Essays in Criticism*. New Delhi: Sahitya Akademi, pp. 153–76.

Parekh, B. C. (1999), *Colonialism, Tradition and Reform: An Analysis of Gandhi's Political Discourse*. New Delhi: Sage. (Rev. ed.)

Park, M. (1799), *Travels in the Interior Districts of Africa . . . in the Years 1795, 1796, and 1797*. London: W. Bulmer.

Parkes, F. (1850), *Wanderings of a Pilgrim in Search of the Picturesque*. London: P. Richardson, 2 vols.

Partnoy, A. (1998), *The Little School: Tales of Disappearance and Survival* Tr. Alicia Partnoy with Lois Althey and Sandra Braunstein. San Francisco: Cleis Press.

Petersen, K. H. (1999), 'First Things First: Problems of a Feminist Approach to African Literature', in B. Ashcroft, G. Griffiths and H. Tiffin (eds), *The Post-colonial Studies Reader*. 1984. London and New York: Routledge, pp. 251–4.

Peterson, K. H and Rutherford, A. (eds), (1986), *A Double Colonization: Colonial and Post-Colonial Women's Writing*. Mundelstrup, Denmark: Dangaroo.

Pettitt, G. (1851), *The Tinnevelly Mission: Of the Church Missionary Society*. London: Seeleys.

Phillips, R. (1997), *Mapping Men and Empire: A Geography of Adventure*. London and New York: Routledge.

Pollock, S., Bhabha, H. K., Breckenridge, C. A. and Chakrabarty, D. (2000), 'Cosmopolitanisms', *Public Culture* 12, 3, 577–89.

Prato, P. and G. Trivero. (1985), 'The Spectacle of Travel'. Tr. Iain Chambers. *Australian Journal of Cultural Studies* 3, 2, 26–43.

Pratt, M. L. (1992), *Imperial Eyes: Travel Writing and Transculturation*. London and New York: Routledge.

Puri, J. (2004), *Encountering Nationalism*. Oxford: Blackwell.

Rabasa, J. (1999), 'Allegories of Atlas', in B. Ashcroft, G. Griffiths and H. Tiffin (eds), *The Post-colonial Studies Reader*. 1993. London and New York: Routledge, pp. 358–64.

Raghuramaraju, A. (2009), 'Internal Criticism in the Democracies Outside West', *Alternatives* 34, 339–58.

Rao, R. (1963), *Kanthapura*. New York: New Directions.
—(1996), *The Meaning of India*. 1972. New Delhi: Vision Books.
Ray, S. (2000), *En-gendering India: Woman and Nation in Colonial and Postcolonial Narratives*. Durham and London: Duke University Press.
—(2005), 'Popular Perceptions of Postcolonial Studies after 9/11', in H. Schwarz and S. Ray (eds), *A Companion to Postcolonial Studies*. 2000. Malden, MA: Blackwell, pp. 574–83.
Raymond, J. G. (1994), *The Transsexual Empire: The Making of the She-Male*. 1979. Boston: Beacon.
Rechy, J. (1984), *City of Night*. 1963. New York: Grove Press.
Reddy, G. (2006), *With Respect to Sex: Negotiating Hijra Identity in South India*. New Delhi: Yoda.
Rennell, J. (1788), *Memoir of a Map of Hindoostan*. London: M. Brown.
Rheingold, H. (1994), *The Virtual Community: Finding Connection in a Computerised World*. 1992. London: Secker and Warburg.
Rhys, J. (1982), *Wide Sargasso Sea*. 1966. New York: Norton.
Robertson, R. (1995), 'Glocalization: Time-Space and Homogeneity-Heterogeneity', in M. Featherstone, S. Lash. and R. Robertson (eds.), *Global Modernities*. London: Sage, pp. 25–44.
Romanowski, M. H. (2009), 'What You Don't Know Can Hurt You: Textbook Omissions and 9/11', *The Clearing House* 82, 6, 290–6.
Rothstein, E. (2001), 'Attacks on U. S. Challenge the Perspectives of Postmodern True Believers', *New York Times* 22 September 2001. http://www.nytimes.com/2001/09/22/arts/connections-attacks-us-challenge-perspectives-postmodern-true-believers.html?pagewanted=2. Accessed 4 November 2009.
Roy, A. (1997), *The God of Small Things*. New Delhi: IndiaInk.
—(2001), *The Algebra of Infinite Justice*. New Delhi: Viking.
Rushdie, S. (1982), *Midnight's Children*. London: Jonathan Cape.
—(1991), 'Imaginary Homelands', in *Imaginary Homelands: Essays and Criticism, 1981–1991*. London: Granta. pp. 9–21.
—(1996), *The Moor's Last Sigh*. London: Vintage
—(2001), *Fury*. London: Jonathan Cape.
—(2002), 'Notes on Writing and the Nation', *Step Across this Line: Collected Non-Fiction, 1992–2002*. London: Vintage, 58–61.
—(2005), *Shalimar the Clown*. London: Jonathan Cape.
Ryan, S. (1994), 'Inscribing the Emptiness: Cartography, Exploration and the Construction of Australia', in C. Tiffin and A. Lawson (ed.) *De-scribing Empire: Post-colonialism and Textuality*. London and New York: Routledge, pp. 115–30.
Safran, W. (2008), 'The Diaspora and the Homeland: Reciprocities, Transformations, and Role Reversals', in E. Ben-Rafael and Y. Sternberg, with J. B. Liwerant and Y. Gorny (eds), *Transnationalism: Diasporas and the Advent of a New (Dis)Order*. Leiden: Brill, pp. 75–99.
Sahgal, N. (1987), *Rich Like Us*. London: Spectre.
—(1988), *A Situation in New Delhi*. 1977. New Delhi: Penguin.
—(1992), 'The Schizophrenic Imagination', in A. Rutherford (ed.) *From Commonwealth to Postcolonial*. New South Wales: Dangaroo, pp. 30–6.

Said, E. (1994a), *Orientalism*. 1978. New York: Vintage.
—(1994b), *Culture and Imperialism*. 1993. London: Vintage.
Saigol, R. (1999), 'Homemakers and Homebreakers: The Binary Construction of Women in Muslim Nationalism', in S. Thiruchandran (ed.) *Women, Narration and Nation: Collective Images and Multiple Identities*. New Delhi: Vikas, pp. 89–135.
Salaita, S. (2005), 'Ethnic Identity and Imperative Patriotism: Arab Americans Before and After 9/11', *College Literature* 32, 2, 146–68.
Sandoval, C. (1991), 'US Third World Feminism: The Theory and Method of Oppositional Consciousness in the Postmodern World', *Genders* 10, 1–24.
Sangari, K. (1991), 'Relating Histories: Definitions of Literacy, Literature, Gender in Nineteenth Century Calcutta and England', in S. Joshi (ed.) *Rethinking English: Essays in Literature, Language, History*. New Delhi: Trianka, pp. 32–123.
Saro-Wiwa, K. (1995), *A Month and a Day: A Detention Diary*. Harmondsworth: Penguin.
Satchidanandan, K. (1997), 'Defining the Premises: Nativism and its Ambivalences', in Makarand Paranjape (ed.) *Nativism: Essays in Criticism*. New Delhi: Sahitya Akademi, pp. 14–27.
Satrapi, M. (2003), *Persepolis: The Story of a Childhood*. Tr. Mattias Ripa and Blake Ferris. New York: Pantheon.
—(2004), *Persepolis 2: The Story of a Return*. Tr. Anjali Singh. New York: Pantheon.
Schipper, M. (1984), *Unheard Words: Women and Literature in Africa, the Arab World, the Caribbean and Latin America*. London: Allison and Busby.
Schultheis, A. W. (2004), *Regenerative Fictions: Postcolonialism, Psychoanalysis and the Nation as Family*. London: Palgrave-Macmillan.
Selvadurai, S. (1994), *Funny Boy*. New York: Harvest.
Semmel, B. (1962), *Jamaican Blood and Victorian Conscience: The Governor Eyre Controversy*. Westport, CT: Greenwood.
Senghor, L. (1994), 'Negritude', in P. Williams and L. Chrisman (eds), *Colonial Discourse and Postcolonial Theory*. New York: Columbia University Press, pp. 27–35.
Senna, D. (2004), 'The Mulatto Millenium', in J. O. Ifekwunigwe (ed.) *'Mixed Race' Studies: A Reader*. London and New York: Routledge, pp. 205–8.
Serres, M. (1982), *The Parasite*, Tr. Lawrence Schehr. Baltimore: Johns Hopkins University Press.
Seth, V. (1987), *From Heaven Lake: Travels through Sinkiang and Tibet*. 1983. London: Chatto and Windus.
—(1999), *An Equal Music*. Delhi: Viking.
Sharpe, J. (1993), *Allegories of Empire: The Figure of Woman in the Colonial Text*. Minneapolis: University of Minnesota Press.
Shome, R. (2006), 'Thinking Through the Diaspora Call Centers, India, and a New Politics of Hybridity', *International Journal of Cultural Studies* 9, 1, 105–24.
Sidhwa, B. (2001), *Cracking India*. Minneapolis: Milkweed Editions.

Silko, L. M. (1986), *Ceremony*. New York: Penguin.

Silva, N. (2004), *The Gendered Nation: Contemporary Writings from South Asia*. New Delhi: Sage.

Singh, K. (1999), Reference.com/Encyclopedia/Wikipedia. http://www. reference.com/browse/wiki/Vikram_Seth. Accessed 22 January 2007.

Sleeman, W.H. (1995), *Rambles and Recollections of an Indian Official* 1893. V. A. Smith (ed.). New Delhi: Asian Educational Services, 2 vols.

Smith, A. D. (2003), *Chosen Peoples*. Oxford: Oxford University Press.

Soyinka, W. (1984), *Death and the King's Horseman*, in Wole Soyinka (ed.), *Six Plays*. 1975. London: Methuen. pp. 144–220.

Spillers, H. (1991), *Comparative American Identities: Race, Sex and Nationality in the Modern Text*. London: Routledge.

Spivak, G. C. (1985), 'Three Women's Texts and a Critique of Imperialism', *Critical Inquiry* 12, 1, 243–61.

—(1988), 'Can the Subaltern Speak?', in C. Nelson and L. Grossberg (eds), *Marxism and the Interpretation of Culture*. Urbana: University of Illinois Press, pp. 271–313.

—(1988), 'Subaltern Studies: Deconstructing Historiography', in R. Guha and G. C. Spivak (eds), *Selected Subaltern Studies*. New York and London: Oxford University Press, pp. 3–32.

Srivastava, N. (2008), *Secularism in the Postcolonial Indian Novel: National and Cosmopolitan Narratives in English*. London and New York: Routledge.

Stepan, N. L. (2001), *Picturing Tropical Nature*. Ithaca: Cornell University Press.

Suleri, S. (1992), *The Rhetoric of English India*. Chicago and London: Chicago University Press.

—(1996), 'Woman Skin Deep: Feminism and the Postcolonial Condition', in P. Mongia (ed.) *Contemporary Postcolonial Theory: A Reader*. 1992. Delhi: Oxford University Press, pp. 335–46.

Sunder Rajan. R. (2001a), 'Dealing with Anxieties', *The Hindu* 25 February 2001, http://www.thehinduonnet.com//2001/02/25/stories/1325067a.htm. Accessed 2 September 2009.

—(2001b), 'Writing in English in India, Again', *The Hindu* 18 February 2001, http://www.thehinduonnet.com//2001/02/18/stories/1318067m.htm. Accessed 2 September 2009.

—(2003), *The Scandal of the State: Women, Law, and Citizenship in Postcolonial India*. Durham and London: Duke University Press.

Tagore, R. (1985), *The Home and the World*. Tr. Surendranath Tagore. 1915. Madras: Macmillan.

Takagi, D. (1996), 'Maiden Voyage: Excursion into Sexuality and Politics in Asian America, in L. Russell (ed.), *Asian American Sexualities: Dimensions of the Gay and Lesbian Experience*. New York and London: Routledge, pp. 21–35.

Tati-Loutard, J.-B. (1988), 'Return from Ethiopia', in J. Reed and C. Wake (eds), *A New Book of African Verse*. 1963. London: Heinemann, p. 102.

Taylor, M. (1986), *A Student's Manual of the History of India*. 1870. New Delhi: Asian Educational Services.

Taylor, P. and Bain, P. (2005), ' "India Calling to the Far Away Towns": The Call Centre Labour Process and Globalization', *Work, Employment and Society* 19, 2, 261–82.

Terranova, T. (2000), 'Free Labor: Producing Culture for the Digital Economy'. *Social Text* 18, 2, 34–58.

Tharu, S. and Lalita, K. (eds), (1993), *Women Writing in India: 600 B.C. to the Early Twentieth Century.* Delhi: Oxford University Press, 2 vols.

Tharu, S. and Niranjana, T. (1994), 'Problems for a Contemporary Theory of Gender', *Social Scientist* 22, 3–4, 93–117.

Thomas, N. (1994), *Colonialism's Culture: Anthropology, Travel and Government.* Cambridge: Polity.

Thumboo, E. (1993), *A Third Map: New and Selected Poems.* Singapore: UniPress-Centre for the Arts, National University of Singapore.

Trevelyan, C. (1838), *On the Education of the People of India.* London: Longman, Orme, Brown, Green and Longmans.

Trivedi, H. (1991), 'Reading English, Writing Hindi: English Literature and Indian Creative Writing', in S. Joshi (ed.) *Rethinking English: Essays in Literature, Language, History.* New Delhi: Trianka, pp. 161–80.

Trollope, J. (1983), *Brittania's Daughters: Women of the British Empire.* London: Hutchinson.

Tucker, S. (1842–1843), *South Indian Sketches.* London: James Nisbet, 2 vols.

Turkle, S. (1995), *Life on Screen: Identity in the Age of the Internet.* New York: Simon and Schuster.

Updike, J. (2006), *Terrorist.* New York: Alfred A. Knopf.

Upstone, S. (2009), *Spatial Politics in the Postcolonial Novel.* Surrey: Ashgate.

Vanita, R. (ed.), (2002), *Queering India: Same-Sex Love and Eroticism in Indian Culture and Society.* New York and London: Routledge.

Vanita, R. and Kidwai, S. (ed.), (2000), *Same-Sex Love in India: Readings from Literature and History.* New York: St. Martin's.

Varghese, L. (2003), 'Will the Real Indian Woman Log-On? Diaspora, Gender, and Comportment', in R. C. Lee and S.- L. C. Wong (eds), *Asian America.Net: Ethnicity, Nationalism, and Cyberspace.* New York and London: Routledge, pp. 235–48.

Vassanji, M. G. (1985), 'The Postcolonial Writer: Myth Maker and Folk Historian', in M. G. Vassanji (ed.) *A Meeting of Streams: South Asian Canadian Literature.* Toronto: TSAR, pp. 63–8.

Venn, C. (2006), *The Postcolonial Challenge: Towards Alternative Worlds.* London: Sage.

Vertovec, S. (1999), 'Three Meanings of "Diaspora", Exemplified by South Asian Religions', *Diaspora* 6, 3, 277–300.

Vikram. (2000), 'A Reason to be Glad: India's First Anthology of Gay Writing'. *Trikone* 15.1, 16.

Viswanathan, G. (1990), *Masks of Conquest: English Literary Studies and India.* 1989. London: Faber and Faber.

—(1998), *Outside the Fold: Conversion, Modernity, and Belief.* Delhi: Oxford University Press.

Voet, R. (1998), *Feminism and Citizenship.* London: Sage.

Waipuldanya. (1962), *I, the Aboriginal*. Douglas Lockwood. Adelaide: Rigby.
Walcott, D. (1986), 'A Far Cry from Africa', in *Collected Poems, 1948–1984*. New York: Farrar, Straus and Giroux, pp. 17–18.
—(1986), 'The Schooner *Flight*', in *Collected Poems, 1948–1984*. New York: Farrar, Straus and Giroux, pp. 345–61.
—(1996), 'Ruins of a Great House' in J. Thieme (ed.) *The Arnold Anthology of Post-colonial Literatures in English*. 1993. London: Arnold, pp. 498–9.
—(1998), 'The Muse of History', in *What the Twilight Says: Essays*. New York: Farrar, Straus and Giroux, pp. 36–64.
Walder, D. (1998), *Post-colonial Literatures in English: History, Language, Theory*. Oxford: Blackwell.
Waldron, J. (1995), 'Minority Cultures and the Cosmopolitan Alternative', in W. Kymlicka (ed.) *The Rights of Minority Cultures*. Oxford: Oxford University Press, pp. 93–119.
Walker, A. (1983), *In Search of Our Mothers' Gardens: Womanist Prose*. San Diego: Harcourt Brace Jovanovich.
Walker, K. (1996), 'We are Going', in John Thieme (ed.) *The Arnold Anthology of Post-colonial Literatures in English*. 1993. London: Arnold, pp. 223–4.
Walsh, J. E. (2004), *Domesticity in Colonial India: What Women Learned When Men Gave them Advice*. Lanham: Rowman and Littlefield.
Ware, V. (1992), *Beyond the Pale: White Women, Racism and History*. London: Verso.
Warschaeur, M. (2000), 'Language, Identity, and the Internet', in B. Kolko, Nakamura, L. and G. B. Rodman (eds), *Race in Cyberspace*. London and New York: Routledge, pp. 151–70.
Watson, C. W. (2002), *Multiculturalism*. New Delhi: Viva.
West, C. (2002), 'A Genealogy of Modern Racism', in P. Essed and D. T. Goldberg (eds), *Race Critical Theories: Text and Context*. 1982. Oxford: Blackwell, pp. 90–112.
West, L. A. (ed.), (1997), *Feminist Nationalism*. New York: Routledge.
Wolf, B. H. (1998), *The Ways of My Grandmothers*. New York: Harper.
Wong, S.- L. C. (1993), *Reading Asian American Literature: From Necessity to Extravagance*. Princeton, NJ: Princeton University Press.
Wright, J. (1972), 'Nigger's Leap, New England', in *Collected Poems: 1942–1970*. Sidney: Angus and Robertson, p. 15.
Yeğenoğlu, M. (1998), *Colonial Fantasies: Towards a Feminist Reading of Orientalism*. Cambridge: Cambridge University Press.
Young, R. J. C. (1995), *Colonial Desire: Hybridity in Theory, Culture and Race*. London: Routledge.
—(2001), *Postcolonialism: An Historical Introduction*. Oxford: Blackwell.
Yuval-Davis, N. (2002), *Gender and Nation*. 1997. London: Sage.

INDEX